# JAPANESE MANAGEMENT

# JAPANESE MANAGEMENT

## Cultural and Environmental Considerations

Edited by

### Sang M. Lee
### Gary Schwendiman

University of Nebraska – Lincoln

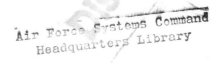

PRAEGER

PRAEGER SPECIAL STUDIES • PRAEGER SCIENTIFIC

**Library of Congress Cataloging in Publication Data**
Main entry under title:

Japanese management.

Based on the selected papers presented at the
Japan-United States Business Conference, held
Oct. 4–7, 1981 at the University of Nebraska–Lincoln
campus.
Includes bibliographies and index.
1. Industrial management — Japan — Congresses.
2. Comparative management — Congresses. 3. Industrial
management — United States — Congresses. I. Lee,
Sang M., 1939–          II. Schwendiman, Gary.
III. Japan-United States Business Conference (1981 :
University of Nebraska, Lincoln campus)
HD70.J3J394   1982              658              82-10116
ISBN 0-03-061773-1                               AACR2

Published in 1982 by Praeger Publishers
CBS Educational and Professional Publishing
a Division of CBS Inc.
521 Fifth Avenue, New York, New York 10175 U.S.A.

© 1982 by Praeger Publishers

23456789   052   987654321

Printed in the United States of America

To Laura and Jill

# Preface

Corporate white papers dealing with international business consistently report the absence of cultural understanding on the part of personnel from nations participating in reciprocal commerce. This condition exists especially in American-Japanese relationships and is extremely serious in view of the fact that the United States and Japan are the two principal international trade partners in the free world. With the relationship growing exponentially, it is vital to the successful completion of business ventures that persons of each nation show an appreciation and an understanding of each other's economic and business practices.

There has been wide publicity about the "economic and social miracle" of Japan. The gross national product exceeds $1 trillion, second only to that of the United States. Crime rates are the lowest in the world. Life expectancy is the highest in the world; infant mortality, the lowest. The unemployment rate is less than 2 percent; population growth, around 1 percent. The Japanese society is said to be built on trust, having an extremely low ratio of the number of lawyers to the total population. Recently, Japan has out-performed other countries in the most sophisticated technological areas, including electronics, camera goods, and the development and utilization of computers.

Behind the economic and social miracle of Japan are its new emerging management philosophy, its operations systems, and its diligent workers. Japanese management systems have turned many failing business organizations around in the United States. American executives flock to Japan to study Japanese manufacturing systems, quality control methods, and employee relations policies. Could Japan's formula for success be transplanted to the United States? It is doubtful whether its formidable combination of virtues could be grafted onto the somewhat disheveled fabric of the declining industries in the United States without a gallant effort. This book is intended to be a provocative stimulus for such an effort.

Until recently, management has been characterized by what we would like to call the information-driven process of management. Management by information certainly makes sense since we live in such a complex and technology-based society. However, management by information has the following general characteristics: a high degree of organizational instrumentation, emphasis on measurable short-term objectives, a top-down communication of objectives, a technology-based functional structure, and an impersonal work environment.

An emerging concept of management is the ideology-driven process of management. Management by ideology emphasizes superordinate organizational values and philosophies, long-term strategic goals, a two-way (i.e., top-down and bottom-up) communication system, cooperation- and harmony-oriented functional structures, strong commitment to the organizational values on the part of the members, and decision making by consensus.

The Japanese management system is closely related to management by ideology. Under this system, the superordinate organizational values and philosophies are clearly communicated throughout the organization. The basic approach of management is to pursue long-term achievement of the organizational purpose. Based on this stable management approach, middle and lower management personnel are encouraged to exercise their creativity in developing intermediate objectives, such as profit, market share, research and development, human resource development, operational efficiency, and the like. These intermediate objectives are simply means to achieving the superordinate organizational purpose.

Under the management-by-ideology framework, employees are recruited based on their commitment to the same basic values of the organization. Thus, organizational commitment of the employee is the foundation of the organization's strength. Also, since the organization attempts to achieve harmonious working relations and consensus decision making, isolated, secretive, or hasty decision making is not likely.

U.S. managers often scorn Japanese managers for their slowness in decision making. Japanese managers apologize for their slow decision-making style. But they also point out that U.S. managers take forever to implement the decisions they make so promptly.

Professors Hayes and Abernathy of Harvard University contend that one of the problems behind financial and productivity woes of many large U.S. firms is their emphasis on short-term monetary objectives, often at the expense of long-term organizational goals. We believe that management by ideology, supported by modern technology and scientific analysis, should replace the management-by-information-only approach pursued by so many U.S. organizations.

In order to facilitate our understanding of Japanese management systems and also provide a forum to study the transferability of these systems to the United States, a first international conference was organized. The

Japan-United States Business Conference, held October 4–7, 1981 on the
University of Nebraska–Lincoln campus, attracted about 300 leading management scholars, business executives, and administrators of schools of business administration from the United States and Japan. Some of the best
known experts in this field of study who participated in the seminar are:

Professor Ezra Vogel, Harvard (Author, *Japan as Number One*)
Professor William Ouchi, UCLA (Author, *Theory Z*)
Mr. Leighton Smith, Arthur Andersen, Tokyo
Professor Motoo Kaji, University of Tokyo
Dean Eugene Kelley, Penn State University
Professor Jinichiro Nakane, Waseda University, Tokyo
Dr. Dick Nanto, Library of Congress
Mr. Edward Hay, Fram Corporation
Professor Toshiyuki Tamura, Tokyo Metropolitan University

This book is based on the best original papers presented at the conference and those specially written for this volume. Currently, there is no
book that deals exclusively with Japanese management systems. This particular volume emphasizes the following key issues in understanding the
Japanese management systems:

• What can we learn from the Japanese?
• Socio-cultural aspects of Japanese management.
• The Japanese management environment.
• The relationship between the United States and Japan.

This book includes a number of empirical as well as conceptual studies that are written by well-known Japanese or U.S. scholars. Their insights
are based on broad and profound understanding of Japanese management
systems. We believe the most important contribution of this book lies in the
discussion of transferability of Japanese management approaches to U.S.
corporations.

This book is directed toward two basic markets: (1) as a text for management theory, comparative management, and organization theory and
practice at the upper undergraduate and graduate levels; and (2) as a reference book for the practicing manager and staff personnel in various organizations.

We would like to express our thanks to all of the contributors to this
book. We are especially grateful to those who made the first Japan-United
States Business Conference a big success: President Ronald Roskens, Chan-
cellor Martin Massengale, and Vice President Alan Seagren of the University of Nebraska; Governor Charles Thone; Ambassador Yoshio Okawara;

Chairman of the Board Mr. T. Takeshita, President Kichiro Ando, and Mr. Robert Summers of Kawasaki Motors Corporation, USA; Dr. Carl Halvarson of CUPP; our Japanese colleagues Professors Motoo Kaji, Motofusa Murayama, Toshiyuki Tamura, Jinichiro Nakane, Norio Ayoama, and others; and other distinguished colleagues in the profession.

We express our sincere thanks to our efficient office staff who made all arrangements for the conference and typed many different versions of the papers: Joyce Anderson, Jane Chrastil, Cindy LeGrande, Angela Sullivan, Billie Lefholtz, Linda Rock, and Mary Best. We give our love to our family members who shared the burden of long hours with us throughout the process of this project.

Sang M. Lee
Gary Schwendiman

# Contents

## Part III
## THE JAPANESE MANAGEMENT ENVIRONMENT

Contents

# JAPANESE MANAGEMENT

# Part I

# WHAT CAN WE LEARN FROM THE JAPANESE?

The three chapters in part one were first presented as papers at the Japan-United States Business Conference. The first chapter, "Japan-United States Business Relationships" by Ambassador Yoshio Okawara, presents far-reaching personal observations about business relationships and mutual interdependence between Japan and the United States.

The second chapter, "Japanese Lessons for America," by Professor Ezra Vogel of Harvard University, presents a provocative challenge to America based on his vast and intimate knowledge of Japanese society and culture. He points out many factors fundamental to Japanese economic growth. In order to meet the Japanese challenge, Professor Vogel submits, the United States must coördinate its own efforts in many different sectors of society.

The third chapter, "United States-Japan Relations in the 1980s: A Maturing Partnership," by Mr. Robert Angel, president of the Japan Economic Institute of America, develops a convincing argument that the United States and Japan are the two countries whose policies will jointly and independently determine the fate of the free world. In order to develop a maturing relationship with Japan, Mr. Angel believes that we must first better understand the attitudes of the new generation of Japanese, as well as their changing social and political environment.

# 1

# Japan-United States Business Relationships

YOSHIO OKAWARA

The Japanese-American economic relationship has developed and matured in recent years and our economies have become intertwined and interdependent. Both countries increasingly depend upon each other for economic prosperity. Japan and the United States are the world's two largest transoceanic trading partners, in a two-way commercial exchange which is doubling in value every five years. Investments in each other's markets are expanding rapidly, and are fast approaching, in aggregate value, the $10 billion mark.

Now, as never before, the two nations are exerting a powerful economic impact upon each other and are focusing on the most timely and important questions: What do our respective private sectors need to know about each other and what can we learn from each other.

It is no secret that Japanese management has for years been looking at, listening to, and learning from U.S. business, for U.S. business has and continues to be the world's most dynamic and innovative. In fact, when you probe some of the strengths of Japanese industry today, such as in quality control and productivity, you will find that much of the original inspiration was derived from U.S. industry.

For the United States, though, the interest in studying Japanese management policies and business practices is rather new. Americans today are taking note of the sizeable inroads of Japanese imports in this market and are asking, "What makes these Japanese tick? Why are their products so competitive? What are their secrets? What can we learn from Japan?" These are, of course, questions which only Americans can ask and answer. But since they are apropos to this conference, I should like to offer a few personal observations.

In putting Japanese business practices under the microscope these days, it seems popular for U.S. and other observers to identify certain practices, such as lifelong employment and consensus decision making, as key factors that account for Japan's strong competitiveness in world trade.

Such elements are very much a part of Japan's business topography, but their importance can be overstated. I know many Japanese business executives who complain occasionally about the inefficiency of such practices, and who admire the more "rational" U.S. approaches of merit hiring and firing, and individualistic decision making. Indeed, such factors in Japan are part myth, for life-long employment covers only about one fourth of the labor force, while our consensus approach to decision making can be often more individualistic than meets the eye.

I suspect that Americans may find the Japanese business experience more useful as a stimulus in identifying problem areas and concerns for management action, and less so as a source of solutions to specific problems. As we Japanese know well from our experience, concepts and practices from a foreign cultural milieu must be adapted and assimilated to one's own circumstances and requirements.

Adaptation and assimilation are, of course, at the heart of our direct investment efforts in each other's countries — successful case studies which you will be examining closely. Direct investment is not just one of the most dynamic, creative aspects of our economic relationship; it is also one of the most challenging, for it requires both investor and host to cross cultural boundaries, to achieve an effective interfacing of differing approaches to the workplace. Indeed, it may well be that this interfacing of differing approaches — this hybridization of management practices — offers the most relevant lessons for our respective business communities.

If we bear in mind that our respective experiences are not necessarily panaceas to our own particular problems, I am convinced that there is, and will always be, much to be learned from each other, in business and all other endeavors.

Basically, the problems of private enterprise in our market-oriented economies are the same: How to mobilize our economic assets most effectively and efficiently to meet the needs of society. Our two countries share a common commitment to entrust the wealth-creating task to the private sector and to individual initiative, with a minimum of government interference. This makes our study of each other — the sharing of experiences and knowledge through such conferences as this one — all the more meaningful and valuable.

Let me offer one final observation. What we can learn from each other is not confined to the field of business management. There is much to be learned in the field of macroeconomic management as well.

As the world's two most productive, dynamic market economies, Japan and the United States stand together at the frontiers of industrial technology and economic development. And for us, the problems of economic growth are complex. Our challenges include utilizing our natural, technological, and human resources most productively to create new wealth, to raise living standards, and to enrich the quality of life of our own and the world's people.

For us, growth cannot be just a function of new business investment, but also of business disinvestment. It cannot be just a question of what industries we want to be in, but also of what industries we can be competitive in, in home markets and in overseas markets, in an increasingly competitive world economy. It cannot be just a problem of short-term profits, but also of long-term return and market share.

Our two countries, by fate and by choice, are destined to be both economic partners and competitors. Our competition with each other, and with the rest of the world, does and will continue to pose difficult challenges for us. If competition with Japan is having a positive impact on the U.S. automobile industry, helping it restore itself to world competitiveness, then so too is efficient American production having a positive impact on Japan's aluminum and petrochemical industry, forcing them to restructure themselves.

This is the way it should be. The problems of industrial adjustment are painful, but they can be managed, if we approach them patiently, responsibly, and sensitively — with confidence in the future. And if we do not look for panaceas, we can learn much from our respective responses to this on-going need to upgrade our industrial structures.

If I may suggest it, perhaps a topic of this kind could be the subject of a future Japan-U.S. Business Conference. I wish to congratulate the College and University Partnership Program, the University of Nebraska and Kawasaki Motors Corporation, U.S.A., on the leadership you have displayed in initiating and conducting this year's conference. You are laying new cement to the foundations of Japan-U.S. relations.

# 2

# Japanese Lessons for America

EZRA VOGEL

During a sabbatical year in Tokyo in 1975–76 I was so impressed by all that I saw in Japan, that I now visit Japan almost every year. I am convinced that the United States ought to be doing more to catch up with the Japanese and that we ought to take all the things Japan has done into consideration.

So, when I came back I decided to write a book, which I entitled *Japan As Number One*. My thought was to try to provoke a powerful response in Americans. If I had just used a title like *Japan's Strengths*, I thought it would have no market in the United States. I really wanted to shake up people. When the book first came out, I traveled around this country and spoke frequently to businessmen with experience in Japan. I would say the general reaction I received to the book was: "That's very interesting and it has many cute things to say about Japan, but that professor has spent a little too long in the East and it's affected his mind a little bit. It's like Americans who study Zen and get caught up in the spiritual things; they get a bit carried away with the subject and lose their sense of balance." Recently, however, Americans have begun to take an interest in learning from Japan, a development that delights me and vindicates my efforts over the years. In this chapter, I will discuss why Japanese successes are likely to continue through the 80s, and then summarize my reasons for thinking so.

To begin with, is the Japanese success likely to continue in the 1980s? Or are the Japanese finally getting affluent and overconfident and is the population aging so they will lose the urge and the capacity to continue to grow? My answer is quite clear. I think that Japan is going to continue to be the fastest growing of the major industrial countries in the 1980s. If one looks at the reason for growth, there is no reason to expect that their growth rate will average anything less than about 4 to 6 percent. That is much faster than the predicted growth rates of all the other major industrial powers. Let me just try to pick off three or four different kinds of things we usually think about when we look at the overall growth rate.

First of all, do they have the capital to carry on this kind of growth rate? As you know, the United States personal savings rate has been running about 6 percent a year and is now down to about 4 percent a year. Japan's personal savings rate has been running about 20 percent a year and it is now up to about 23 percent a year. The overall size of the Japanese economy is already about half that of the United States. Given the fact that we have about twice as many people, that means about the same per capita product that we have in the United States. But breaking that down simply on the basis of industry, by 1978 the U.S. was already importing $5 billion more of industrial goods than it was exporting, while Japan was exporting $76 billion more than they were importing. By that time, the Japanese already had about three quarters as much overall industrial output as we did. These figures are provided by Bill Wrap, a specialist on the Japanese economy at Morgan Bank.

Now, as Japan continues to develop capital, and their savings rate continues to be much higher than the United States, their overall level of investment in industrial plant and equipment is already close to the same absolute amount that ours is here. Let us look at the figures on the largest banks in the world. The last time I looked at a list of the top 300 banks, there were 58 American banks and 60 banks from Japan. The top 25 were even more striking; 4 of those banks were American and 11 were Japanese. Now, to be sure, Japanese banks tend to be national where many more of ours are regional. That means that they have a tremendous amount of capital in very large organizations that are able to spread out into the world. I think we can expect that Japanese capital will begin to come onto the world scene during the 1980s in a very major way.

If one takes the availability of special government funds to aid industrial development, the Japanese postal savings bank is the single largest bank in the world in terms of assets. Every little, local post office is connected by a computer system so that anybody can go into his local post office and deposit or withdraw money from any post office throughout the country. It is all neatly organized and computerized and they have more savings in the postal savings system than any other bank in the world. That money is recycled through the finance ministry into banks like the Development Bank, Export-Import Bank, Small Business Bank, and so forth. Therefore, they have tremendous amounts of funds available at low and special interest rates that aid the development of their economy. Also, because the discount rate is so low in Japan, the rate of inflation is expected to be very low, something like 3.8 percent during this next year. They have really got inflation under control. Thus, bank loans are available at a very low cost. This means that there will be a tremendous amount of capital available to Japanese companies at low costs in a relatively stable environment.

Second, what about personnel? Those who have read my book know that comparable data on international tests in fields like mathematics and science show that Japanese youths have done as well as any in the world. National samplings based on general population data seem to agree; the estimates are that Japanese training in mathematics and science is as good as or better than that of any other country. The Ministry of Education issues guidelines for what has to be covered in every school throughout the country. Therefore good training is not limited to certain schools; the same standards are applied everywhere. There also tend to be no great differences in the economic condition of schools or in the amount of money available to them to hire quality teachers. And almost every Japanese child (something like 99 percent) gets through nine grades of education. If we look at high school graduates, a little less than 85 percent graduate from high school in the United States, but 93 percent graduate in Japan. Thus not only is the average quality of junior and senior high school students in science and mathematics much higher in Japan, but more of them actually graduate.

Then, if we think about the areas that are going to be really important for high technology growth in the years ahead, perhaps none is more important than engineering, especially electrical engineering. In 1980 the Japanese produced 20,000 more engineers than the United States did. That's an absolute figure; it means that, since we have twice as many people, they produced almost three times as many engineers per capita. In electrical engineering alone, the United States produced 14,000 electrical engineers in 1980; Japan produced 20,000. About 40 percent of Japanese graduate students are in engineering, as compared to a very tiny percent in the United States. Among undergraduates, about 20 percent are in engineering. This means that they have a very high level of trained manpower moving into engineering.

One of the implications of the new program to strengthen military defense in the United States is that a certain number of engineers from civilian-oriented projects will be working for the federal government. This means that the availability of engineers for commercial enterprises will be seriously curtailed. By contrast, Japan seems to be in a very good position.

Now, what about technology? In general, Japan has had a different approach to technology than we have. We have been much more involved in basic research, and Japan has been much more interested in learning research, buying technology, developing licensing arrangements, buying patents and so forth to acquire technology from abroad while concentrating their R&D money on development. They have been taking a product, improving it, engineering it and mass-producing it so they can market it at lower costs. However, that is beginning to change because Japan recognizes that as they get up to world standards they're going to have to invest a great deal more in their own basic research. And, just as after World War II, when in setting up new steel plants the Japanese built the most modern kind, now they will build the most up-to-date, state-of-the-art R&D laboratories.

In 1970 the U.S. was spending about 3 percent of its GNP on R&D; now, in 1981, it's 2 percent. Japan was spending, I think, something slightly less than 1 percent of its GNP on R&D in 1970; by last year it was 2.15 percent. The Japanese aim to get that up to 2.5 percent very shortly and to 3 percent by 1990.

Given the fact that their total level of investment in plant and equipment is already close to that of the United States and that they are beginning to invest very heavily in R&D in new plants and equipment, I think one has to assume that they are going to be acquiring a lot of technology. Now, to be sure, they have not yet made a big onslaught in the basic research. But I think we would be underestimating them to assume this was not going to happen. In the 1930s, when they became somewhat separated from world standards because of the war preparations, they started a research center that developed very advanced research and the Nobel Prize winning scientists at that time mainly came out of that research center. They are beginning again now to put money into basic research and I have no doubt that as a result they will soon begin developing new kinds of creative technology and science.

To give just one example, the head of the mathematics department at Harvard happens to be somebody who grew up in Japan and was educated in Japan, Professor Hiranoka. He came to the United States as a young graduate student and has been in the United States ever since. Japanese businessmen have now approached him with the idea of getting a number of talented young Japanese in mathematics to come to the United States where they would have a number of years of close contact with the highest-level mathematicians so that they could go back to Japan as some of the leading talents in mathematics. These businessmen have already invested approximately half-a-million dollars for such projects. What they would like to do is be able to identify a number of promising young grade school-age children, bring them to the U.S., and while they're going to junior and senior high schools here have them in close contact with America's leading mathematicians. By the time they're 18 or 20, the age when most mathematicians begin to make their first creative breakthroughs, they would have had some of the most advanced training at their level.

Now it may be that the program will never come to fruition in precisely this form, but I mention it as an example of the bold way the Japanese are thinking about investing in R&D. They are beginning to participate in new technological developments around the world. If I remember correctly, something like 25 percent of the new patents come from the U.S. and about 20 percent of the new patents now come from Japan. To be sure, these figures can't be taken as a simple reflection of the level of scientific achievement in these countries because I think there are still many areas where the United States is substantially ahead in basic research. But I think we would be underestimating Japan's capacity if we didn't realize that they could substantially increase their number of patents and make a big difference in the years ahead.

A fourth area we sometimes use to make predictions of how well people will be doing concerns their energy resources. I think the conventional wisdom was that Japan was going to be in a worse situation in the 1980s than other countries because Japan is an island without many natural resources, virtually no oil, high quality coal, or other mineral resources. I think it could be argued now that precisely because Japan is so vulnerable the country has moved more rapidly to ensure a system that will give them a safe supply of raw materials. For example, they have undertaken enormous oil conservation programs and converted a number of plants from electrical power, cement, and so forth to coal. One American oil company official in Japan told me recently that it's actually hurting their business because the Japanese have been so rapid in practicing conservation.

Also, they have developed long-term contracts with oil-producing countries in the Middle East and Indonesia. When Mexico discovered more oil, the Japanese expanded their diplomacy and friendship with the Mexican government. In dealing with the Middle East, they aren't bound by a close relationship with Israel the way the United States is. And they have all the natural advantages for good cultural contacts with other countries. They maintain ties with the Soviet Union and China in case those countries become oil exporters. Japan also has about six months storage facilities for petroleum so that they are insulated from the kind of short-range disasters or interruptions that occurred during the Iranian crisis.

In coal development they've arranged very long-range contracts with Australia and Western Canada. I think they would like to move even faster with the United States, if the American companies had the kind of facilities, the transport networks, and the port facilities that would enable the rapid exportation of coal to Japan. Now, if any country is able to buy petroleum and coal in the 1980s, it is probably going to be Japan because they have a much more positive trade balance than any other major country. Even in 1981, not only will the trade balance be favorable but the current accounts balance is estimated anywhere from about $5 to $10 billion in the black. I think one has to assume that oil-producing countries and coal-producing countries will want to be selling their products, and it is difficult to imagine that any country is going to be better able to pay for those products than Japan.

In short, I agree with the conventional wisdom that says Japan is in a very vulnerable position because of its inability to produce its own energy resources. Still I think the chances are great that Japan is going to remain in a very favorable position to obtain these resources during the 1980s.

Now, given such favorable factors, what are some of the deeper reasons why Japan has been so successful? One that I keep coming back to and that I put high on any list is their search for information around the world. Since the late nineteenth century, the Japanese have gotten into the habit of going anywhere to study anything. If something is going to be useful, they will send their scholars to the laboratories for years to learn about it. When biogenetic engineering becomes popular, you can be sure there are going to be well-trained Japanese over here very quickly, picking up all the latest bits of information. There will be special delegations coming over, most of which will be well-briefed beforehand. They will have read the literature and know what they are looking for so they can make good use of the time. When they go back to Japan and they talk about it and report it in various journals, the information will be assimilated very widely.

The Japanese can also assume that their foreign correspondents will automatically bring back information useful for the growth of the country. Ever since the late nineteenth century, when Japan decided they had to get caught up, one of the important functions of the newspapers was not only to carry the interesting crime and sports news and so forth from other countries but to bring back ideas that would be useful for building up the country. Therefore, the reporters who are sent to other countries almost automatically do this. In Washington, there are now about 45 Japanese reporters, all of whom handle the English language at least passably; they can speak and read English. In Tokyo, the U.S. now has perhaps two or three reporters who can handle Japanese adequately, and of course, they're not ordinarily interested in bringing back ideas from Japan about how to improve America. I'm happy to say I think that's beginning to change.

The habit of learning from other countries, however, is a national one for the Japanese, and almost any tourist (out of 100 million people, Japan is now sending 4 million people abroad each year), is constantly thinking of ways to apply foreign ideas in ways that will help Japan. One of the problems in the United States, I think, is that in the last 20 years we have so dominated international business and science that we've gotten out of the habit of following developments abroad. Times have now changed and we haven't yet fully adjusted to that fact. In the 1920s and 1930s, when German science was so outstanding, U.S. science students at the graduate level studied German, and many of them went to Germany; they kept very much on top of the German literature. Yet today we don't have Americans going to Germany and Japan to study engineering in order to keep up with their latest developments in this area.

A few months ago when I was in Tokyo I asked the U.S. science attaché there if he knew approximately how many American engineers were studying in Japanese universities or Japanese research centers. He scratched his head and said he thought that there were first- or second- or third-generation Americans who were over there and he thought that perhaps there were a handful of engineers in the U.S. who could handle the Japanese language and follow the literature. Well, when you think of all the thousands of Japanese engineers who constantly follow U.S. ideas and developments, it's just a very different order of magnitude. Not only are they studying our science and technology, they're studying our management, our organization, and our ways of doing things.

One of the biggest and most systematic information-collecting devices in Japan is the general trading company. Since the late nineteenth century, when Japan felt its disadvantage in international trade because shipping costs and insurance costs and so forth were quite high for them, they tried to concentrate their manufacturing into a small number of Japanese companies to cut down on carrying costs. This was the origin of the general trading company. These, of course, have continued to grow very rapidly since World War II, and right now the six largest general trading companies in the world are all Japanese trading companies. As of last year, these have annual sales between 30 and 60 billion dollars each, which is really quite an enormous amount. Each of the general trading companies has offices in over a hundred countries, and in all the major countries they have several offices.

The general trading companies have become information-collecting devices as well. The people working for them have both a regional and functional specialty; they can specialize in product lines and geographic regions. They have the most modern telex equipment so that they can photofacsimile and send back thousands of telexes each day to their home offices. In this way the latest economic information becomes available not only to the large companies but to middle-size and small-size companies.

The U.S. middle-size and small-size company, say, in the manufacturing area, finds it much more expensive to break into the international market. From its connection with the general trading company, a middle-sized Japanese company already has access to the kind of information it needs to develop a global marketing and production strategy; it can produce specialized products with economies of scale for a large number of products that are geared toward international marketing. And of course, economies of scale of this sort will give them an advantage in the long run.

But aside from being the source of new ideas and understanding about market penetration, one of the most important functions of the general trading company is that it provides a sure environment. When a company wants to make an investment or wants to decide how to carry on a certain process it can send people to the place in the world most advanced in that area, and it can invest with a greater degree of certainty and a greater probability of success. In short, it reduces risk, which is really terribly important.

For all these reasons I would rate the systematic gathering of information around the world as one of the most significant activities in which the Japanese are engaged.

A second area of involvement is business coöperation and government strategy. Now people will say that the United States government does not have a strategy for dealing with business. It leaves it with the market forces. But, unfortunately, that is not the way it actually works because ailing industries, sometimes representing large areas of the country, often go to the federal government for support. For example, when U.S. textiles were in difficulty, the people of the southeastern U.S. went to the government for support. When a major automaker — like the Chrysler Corporation — is in trouble, it goes to the government for support. When a city like New York is in trouble, it goes to the government for support and often has the political clout to get that support. In fact, because our government does not have a conscious economic strategy, it often ends up supporting industries and municipalities that are already in trouble.

In Japan, because there is a conscious strategy, they try to make available low-cost loans and so forth in areas that are going to be important in the future. And they try to concentrate that money in areas where it will make a difference. They do not just give huge grants to industry; they first sit down with industrial leaders. It is not that the Japanese government is so brilliant. People say, "Well, how can the U.S. government make correct decisions — they are not smart enough?" Well, Japanese government leaders aren't any smarter. The reason they are perhaps able to make better decisions in this area is, number one, because they have organized advisers selected from business leaders representing the various industrial sectors who sit down and engage in careful discussion. They use the best information at their disposal and make their decisions accordingly. Also, it does not take any special genius to predict that computers and telecommunications are going to be among the more important areas in the future and cotton textiles is going to be among the less important. The Japanese government utilizes the best information it can to choose industries of the future. They try to do the best they can at any given time and that is certainly considerably better than leaving it to chance or, even worse, leaving it to political forces that tend to end up supporting only the industries that are in trouble.

I have mentioned the problem of our auto companies. Part of their problem, of course, was that they did not adapt quickly enough to changing markets. But part of the problem was caused by the fact that our government did not let the oil price rise flow through the gasoline to the consumer after the first OPEC price rise. Any businessmen who was running an automotive company at that time would have to try to make future plans accordingly. For the second OPEC price rise, however, our government made the decision to let the price rise flow through to the consumer, and it was in that quick crunch that our automobile companies were caught. It would take several years before they would be able to produce the kind of cars best suited to the new situation.

Now if Japan had been involved in a similar kind of decision, if the government had been involved in letting the price rise flow through, they would have provided special adjustment assistance right away to those companies, either through low interest loans or special tax exemptions. They would realize that the government's decision was partly responsible for that situation and then they would come in and try to help. That kind of governmental responsiveness creates a business environment and a security that makes it much easier for business to move ahead.

A third area that I think is very important is the businesses' commitment to their employees. There are different ways that people have of stating this basic idea. Some say it's the Japanese permanent employment system or the Japanese seniority system. I think, sometimes, that the two are very close to being the same thing. I also think, however, that for many Americans who hear such remarks, there are certain nuances that are not quite right. One of the main problems is that we seem to assume when we hear the term "permanent employment" that it means a kind of contractual obligation exists to prevent the company from getting rid of the employee. In fact, if the Japanese employee does a lousy job — if he's not conscientious, doesn't do his job well, or is often absent — there's no difficulty at all for the Japanese company to get rid of him. The company is committed to that person who does his job responsibly and gives his best and all. And they see a very big difference between one who works hard and one who does not. The U.S company, when it goes in the red, is most likely to lay off a person quite quickly or to fire him. In Japan, the company would do much more to see that person through if it was a structurally depressed industry. With the government's help, it would try to work out a plan over a period of several years to allow for a more gradual readjustment. Even though the companies must bear a considerable part of the responsibility, the fact that the government is willing to support and stand behind them gives them a greater degree of assurance. And the fact that the company will do that for the person in time of difficulty gives the employee the feeling that the company is trying to help him and he should do what he can to help the company. Because he expects to be at the company 20 or 30 years, he knows it is in his personal interest for the company to do well. Take a thirty-year-old person. He knows that if his company is doing well 20 years from now his salary is going to be better because he is still going to be with that company. So he is willing to make short-range sacrifices for the company.

My personal conviction is that the reason the employee is willing to work hard in Japan for the company is not because he sings the company's songs in the morning or because of some mystical feeling that goes back to the Tokugawa period but simply because the company and the company leaders do try, on the average, to show interest in the success and the development of the employee, and reward the employee who works hard. The employee knows that and responds to that basic fact.

Some people ask me why Japanese work harder or if there is a basic difference in the work ethic between Japan and the United States. My personal conviction is that there is not a big difference. The basic principle of the Protestant Ethic is not laziness. I think there is a lot in our ethical tradition that emphasizes hard work just as Japanese tradition does.

Recently, I came across a marvelous report by the Australian Trade Commissioner in 1914 describing his visit to Japan, and the condition of Japanese industries. He says, "It is true that Japanese workers are paid very low wages, but there is very good reason for this because they do not put out very much work. They are very disorganized and very sloppy; I have never seen a more disorganized and lazy bunch of people. And if we really want to shape them up we will have to send in many managers and at best it will take several years before we can really get these people to really work properly. And I don't know how we can possibly get this done within the course of several years." In short, I do not believe that the Japanese work hard because of some mystical, historical tradition.

I think that the U.S. farmer works as hard as anybody and I think that there are many American executives and many American people, even in Washington, who are not given adequate credit for their dedication in putting in tremendous numbers of hours. I think at the present time that, proportionally, Japanese work harder than Americans, but I don't think it is because of some basic ethic. Rather, it is due to the conditions of employment and the desire and the motivation to carry on with the work.

There are many challenges that the United States faces in the years ahead. I think we can compete effectively with the Japanese but what I have been trying to suggest is that we have an enormous amount of homework to do in this country. If one thinks about the challenge we face from the Soviet military, the response it leads to is more troops, more arms, and so forth, which is not very helpful to the U.S. But if one thinks about the economic challenge that we confront from Japan, it seems to me that it provides a terrific opportunity for improving our country. The kinds of things it ought to lead to are the improvement of management-worker relations and better coöperation between government and business. There is no reason why it could not also lead to improving the quality of our products, the efficiency of our industries, and the motivation of the individual worker. In short, I think the challenge from Japan is dangerous if we do not respond to it, because we could become even more protectionist and backward-looking. But I think it has the potential for doing a great deal to revive our country.

# 3

# United States-Japan Relations in the 1980s: A Maturing Partnership

ROBERT ANGEL

When examining the relationship between Japan and the United States, it is useful to think about what that relationship is likely to look like during the rest of this decade. Beginning with the postwar occupation of Japan, perhaps the most successful effort of that sort the world has ever seen, U.S.-Japan relations throughout the 1950s and 1960s were very much a big brother/little brother affair. Japan realized that it was quite dependent upon the United States for its economic well-being and its national security. Japanese government and business leaders worked hard to maintain good relations with America using all the diplomatic instruments available for that purpose. Good relations with the United States continued to characterize foreign policy for a long time and I hope they still do today. On the other hand, during the 1950s and 1960s, Japan wasn't as important to us as we were to Japan. Our strategic planners were primarily interested in maintaining Japan as an Asian outpost of the free world, and during the Korean conflict we were pleased to be able to use bases in Japan to support our coöperation in the defense of South Korea. In fact, we continue to use those bases even today.

But the sense of importance attached to the relationship by the U.S. side never reached the level felt by the Japanese, especially in the case of economic relations between the two countries. By and large, as the senior partner in the relationship, we were content to go along with Japan as long as they took care not to cause us too many problems, especially economic problems. This rather passive economic attitude toward Japan wasn't unique at all. For most of the 1950s and 1960s the United States considered its participation in international trade to be a charitable act, the purpose of which was to strengthen the economies of other countries. We allowed them to buy things from us and to sell things to us. And throughout that period, foreign demand for our products was usually more than sufficient to cover the cost of the goods that were exported to us and to spill over a little bit and fill in the holes in other areas of the international payments account. During that period, the United States' international trade, compared to that of other countries of the world, comprised only a small proportion of the total gross national product.

Of course, as the years went by, U.S. agribusinessmen began to realize that the Japanese consumers could increase American farm income through their purchases of wheat, corn, and other commodities. And, as Japan's economic strength increased, our high-technology industries also began to find in Japan an important additional market for their products. Computers, semiconductors, aircraft energy initiatives, and a variety of endeavors began to be increasingly important to us as well as to Japan.

Now U.S. companies are very interested in foreign business. Even firms that once were content to focus their efforts during the postwar period on the huge U.S. domestic market have recognized that while the decision made *micro* sense, it may not have made *macro* sense. And we may have to pay the price for that discrepancy today and throughout the decade. The United States, too, has become increasingly dependent on good international economic relations to help maintain a healthy domestic economy and to provide jobs and profits for Americans. We can no longer afford to remain passive, depending on our international trading partners to initiate growth by buying our products and selling us theirs. To do so will mean becoming little more than an exporter of raw materials and foodstuffs. Not that there is anything wrong with exporting raw materials and foodstuffs, but today an industrial nation cannot afford to sell only raw materials. Actually, agricultural products are a very large percentage of our total exports, and I believe that in part it is because, in international trade as in domestic trade, primary products tend to be bought, whereas manufactured goods have to be sold. You know that if a nation requires food supplies it will go out and buy food. Whereas if a nation or an individual wants to acquire manufactured items, it will sometimes find the raw materials to manufacture the product itself, and once the product is manufactured at home, the situation changes.

By and large, U.S. manufacturers do not compete effectively in the international arena, at least when compared with primary products. In order to increase the percentage of our manufactured exports, we have to get down to business in the 1980s. Business has to learn how to sell its products in the world markets. There are both political and economical demands for an increasing international presence. Japan, with the second-largest economy in the world conveniently concentrated on four small islands, will be our most attractive target for that effort during the 1980s. Moreover, given Japan's highly visible penetration of the American economy and the potential for resentment that it incurs, a failure to more effectively exploit Japan's market will guarantee a continuation of U.S.-Japan political frictions of the very worst sort.

Later in this chapter, I will comment on that effort, especially in regard to the role of business schools, but first, I would like to consider some other factors that are likely to cause increased friction in our relationship during the 1980s as our free-world partnership matures, even if we do increase our markets in Japan. I don't want to sound pessimistic, but I think we should be realistic and face up to the problems and consider how we can deal with them. Throughout the 1970s, bilateral irritation piled upon bilateral irritation. Each incident was resolved with varying degrees of success, but not forgotten. People remember the textile dispute. What about the 1971 international monetary fracas? Do you remember the soybean boycott? I think we all do and it is remembered in Japan as well. Regrettably, the 1980s seem to be headed in the direction of more severe conflicts, unless we pay close attention to this important relationship on both sides of the Pacific.

Let's look at some specific factors. First, on the Japanese side, I believe that one of the most important and least understood potential sources of friction is the generational change. Japanese government officials and businessmen assuming leadership positions today did not start their working life until after the U.S. occupation began or even after it ended. As you might imagine, this fact makes a difference in the way that they view America and the way they shape their working relationships with us. These post-occupation officials and businessmen, I believe, tend to feel less gratitude toward their former benevolent occupiers than did their predecessors. They tend to have less patience with insensitive and poorly informed Americans of the sort that still fill their briefcases with Hershey bars in preparation for a trip to Japan and who have been schooled to expect the Japanese side to make the first concession in all negotiations. This new generation tends to be less burdened with guilt over Japan's role in World War II and is taking a fresh look at Japan's place in the world. This reassessment is a little difficult for many U.S. government and business officials, and even scholars, to understand and to accept. Especially if they have been accustomed to dealing with former Japanese counterparts who were more understanding and deferential. Americans often interpret this mood as a resurgent nationalism or worse, rather than as a return to a more balanced partnership.

I remember that about two years ago I was in the Hotel Okura in Tokyo and a very senior U.S. businessman was talking to me. It was, I think, his second trip to Japan, and while there were gaps in his knowledge, he had been told what to expect. But it became clear that Japan was nothing like what he had been told by old Japan-hands and he was furious, raging that ". . . they are worse than the French!" And I think that sums up the problem. Increasingly, Japanese representatives in this new generation will be reluctant to sit at the table down below the salt. I believe that their more assertive posture will surely ruffle the feathers of the Americans and perhaps contribute in a small way to increasing bilateral frictions.

A second problem is the gradual dispersion of power within Japan's political community. Throughout the postwar period the Liberal Democratic Party (LDP) has been the dominant force in Japanese politics. It still is today; the last election returned the party's candidates to office in record numbers. But the recent electoral success notwithstanding, I believe that during the 1980s the LDP is likely to be forced into some sort of a coalition. They stand to lose their absolute majorities in both Houses of the diet, not so much because of the skill and resources of the opposition, but simply because the party has been in power for a long time and it may fail to respond adequately to changing social and political movements. Whether or not this fundamental change in Japanese politics will be good or bad over the long term is too difficult a subject to tackle. But if it happens, it will lead to increased frictions in U.S.-Japan relations by making political coördination on the Japanese side even more difficult than it is now.

Conventional wisdom about the Japanese confirms their tendency to make decisions by a slow consensus process. Interestingly, numerical majorities just don't seem to have the legitimacy in Japan's political process that they do in our own. I believe that coalition government, when it comes, is likely to slow up the consensus process even more, especially in foreign policy decisions. And this will frustrate U.S. negotiators and help to heat up the relationship. It is likely the opposition party members will have different views of the U.S.-Japan relationship than their LDP predecessors, specifically vis-à-vis economic policies.

Another domestic factor that will complicate U.S.-Japan relations is the growing tendency of the Japanese public to demand more for themselves from government economic policy and to be less willing than in the past to defer consumption for the sake of national gain. In the postwar period, perhaps the most important factor in Japan's miraculous recovery was the fact that Japan had a ready-made and universally accepted national goal. What was that goal? To catch up. Everyone believed it. In the 40s and early 50s, the goal was to revive the Japanese standard of living to the level that the Japanese people enjoyed before the war. By the 1950s and the early 1960s the goal was to bring the Japanese standard of living — the Japanese gross national product — up to the level of some of the less prosperous European countries. But by the 1970s that goal had changed to achieving a Japanese standard of living equivalent to what Japan's news media portrayed as the U.S. standard of living. There may have been a little idealization there, but that was what they wanted to do. And they have pretty well caught up.

Another source of bilateral friction in Japan that we may see in the next ten years is a phenomenon that U.S. observers are familiar with — economic protectionism. Protectionism is not new in Japan. It was quite widely practiced during the 1950s and the 1960s and, as in all other countries, including our own, it remains in Japan to a limited degree. But when we look at Japan's past protective behavior, we notice that it was primarily devoted to infant industries. Specifically, those industries that the government and business community expected would prosper in the future. In other words, it was an attempt to become more internationally competitive rather than less. I suspect that during the 1980s Japanese protectionism will change in character and will come to look a little more like its U.S. counterpart. In other words, it will attempt to defend domestic industries in sectors with declining competitiveness that face real or perceived threats to their market from foreign competition. For the reasons outlined today, I think that it will be increasingly difficult for the government of Japan to resist the demands from industry and union representatives for protection. During the 1950s and 1960s, Japan was able to internalize some of these economic tensions and avoid the consequences of their impacting on international economic relationships. But during this decade, I think they will tend to spill over and that we will have our share of problems with them.

One final point that may cause more friction in Japan is a reëvaluation of its national defense situation and military capability. Since the 1970s, Japan's confidence in the United States as the leader of the free world has been declining. Throughout the postwar period, Japan has been greatly dependent on America for its security under the bilateral defense treaty. Shortly after the late occupation period, the self-defense forces began to grow and increase their capability, but only slowly. Americans should not underestimate the importance of that sense of security dependence in blunting the edge of Japanese resentment for some of our more blatant diplomatic pressures in the past. Partly at the insistence of the United States, Japan is very likely to substantially improve its self-defense capability. Therefore, its dependence, both real and psychological, will decline. And that will mean further problems.

Now let's look at the United States. I think that we, too, will contribute our fair share of fuel for the fire. First, we may not come to fully realize in this or the next decade the importance of the international sector of our economy. Many important Americans in government and the business community will continue to consider international trade as a charitable act — one we permit for the benefit of other countries but do not consider important enough to justify great effort on our part. Of course, our attitudes are changing; the fact that we are meeting in Lincoln, Nebraska to discuss this subject is evidence of that change, but we may not be moving fast enough to have an impact on the figures. And that's what we're talking about, isn't it? We may not be able to permanently remove balance of payments problems from the political agenda in the 1980s. Yet another factor on the U.S. side that may prove to be a problem is our tendency throughout the 1970s to almost totally externalize the causes of our current account deficits. U.S. government agencies responsible for trying to maintain some balance in our trade statistics have argued that if only our trading partners — especially Japan — would play fairly we would not have trade deficits. Given that assumption, the logical thing to do is dispatch negotiators to warn other countries to play by the rules so that the United States will not have a trade deficit. In that spirit, we dispatched wave after wave of international economic negotiators around the world on these tours of theatrical diplomacy. It was the 1970s version of an earlier theme called gunboat diplomacy. We called it economic diplomacy and we instructed our spokesmen to inform our trading partners in no uncertain terms to shape up. Now this approach to the deficit problem proved wonderfully attractive to the politicians. And it helped the Executive Branch and the Congress to avoid the hard political decisions that would have been required to really strengthen international U.S. competitiveness. And it had another short-term gain: it won elections and kept bureaucrats out of trouble.

The problem is that on examination, the argument somehow lacks intellectual appeal. How can we explain our huge surpluses with Europe — surpluses which continue to this instant — if we consider Japan's surpluses with us a result of devious dealings? I think this tendency to externalize the causes of our deficits diverts national attention and energies in the United States from the real problem, which would involve strengthening our competitiveness. In this context, I would mention one culprit — the limited knowledge in the United States about Japan. When you think about it we suffer from an information vacuum when it comes to Japan. For one thing, we do not have too many Japanese-Americans. Moreover, the language is very difficult, and the Japanese are not the most effective international communicators. This information vacuum makes it far more difficult for Americans in a decision-making capacity to make rational choices about how to deal with Japan. Very few people in the government can even read a Japanese newspaper, let alone do any substantive research on the Japanese economy. Certainly we ought to do something about that.

Nonetheless, it is possible that the pace of international economic awakening in the United States that I think we have seen over the last two years may bring sufficient American penetration of Japan's economy to reduce the temperature of bilateral relations during the 1980s to a more manageable level. As you know, there is no more effective diplomatic glue than mutual economic gain sweetened by the prospect of even greater gains in the future. For many years the U.S. academic community has played an important role in improving our ability to deal as a nation with Japan and assisting us in our efforts to take advantage of the economic opportunities. Generations of students — too few, but still generations of them — were trained to communicate in Japanese and taught to understand the cultural, social, and political forces behind Japanese reactions to our efforts and initiatives. Liberal arts programs channeled funds for travel fellowships enabling people like me to live and study in Japan for long periods of time and return with a better understanding of that society. Many of the recipients have applied training to the economic side of the U.S.-Japan relationship and are working to improve U.S. penetration of economic Japan. But the percentage of Japan studies students from the liberal arts programs who venture into the economic realm is far too small; we have too few trained people working on bilateral economic relations.

One reason seems to be the initial motivation of students who enter Japan studies programs in the liberal arts faculties. Many are interested in Japanese literature, history, arts, religion, or even politics. And only a few are really interested in economics or business. When the job market in the literature-history-politics spectrum dries up, we have some cross-overs to the business and economics side, although some of these are ill-prepared and sometimes even ill-disposed to perform well in business. Having spent 10 or 15 years of their lives learning how to read ancient Japanese text that the Japanese themselves can't read, or becoming acquainted with every major or minor Japanese political figure, they are hesitant to shift into the business world. They more or less resign themselves and decide to make the sacrifice in order to keep things going until a teaching position opens up in liberal arts. In the meantime, we meet them on the business side.

This does not mean that I disdain liberal arts Japan studies — far from it. However, I am suggesting that during the 1980s the business schools of our campuses can and should be more involved in preparing their students to deal effectively with Japan. It is too late to begin with a student who has graduated and is in his first job. But opening a department of Japan studies that is adequately staffed and financed is a luxury that even the largest business schools can ill-afford. In this context, a partial answer may be for all of us to work for more effective cross-campus coöperation between business schools and the established liberal arts Japan studies programs. Both business schools and liberal arts centers need more funding and I think there are great opportunities for coöperation and grantsmanship between the two. Presenting the potential donor with jointly sponsored projects that will bring business students opportunities to learn more from the Japan studies centers and prepare them to do business in Japan should be an attractive option. Japanese language training is just one example. While two years of Japanese language training together with a full business course load won't be enough to achieve fluency, if it is handled with the close coöperation and coördination of the business and language faculties, two years can bring that student to the point where three to six months of intensive training after graduation could bring him to fluency.

Language training is just one example. Sociologists or anthropologists specializing in Japan can participate in business school programs to prepare students to deal with the social and cultural environment in which business is done in Japan. Political scientists might teach business school students something about the lobbying procedures in Japan. The arts and literature specialists can help make our business school graduates who have decided to deal with Japan more literate citizens so that they have more social and cultural confidence in dealing in that highly competitive society.

My conclusion is that the business school side of the campus ought to initiate this cooperative effort. And as all of the graduates will need jobs, a parallel effort should be to encourage U.S. companies to look at the potential Japanese market and the possibilities of doing business there if they had the properly trained personnel. Where will they find personnel? They will be graduating from programs established especially for that purpose.

# Part II

# JAPANESE CULTURE AND JAPANESE MANAGEMENT

Japanese management is not created in a vacuum. To learn about the basic philosophy and values held by Japanese, we must study the broad cultural environment of their country. Martin H. Sours, in his "The Influence of Japanese Culture on the Japanese Management System," argues that an historical/cultural perspective is necessary to an understanding of Japanese management. He supports this thesis with a short descriptive section on the evolution of Japanese management within the modernization process of the Japanese society. He also acknowledges that a comparative management framework indicates the existence of parallel assumptions in Japanese management theory and the "human relations" school of U.S. management, but cautions against the indiscriminate application of Japanese managerial techniques in the U.S. in an effort to solve indigenous American managerial problems.

Lane Kelley and Reginald Worthley address the question of the relationship between Japanese culture and Japanese management attitudes. This is accomplished by (1) employing a research design that aids in isolating the impact of culture, (2) applying an ideal organization construct to detect changes in Japanese management attitudes, and (3) comparing and discussing Japanese managers' work motivation profiles as they pertain to the "desire for competitiveness" and "desire for security" in the job situation.

In his chapter, Magoroh Maruyama compares the covert cultural and epistemological bases behind overt forms of management practices in four cultures. Superficially similar behavior in several cultures may be anchored on very different perceptual and cognitive structures. A surface conversion to an imported method does not alter the cultural and psychological understructure, and may eventually fail like a heart transplant. A new solution, which is neither Japanese nor traditionally American, is proposed for U.S. firms.

In "Japanese Values and Management Processes," David M. Flynn explores personal values as significant affecting constructs in the behavioral expression of culture. The Japanese people are characterized as a culture with both traditional (Oriental) and modern (Western) values. Japanese management processes express Japanese values within this duality. The Japanese people are also considered to be highly adaptable to diverse situations. This adaptability may affect their traditional set of values. Their traditional family-based values, however, are expected not to change. These values are associated with nurturance and the primary importance of group goals.

"Individualism in the Japanese Management System," by C. S. Chang, analyzes the conflict between the group-oriented work behavior and individualism in Japanse organizations. Individualism in Japan has been overshadowed by this group-oriented behavior. Nonetheless, individualism does exist in Japan, and many managers and workers strive to achieve their personal goals. Japanese workers nevertheless understand well that they cannot pursue their individual aspirations openly in the system. Thus, they attempt to accomplish them within the framework of the group. There is no guarantee, however, that individual goals will be in accordance with group goals. As a result, a conflict sometimes develops in the system, and the Japanese managers try to solve it through a special type of informal gathering.

In "The Japanese Business Value System," Motofusa Murayama attempts to characterize Japanese business ethics as an integrated doctrine that can be viewed as a cause factor as well as an effect factor. To do so, the author analyzes four value dimensions: group, individual, behavioral, and philosophical values.

Finally, Robert Lange suggests in his chapter that the acceptance or rejection—hence, the success or failure—of participative management systems depends greatly upon the cultural imperatives within which these systems work. To support this idea, he has compared the traditions of northern Europe (specifically West Germany), the United States, and Japan in reference to their respective responses to feudalism and industrialism as a means of explaining their present participative and "humanistic" posture in organizational life. The author expresses concerns about a lack of "humanism" seen in the U.S. system and its ultimate effects upon U.S. organizational success, as presently manifested in a productivity crisis.

# 4

# The Influence of Japanese Culture on the Japanese Management System[1]

MARTIN H. SOURS

## INTRODUCTION

It seems self-evident that U.S. management, whether viewed from the perspective of the business administration academic or the practicing U.S. businessman, has a concern with Japanese management today. An informational overload exists consisting of materials dealing with the general subject of "how the Japanese do it" which, in turn, reflects a general awareness that productivity in Japan is higher than in the U.S. and that selective imports from Japan are more competitive in U.S. markets than domestic manufactures. The resultant impacts have created economic sectoral crises in such U.S. industries as automobiles and steel, and some U.S. industries have ceased to manufacture certain products such as color televisions, altogether.

There are two general schools of thought with regard to analysis of Japanese management. One may be called the universal or "organizational" approach, which stresses the universality of organizational principles, and concurrently hypothesizes that Japanese business has succeeded in utilizing these universal organizational and business principles in more effective ways than have U.S. corporations. The bulk of the academic analysis of the Japanese economy done by economic and business administration scholars falls into this approach. It is most susceptible to formal comparative analysis, by virtue of the analytic frameworks already established through the general study of comparative administration. For example,

William Ouchi's book, *Theory Z . . .* , is best known for its thesis "that the Japanese approach could be found among some American companies," [9, p. viii] which supports the universality of organizational principles.

The present analysis, however, proceeds from the second or "historical/cultural" approach, which posits that the Japanese managerial system is an outgrowth and reflection of the Japanese historical experience, which molded a cultural tradition quite different from that of the West. The major proponent of this approach is Edwin Reischauer of Harvard University, who comes to this subject from the discipline of history, rather than the contemporary or empirical social sciences. The differences in the two approaches, therefore, are partly a reflection of academic orientation and training, in addition to genuine differences in methodology and conclusion.

By stressing the importance of the impact of Japanese culture on Japanese management, I hope to highlight the critical differences between Japanese and U.S. management systems. The rationale for this orientation lies neither in a rejection of universalistic management principles, nor in an intent to perpetuate an irreconcilable notion that "East is East and West is West." Rather, a more balanced assessment of the particular nature of the Japanese management systems, when contrasted with that of the United States, is viewed herein as the first step toward a more fundamental understanding of Japanese management *per se*. From this perspective, two widely differing conclusions may emerge below. On the one hand, a culturally based management system, such as Japan's, ironically may be well suited to the post-industrial, information age of high global interdependence. At the same time, Japanese management, like all management systems, carries inherent limitations that require continued refinement, leaving open the possibility for U.S.-Japanese mutual benefit based upon collective learning and mutual respect for the strengths and weaknesses of each system.

The methodology utilized below will consist of two parts. First, a descriptive section will lay out the elements of the Japanese management system that are derived from the Japanese historical and cultural experience. Second, an analytic section will compare and contrast these elements with those to be found in American management practices. In the conclusion, some common Japanese and U.S. management concepts will be presented, with the aim of indicating some possible compatible areas in the management styles of the two systems.

## JAPANESE MANAGEMENT – AN HISTORICAL PERSPECTIVE

A system of Japanese management existed during the feudal *Tokugawa* era in Japanese history (roughly from 1600 to 1868), but its roots may be traced to prehistoric times. While the exact origins of the Japanese people are unknown, it is commonly believed that they go back at least 6,000 years [5, p. 327]. The earliest settlers apparently came from the northeast Asian mainland by way of Korea, and were fused with northward-bound migrants from southeast Asia who arrived in the Japanese islands by way of the China coast. Yet the island nature of Japanese geography created a barrier to continuous in-migration, and at the same time promoted the development of a homogeneous culture within the islands. Moreover, the islands of Japan are mountainous, giving rise to separate village-based populations with strong loyalties to local and regional hierarchies.

This indigenous Japanese culture was influenced over time by periodic visits by Buddhist missionaries from China, which contributed to the codification of basic assumptions about life and ultimately resulted in the development of a philosophical tradition based, in part, on Chinese Confucianism. The Confucian tradition valued external order and harmony within the society, while at the same time emphasizing the collective aspect of the social order. This point is extremely important in understanding the root philosophical foundation of Japanese management, which rests ultimately on a rejection of Western individualism. Its tradition stresses a living human society, rather than salvation of the individual in life after death, and within that society, the natural order as represented by people living in a human community, rather than by individuals living in a "state of nature" (as suggested by the individualist Rousseau, who believed that society corrupted the individual).

Returning to the formative *Tokugawa* period (1600 to 1868), M. Y. Yoshino has identified a set of values which came to form the particular value system for the Japanese leaders [11, Chap. I]. These leaders were the hereditary *samurai* class, a group of warrior-knights for whom the highest virtue was loyalty. Their code may be summarized by three terms: *giri*, a complex notion of duty; *on*, the concept of benevolence, and thus obligation to those of lesser status; and *ninjo*, or human feeling — a kind of tolerance for human nature. Greatly simplified, these values created in the *samurai* class what would be today classified as a professional code of ethics.

The *samurai* were viewed as inherently superior, but they had to perpetually justify this preferential status by being loyal to their feudal leaders, executing their duty, and caring for those subordinate to them. With the abolition of the feudal order in 1868 by the Meiji Restoration and the establishment of a constitutional political order under the Emperor Meiji, these values were transferred to the managerial class in industrializing Japan, and so from the beginning of Japanese modernization, those Japanese who led the industrialization process had a self-image of a highly professionalized occupational group. They transferred their loyalty, which had previously been directed toward the feudal lords, to the corporations to which they attached themselves for their entire lives. Thus, their own professional development became synonymous with the development of the firm, and they were rewarded for this dedication by a system of benefits which set them apart from others in the society. Ultimately, the Japanese society as a whole acceded to this system, because general societal values accepted the notion of hierarchy and privilege as long as this form of elitism justified itself through legitimate behavior.

The specifics of the Japanese management system flow from these historical roots. Today the "ideal" Japanese manager is a generalist, that is, a person who is initially hired because of the overall personal characteristics he possesses, rather than technical, specific skills. These general, personal qualities, in turn, are determined or assumed by the college attended rather than the specific major subject studied. If a person is admitted to a "good" school — it must be located in Tokyo, the national capital, and have a very difficult entrance examination — then the individual is assumed to be "good." Since a manager will remain with a single company for his entire career (a fact guaranteed by the common personnel practices of *all* companies, as well as the values of the society itself), there is little concern about specific managerial skills, for these are assumed to be teachable, and the return to the company for in-house training in the tools of analysis is systematically guaranteed by the life-time employment of the manager. In brief, Japanese firms recruit managers almost exclusively on the basis of potential.

Also, managers of firms relate to each other and to managers of other firms in what would be considered a traditional manner. Japanese firms tend to be highly specialized, yet concurrently form into loosely organized conglomerates. Relations between member firms are continuous, harmonious, and ongoing, as are the relationships among the management groups in each member firm of the conglomerate. These relationships are based on close face-to-face contact and rarely rely on formal written contracts and/or other forms of memoranda. Robert Reich of the U.S. Federal Trade Commission has been quoted as saying that one Japanese lawyer exists for every 10,000 Japanese citizens, while the U.S. ratio is 20 lawyers to each 10,000 U.S. citizens [8, p. 4]. This reliance on professional, full-time "interpreters" is reflective of "paper entrepreneurialism" in the United States, but also demonstrates, by contrast, the high degree of unspecified trust and obligation assumed by Japanese managers in their mutual dealings, both intra-firm and inter-firm.[2]

Another historically determined characteristic is the relatively long time line used in developing managerial decisions. Within the Japanese setting, there is not the same compulsion to demonstrate decisiveness by making sharp, clear, individual decisions in a condensed time period. On the contrary, the "good" Japanese manager is deliberate and consultative and, therefore, leads more by example than by hierarchical authority. These characteristics result both from a sense of a long historical tradition in Japan which implies that problems will be around forever, and the need to consult and bring many minds to bear upon a problem, again a negation of the concept of individual responsibility. The result is the well-known Japanese *ringi* consensus decision-making system.

The *ringi-sei* is a document circulated from the bottom levels of management to the top and requires the signature or "seal" of each manager at each level involved before a decision can be implemented. The role of top management in this process is to create an atmosphere in which the relevant levels and departments can reconcile their differences and reach a consensus as to the proper course of action.

Several important principles emerge from this approach. First, participation at all levels is automatically sought, and no one can be bypassed. Second, each participating department is involved in a project from its inception; therefore, those "closest to the action," who will ultimately be responsible for the project's implementation, have an opportunity to provide initial input. Third, *all* relevant elements within an organization, even those not directly participating, are informed of an anticipated action from the beginning. Finally, the approach puts into practice the theory of positive and active staff and personnel development, in that people at all levels must get involved in a project and thus gain experience in a collective setting.

The emphasis in this process is not the relatively long lead time necessary to generate a project, but the extremely rapid implementation phase once a project has been agreed upon. This stands in contrast to the practice of "Theory X" in U.S. management, wherein decisions are made at the top and communicated from the top to the bottom. Using the latter method, rapid decisions are possible, but resistance may develop to a decision made at the top of an organization at one or several levels, and this may result in delays, resistance, or even obstruction. Thus the Japanese consensus decision-making system may be said to be characterized by the need for feedback and control *before* a decision is reached, while the American managerial philosophy stresses the need for feedback and control *after* a decision is communicated, i.e., in the implementation phase.

Having structured a decision-making system which maximizes involvement and participation, the Japanese society developed a work ethic to complement it. Much of the current U.S. social and business commentary on Japan focuses on the propensity of Japanese to work hard and long hours. Two major factors account for this trait. The first, already suggested above, is that since all participants are involved in any project from its inception, each individual's status and reputation rests, in part, upon the successful completion of the project. This may be viewed as a sort of generalized system of management by objectives, wherein the goals are defined by all in advance, and thus all participating personnel have a direct and ongoing stake in a successful project completion. Thus, there is a natural propensity for all to be totally committed to success, and increased effort is a logical result.

This dedication is reinforced by the fatalistic view of life shared by many Japanese. Japan is a poorly endowed country whose history has been filled with numerous natural disasters (earthquakes and typhoons) and unsuccessful struggles against foreign powers culminating in the forced opening of its borders to Western trade in the mid-nineteenth century and its defeat in World War II. As a result, if one may generalize, the Japanese usually tend to anticipate the worst and see the arrival of bad times as inevitable. Where there is a general belief that a "rainy day" will come, so there is a perceived need to prepare for it, and the historical experience of a poor, agrarian country translates into a cultural norm that has become a stimulus for a work ethic in modern times.

Given the above, the lack of distinction between a manager's private life and his public or working life in Japan becomes more understandable. The long hours spent by Japanese employees at work or with working colleagues are a natural part of a Japanese manager's life. The willingness of Japanese managers to commit themselves in an open-ended way to their companies makes for a different concept of time. Time in Japanese managerial circles is relative and revolves around the notion of "whatever it takes to get the job done." This contributes to the statistically high productivity ratings in Japan, for if productivity is measured and quantified along traditional American lines with traditional American assumptions about the amount of time devoted to work, one finds that the Japanese manager's open-ended commitment to his firm and to his colleagues translates into increased output resulting from essentially hidden costs.

At the same time, the opposite extreme manifests itself within another part of the Japanese society, in that a Japanese manager's personal and family life is considered extremely private and is not brought into contact with the work setting. This results in most business entertaining being done in clubs and restaurants, utilizing company expense accounts. The net result of this dichotomy is a strong, open-ended commitment by the individual manager to the firm with the concurrent acceptance of a reduction in his private life and free time, yet a nearly complete separation of his private from his corporate life.

Finally, Japanese managerial advancement and promotion procedures are derived from classical Asian assumptions about age and seniority. The Japanese promote personnel fundamentally under a seniority system, modified only by considerations of merit based on his work over a long period of time. This means that rank is virtually guaranteed to an individual by his longevity with the firm, as opposed to the concept of a "fast track," wherein a manager may rise rapidly. The job status and security of a Japanese manager allows him the freedom to develop his subordinates and, in fact, a manager is judged in part on his ability to "bring other along" in their own career development. The long time line for promotion to truly top management means that the assessment process is spread over a number of years, during which time promotion is relatively automatic. All this enhances the feeling of job security for the individual manager, and *within the Japanese managerial context* is a motivator for higher productivity.

The contrast between this approach and U.S. management practices is striking. Increasingly, job performance, which in the American context means short-term, measurable performance, has come to determine an U.S. executive's bonuses and stock options. "The trend is unquestionably to put more emphasis than ever on performance," says George A. Goddu, a partner at Peat, Marwick, Mitchell & Co., the New York accounting firm. "Few annual bonuses are discretionary any more, and more long-term stock plans are linked to company profitability in some way." [4, p. 48]

Just as Japanese staff development is viewed as part of an overall managerial process, the Japanese use of quality control circles, or participative management-labor relations, is derived from the foregoing assumptions. Japanese management, being secure both in terms of status and position, is free to interact on an ongoing basis with workers, and thus there are few formal barriers to two-way communication between the quality-control groups — the workers and the managers. Quality control groups are an output of a broader system of management-labor relations and a Japanese managerial philosophy that rests on assumptions intuitively understood and accepted by the Japanese society as a whole.

## COMPARATIVE/ORGANIZATIONAL CHARACTERISTICS

Scholars have identified several structural elements in Japanese management principles that effect the conduct of Japanese managers in ways that contrast sharply with American practices. For example, Vogel's research has convinced him "that Japanese success ha[s] less to do with traditional character traits than with specific organizational structures, policy programs, and conscious planning," [10, p. ix] in other words, transferable organizational skills. His central thesis holds that "if any single factor explains Japanese success, it is the group-directed quest for knowledge." [10, p. 27] Yet, this universalism implies an elitist meritocracy conforming to traditional Confucian principles, and as Vogel himself points out, it manifests itself in life-long training and development programs, the use of in-house consultants and a more total commitment by Japanese management to move into the "post-industrial" or "information" societies hypothesized by theorists such as Peter Drucker and Daniel Bell.

A second systemic element relates to the functionalization of Japanese firms. Each firm tends to specialize in a particular enterprise, and may even specialize within an industry. This high degree of specialization is possible because of the high degree of interdependence among firms, which ultimately rests on the professionalism of the Japanese managers involved. But the key point, identified by Rodney Clark, is that "functionalization lessens the emphasis on financial management within the firm. The language of management in a diversified company necessarily has to be finance . . . "

> Such a method of management helps to ensure the efficient use of the company's —and by extension, the community's—resources. The disadvantage, however, is that while money unites different parts of the organization, it divides different groups and categories of people associated with the company. [2, p. 63]

Thus the managers of Japanese firms tend to be more marketing and production oriented, rather than displaying the concern with accounting and finance that has developed within U.S. management. This marketing orientation ultimately results in higher profits and greater market penetrating because line management talent is concentrated on problem solving instead of protecting against excessive staff oversight.

Finally, Peter Drucker has argued that the financial structure of Japanese firms greatly influences managerial goals and performance [3, pp. 228–48]. Japanese firms are characterized by a large degree of debt financing which, coupled with high fixed costs due to long-term contracts for raw materials and a permanent work force created by life-time employment practices, has created a high degree of both financial and operating leverage. This condition makes it rational to increase production and aim for a high volume of sales in almost any business situation. Drucker's major thesis is that increased production volume translates directly to increased productivity in the Japanese firm.

These ideas provide insights into Japanese corporate behavior, but a more specific focus on management styles shows that elements of the Japanese managerial philosophy outlined above are contained in what may be called the "human relations" approach to management as it is understood in the United States. These elements of management include the principles of (1) harmony, not discord, (2) coöperation, not individualism, and (3) the development of each man to his greatest efficiency and prosperity. Likewise, Henri Fayol's principles of management contained such "Japanese" concepts as order, equity, stability of tenure of personnel, ésprit de corps, and subordination of individual interests to the general interest. Likewise, Lyndall Urwick advocated direct interaction between supervisors and subordinate personnel in order to settle issues and to implement decisions collectively taken.

More obviously, Abraham Maslow's theory of human needs is directly compatible with the concepts of Japanese management. His preference for "problem-centering" is directly linked to the Asian notion of the whole person, and his conceptualization of "self-actualization" is directly related at the theoretical level to the commitment of the Japanese manager to his firm, and through his firm to an achievement greater than a single person. Douglas McGregor's "Theory Y" and Mason Hare's formulation of the "work-centered group" represent Japanese managerial and organizational forms in virtually their pure state. Finally, Harold Koontz's direct theory of control, which advocates the selection of the best and most loyal people and letting them control an operation, explicitly invokes Japanese concepts, yet it does so within an entirely American context.

In sum, it may be noted that the classical writers in Western and American management thought have identified common principles that they have presented as part of their overall conceptualization of "management." The Japanese perspective of management, on the other hand, has placed almost total reliance on the human factors within general management theory and then assumed other elements (planning, control, organization) would "logically" follow. Thus, rather than rejecting formal universalistic and comparative analysis, this author has tended to recognize the commonality of U.S. and Japanese management in the abstract, with regard to the human side of management, and therefore, acknowledges the universality of the human relations principles that are contained in the study of management, generally. At the same time, the differing cultural and historical foundations upon which these common human management principles rest requires differing companion principles. This approach may be more insightful, if less complete, than formal comparative modeling.[3]

## CONCLUSIONS

On one level, two major conclusions concerning the Japanese managerial style have emerged. To be seen accurately, Japanese management must be studied within the context of the society of which it is a part. So much of Japanese managerial behavior is determined by its setting that one is tempted to posit that modern Japan constitutes a social system in the most complete sense of the term, in which cultural norms almost entirely form the system's basis and condition both inputs and outcomes. Concurrently, precisely because of this strong societal base, Japan has been able to adopt and absorb Western economic principles and techniques while retaining its own particular form of managerial organization.

Second, Japanese management is human management. There exists a general consensus throughout all levels of the Japanese society that "Japan's only resource is its people." [6, p. 18] Thus, in any managerial decision, so-called "people questions" are going to receive priority; however, this universal emphasis on human management is only possible because the particular historical experience of Japan has created a consensus of values that allows for such a managerial system. Most obviously, the radically different U.S. historical tradition, let alone that of the West in general, inhibits both compatability with and understanding of the Japanese approach.

This emphasis on management as an activity of goal accomplishment through the efforts of other people has direct implications for post-industrial corporations. In the industrial age, the primary focus of management had to be production and asset management. In post-industrial corporate operations, service functions predominate, in part as a reaction to the scarcity of raw materials (and thus their high cost) and also as a natural outgrowth of technologies which emphasize information management.

The important irony to grasp is the long-standing phenomenon of a social and managerial system in Japan designed to cope with managing scarce resources. Because scarcity has been and is an inherent and natural condition in Japan, Japanese managerial techniques have evolved with an inherent emphasis on information and human management. Now the rest of the world is recognizing scarcity as an environmental factor that impacts upon all business operations world-wide. Thus, there is a natural interest in the U.S. and Europe in Japanese managerial processes explicitly adapted to such conditions.

Much has been written about learning from Japan. Some of the assertions involve U.S. management — advocating more risk-taking, more concern for workers, and the development of a participative system of decision making. The conclusions that emerge from this analysis are of a somewhat different cast. In the first place, American management cannot adopt a longer view until systemic changes that reduce the need to constantly watch "bottom line" short-term matters are implemented. This would involve changes in accounting principles, executive compensation programs, and capital markets. Because such fundamental shifts in the domestic economy appear remote, a different, more incremental approach to integrating elements of Japanese and U.S. management seems more realistic.

One possible area of future research would involve the impact on management of greater job security resulting from a longer evaluative period. Such experiments might be carried out by setting stock options and bonuses aside in trust, to be lost only if the manager left the firm before his multi-year contract expired. Then the manager would have a more extended time period within which to innovate, take risks, develop knowledge-intensive operations, and generally modernize.

Moreover, the adversary system in the United States has in large part created an environment within which risk (generalized) has become too costly. Yet, this adversary system lies at the heart of the individualism which powers and motivates people in America. Thus, managerial tools that "collectivize" adversary relationships need to be developed, so that competitive efforts may be directed outward rather than inward, creating self-destructive forces inside the firm. The *Business Week* analysis calling for a "new social compact" at both the firm and societal levels goes a long way in this direction [1, pp. 86–102].

Finally, given the mass of material available on Japanese business and the amount of discussion the topic has generated, a healthy recognition that Japan is "different" from the United States may be helpful. So much effort has been directed at discovering a nonexistent secret, or manipulating data to prove one or another points in support of the status quo (i.e., "There are no American businessmen who speak Japanese" — if this were a real problem, business schools and corporations would train managers in the Japanese language), that little effort can be expended at real issues.

Simply put, high Japanese productivity has resulted from a system of incentives that rewards productivity. As a result, Japanese managers can structure their operations to become more capital- and knowledge-intensive because such changes do not threaten the vested interests of employees. This conclusion is now supported by detailed research comparing similar enterprises in Japan and the United States. In the case of automobiles, for example, the factory organization of a Ford plant requires twelve layers of management to Toyota's seven [7, pp. 92–97]. These studies do not expand on the underlying theme that Japanese management, rooted in a cultural tradition of corporate loyalty, does not require the excessive staff supervision discussed above in order to assure minimum results.

Rather than creating slothful, disinterested employees, job security in Japan has liberated creative talents which, in turn, have propelled Japanese firms to the forefront of world production. Technology, viewed superficially as the antithesis of an Asian, culturally based management system, has instead been internalized into a culture-bound human management system. Such an approach tends to appear illogical by Western, materialistic, and individualistic standards. Yet, the very success of the Japanese economy demonstrates the validity of such an approach in Japan for the Japanese. By contrast, U.S. "reindustrialization" may need to find an approach compatible with its own historical and cultural experience, rather than simply seek a "quick fix" from abroad.

# FOOTNOTES

[1]The author wishes to express his appreciation to Professor Joseph Schabacker, Department of Management, Arizona State University, for his critical review of an earlier version of this article.

[2]For an in-depth case study on this point, see "Sumitomo: How the 'Keiretsu' Pulls Together to Keep Japan Strong," *Business Week*, March 31, 1975, pp. 43–48.

[3]See, for example, Charles Y. Yang, "Management Styles: American vis-à-vis Japanese," in Harold Koontz, Cyril O'Donnel and Heinz Weihrich, editors. *Management: A Book of Readings.* (New York: McGraw-Hill, 5th edition, 1980), pp. 98–104.

# BIBLIOGRAPHY

[1] "A Solution: A New Social Contract." *Business Week*, June 30, 1980.

[2] Clark, Rodney. *The Japanese Company.* New Haven, Connecticut: Yale University Press, 1979.

[3] Drucker, Peter F., "Economic Realities and Enterprise Strategy," in Ezra F. Vogel, ed., *Modern Japanese Organization and Decision Making.* Berkeley, California: University of California Press, 1975.

[4] "Executive Pay Raises Likely to be Less in 1981: Bonuses and Perks Keyed to Job Performance," *The Wall Street Journal*, November 17, 1980.

[5] Fairbank, John K., Edwin O. Reischauer, and Albert M. Craig. *East Asia: Tradition and Transformation.* Boston: Houghton Mifflin Company, 1973.

[6] Ibe, Kyonosuke. "It Took the Japanese to Build Japan." *Business Week*, October 6, 1980.

[7] "Labor: Japan's Edge in Auto Costs." *Business Week*, September 14, 1981.

[8] *News from Japan*, Washington International Communications. Washington, D.C., September 5, 1980.

[9] Ouchi, William. *Theory Z: How American Business Can Meet the Japanese Challenge.* Reading, MA: Addison-Wesley Publishing Company, 1981.

[10] Vogel, Ezra F. *Japan As No. 1: Lessons for America.* Cambridge, MA: Harvard University Press, 1979.

[11] Yoshino, M. Y. *Japan's Managerial System.* Cambridge, MA: The MIT Press, 1968.

# 5

# Japanese Management and Cultural Determinism

LANE KELLEY and REGINALD WORTHLEY

## INTRODUCTION

At a recent lecture series by the Pacific Asian Management Institute, University of Hawaii, a distinguished researcher in cross-cultural studies negated the value of such work in comparative management during the last two decades. This is a depressing posture to be taken by an individual who has few equals in the area of cross-cultural research in terms of sophistication, size of effort, and reputation. Perhaps this conclusion in part reflects the tremendous difficulties in conducting good cross-cultural research, but then again, because of the attention given to management practices in countries such as Japan (i.e., Ouchi and Vogel), there has recently been a significant demand and pay-off for work done in this area and therefore we have seen a proliferation of "research" articles. The problem seems especially relevant for this conference because of the bombardment of propaganda concerning Japanese management practices and their applicability in the United States.

## CONTINGENCY, CONVERGENCE, CULTURAL, OR WHAT? WHERE ARE WE?

In a 1975 article, Negandhi [16] states that there is increasing evidence to support the contention that management practices, behavior, and effectiveness are as much, if not more so, functions of such contextual variables as size, technology, location, and market conditions as they are of sociocultural variables. In the same year and the same journal, Bedeian [1] stated, "It is a well-established fact that different cultures possess different organizational norms and behavior standards and that they recognize these as legitimate forms of influence." It seems that the role of culture in terms of management attitudes is still not fixed, and the confusion permeates even the most respected research on Japanese management. Marsh and Mannari [15] de-emphasize the role of culture, concluding that the Japanese factory is not fundamentally different from its Western counterpart, "and that the norm of modern, rational, bureaucratic career expectation is well internalized not only among Japanese managerial and staff employees but also among male rank and file workers."

In a study of values, England and Lee [6] report that managers from the U.S., Australia, India, and Japan were "rather similar in terms of the managerial values that were related to success; successful managers having more pragmatic, dynamic, and achievement-oriented values, while less successful managers have more static and passive values."

Harari and Zeira [9] write that there "is a similarity of perception among employees in industrialized countries, irrespective of organization behavior and corporate structure." However, "perception of desirability regarding goal definition and performance evaluation differed." Japanese working in foreign-owned MNC's considered clearly defined goals and evaluation to be more desirable than did Japanese in Japanese corporations.

Tadayoshi Yamada [20], a special executive advisor to a large Japanese corporation, reports that there are basic changes occurring in Japanese management, including more official delegation of authority, increasing number of Japanese organizations utilizing staff management, and self-supporting division systems. The cornerstones of Japanese management — paternalism and group decision making — were also reported as being critically examined by Japanese management. There seems to be basic reasons for the different positions taken by scholars regarding the linkage between culture and managerial attitudes, behavior, and effectiveness. The first problem is the vague definition of culture. In a recent paper, Child and Kieser [4] state: "Cultures may be defined as patterns of thought and manner which are widely shared. The boundaries of the social collectivity within which this sharing takes place are problematic so that it may make as much sense to refer to a class or regional culture as to a national culture." The second problem lies in the methodological difficulties of accurate translation and having a representative sample. Many studies simply do not have samples that can be considered representative. A third problem is that studies reporting to have a culture-free context are actually national studies. A comparative study of French and German managers not only compares the impact of their cultures, but also of other factors such as their political and economic systems. It might be that the cultures have similar attitudes on those variables closely associated with management, but other contextual factors are quite different. For example, the values of U.S. and English managers might be similar, or more similar, than those of Taiwanese and Korean managers. Regardless, the argument can be made that the use of a national sample is not in the strictest sense a sample testing for the impact of culture.

## PURPOSE OF THE STUDY

The purpose of the present research is to contribute to the resolution of differences between two of the most popular theoretical models in cross-cultural management studies — the Farmer-Richman and the Negandhi-Prasad models [7], [17]. The sample design used to isolate the role of culture is depicted in Figure 1.

This design reduces some of the problems associated with many of the cross-cultural studies. Negandhi [16] has said that "it appears that culture, although used as an independent variable in most cross-cultural studies, has a most obscure identity and often is used as a residual factor." An examination of Figure 1 supports his contention. Most empirical cross-cultural management studies do not isolate the impact of culture but are actually national studies that also reflect other factors, such as educational, economic, and legal systems; these factors are identified in both the Negandhi-Prasan and Farmer-Richman studies.

FIGURE 1    Research Design for Isolation of Culture

| $S_1$ CAUCASIAN AMERICAN MANAGERS | $S_2$ JAPANESE– AMERICAN MANAGERS | $S_3$ JAPANESE MANAGERS |
|---|---|---|
| Culture | Culture | Culture |
| Education | Education | Education |
| Economic | Economic | Economic |
| Legal | Legal | Legal |

The sample in this research consists of three groups: Caucasian American, Japanese-American, and Japanese managers. The Caucasian American and Japanese-American have been exposed to the same economic and legal systems, the same educational and cultural variables; the only commonality between the Japanese-American and Japanese managers is a cultural link. If the Japanese-American managers' responses are observed to be more similar to the Japanese than to those of the Caucasian Americans, the cultural link would seem to be the cause. The operational tests are:

1. Tests for differences among the responses of the three groups, with differences between Japanese and both American groups pointing to national differences, and differences between the two American groups not found between the Japanese and Japanese-American groups pointing to cultural differences.
2. Another test supporting an important role for culture in determining managerial attitudes is based on the sequence of responses for the entire set of 15 items, with the predicted positions determined by a review of the literature [3], [5], [6], [8], [9], [18], [19]. It has been postulated that the Japanese-American responses will fall between those of the Caucasian Americans and the Japanese because of their Japanese cultural heritage coupled with a lifetime exposure to the U.S. political, economic, and educational systems.

The second research projection concerns a comparison of the ideal versus the actual organization practices of the three ethnic groups. Questions have been designed to isolate the difference between the "way it is" in the respondents' respective organizations and the "way it should be." Two tests are relevant; the first is for the significant differences in satisfaction with managment practices and the second is for differences between the three groups in terms of the "ideal" organization.

The results of the research are divided into three parts. The first part considers the role of culture in management by isolating cultures in the two different countries. The second part of the findings discusses the statistical results of company "ideal organization" constructs and the respective variances in terms of how it actually is. The results of a previous study encouraged the second part of the research, which basically asks the question "How Japanese is Japanese management?" One answer is found by looking at several contextual factors relevant to management attitudes such as (1) size of organization, (2) education achievement level, (3) management level, and (4) age.

A third research finding discussed in this paper is included to help explain Japanese management practices in terms of Japanese manager attitudes. Earlier research by Borgatta and Bohrnstedt [2] indicates that U.S. managers who desire competition in the job situation are assessed by their companies as having the highest promotion potential. It was predicted that this variable would not be found desirable to Japanese managers, which would indicate that what makes for success in one culture is different from what makes for success in another.

## RESULTS

### Isolation of Culture

Table 1 identifies the management practices and attitudes included in the first study questionnaire. The direction of the hypothesis is based upon descriptive articles and empirical studies of Japanese management. The items cover written procedures (two), centralization of decision making, paternalism, diversified experience, seniority, self-motivation, team work, and company politics.

The first statistical test for difference in responses indicates a dissimilarity of responses between the American managers and the Japanese managers. Of the 11 items that showed significant differences, the Japanese group is separated from at least one American group in all 11 cases and from both American groups on 8 of these 11 items. On only three of the items is a significant difference found between the two American groups. This implies that culture is not strong enough to create significant differences in managerial attitudes but that there are "national" differences. The major obstacle in this case is the smaller sample sizes involved in comparing the two American groups (27 and 41). This is a result of the highly stratified sample needed to obtain Caucasian and Japanese-American managers similar to the Japanese group with respect to industry, management level, and age, which control for contextual factors other than nation and culture. The procedure used, distribution-free multiple comparisons based on ranks, requires much larger differences between the smaller groups in order to be designated "significantly different." In many cases the actual differences between the mean responses of the two American groups are comparable to differences between the American groups and the Japanese group. Also, if a higher level of significance is used, differences will show up between the two American groups on several other items.

The second statistical test, the sequence of responses, supports the role of culture in the formation of managerial attitudes. Nine of the 15

TABLE 1  A Summary of Results from Japanese (1), Japanese-American (2), and Caucasian American (3) Managers on 15 Likert Scale Statements Concerning Managerial Attitudes

|  | ORDER OF SAMPLE RESULTS | SIGNIFICANT* DIFFERENCES |
|---|---|---|
| *Group I Statements: The Predicted Order is 3 < 2 < 1, with the Japanese Managers in Strongest Agreement* | | |
| 1. Self-motivation | in agreement | 3 < 1 |
| 2. Self-development | in agreement | 3 < 2 < 1 |
| 3. Group appraisal (2) | in agreement | 3, 2 < 1 |
| 4. Centralized decision making | in agreement | 3, 2 < 1 |
| 5. Participation in decision making | in agreement | 3, 2 < 1 |
| 6. Long term employment | in agreement | 3, 2 < 1 |
| 7. Coöperation | in agreement | none |
| 8. Group appraisal (1) | 2,3 reversed | 2, 3 < 1 |
| 9. Promotion based on seniority (1) | in agreement | 2 < 3, 1 |
| 10. Promotion based on seniority (2) | in agreement | 2 < 1 |
| 11. Diversified experience | in agreement | none |
| 12. Respect for formal authority | in agreement | none |
| *Group II Statements: The Predicted Ordering is 1 < 2 < 3, with the Caucasian American Managers in Strongest Agreement* | | |
| 13. Company politics and career progress | in agreement | 1 < 2 < 3 |
| 14. Written procedures (2) | in agreement | 1 < 3 |
| 15. Written procedures (1) | 3 < 1 < 2 | none |

*Significant differences were determined with distribution-free multiple comparisons based on Kruskal-Wallis rank sums.

items' sequence of means agree exactly with the predicted ordering. The probability of observing as many as 9 out of 15 sequences in the exact expected ordering is only .00019 (assuming a binomial model with $P = 1/6$, the six possible orderings). Of the six items in which the ordering differs from the hypothesis, only the two American groups differ in five of the cases, and only one of these (#9) reveals any significant difference between the American groups. Item #15 alone shows any substantial difference in ordering than hypothesized, and no significant difference is found on this item among any of the groups. The reader is reminded that in five of the six sequences the Japanese responses are in the predicted position, but not the responses of the Japanese-Americans which, although they are "out of place," are not significantly different than the Caucasian Americans' responses. The reader is also reminded of the very small probability (.00019) of having 9 out of 15 sequences in their predicted position.

It was expected by the authors, and supported by the results, that it would be more difficult to separate the two American groups from each other in terms of managerial attitudes than to show differences between them and the Japanese groups. Of the 11 items that showed significant differences, the Japanese group is separated from at least one American group in all 11 cases and from both American groups on 8 of these 11 items. On only three of the items is a significant difference found between the two American groups. The authors feel that the lack of significant differences between the two American groups, despite the preponderance of items in predicted order, is due mainly to the difficulty involved in obtaining large samples for them that are comparable in terms of education, age, and managerial level in a similar organization.

## Contextual Factors

The questionnaire items used in the first study were prefaced by the phrase "in well-managed companies." The results indicate that culture is associated with managerial attitudes, but to what degree is it associated with other variables such as 1) size of organization, 2) management level, and 3) age? The sample for this study was taken at the Japan American Institute of Management Sciences in Honolulu.

Size of organization would seem to be related to a difference in the formation of ideal management practices. The interpretation of these results is constrained by the fact that of the 97 Japanese managers in the sample, 72 were in organizations larger than 1000 employees, 8 in organizations with 500 to 999, 9 in organizations with 250 to 499, and 8 in organizations with less than 250 employees. (The only variable reaching significance [$x^2 = 40.72859$, with 12 d.f., sig. $= .0001$] was the belief in self-development with the larger organizations managers showing stronger feelings.) (See Table 2.)

Management level is the second contextual factor considered for differentiation of Japanese management styles. The statistical results indicate that the influence of management level is not crucial in terms of eight variables, but is in terms of top and middle management having stronger feelings for 1) formal authority and 2) self-development. (See Table 3.)

The statistical analysis for age as a contributing factor of Japanese manager attitude is no stronger than the other contextual factors, with only self-development indicating a significant difference. The relatively small size of the $x^2$ values suggests that age is not a critical factor in the formation of Japanese manager attitudes and that the idea of rapid changes in what is called Japanese management is not well founded.

TABLE 2   Size of Organization

|  | $x^2$ (12df) | LEVEL OF SIGNIFICANCE |
|---|---|---|
| 1. Coöperation | 14.08331 | .2954 |
| 2. Formal authority | 19.72926 | .0724 |
| 3. Written procedures | 15.35665 | .2225 |
| 4. Paternalism | 5.94842 | .9187 |
| 5. Self-development | 40.72859 | .0001 |
| 6. Group appraisal | 6.22144 | .9045 |
| 7. Nepotism | 15.44776 | .2179 |
| 8. Participation indecisions | 14.88566 | .2477 |
| 9. Promotion via seniority | 4.35737 | .8864 |
| 10. Diversified experience | 13.63226 | .3248 |

## Changes in Management Attitudes

Are the attitudes converging? What are the directions of change? One set of questions was structured to provide an indication of the direction of change by having the first response prefaced by "the way it is" and the second response by "the way it should be." A significant difference would favor future change. The sample for this study was the same as the first research study reported: Japanese, Japanese-American, and Caucasian American managers. Comparing the three group responses, we find that the Japanese managers' ideal organization is more concerned with (1) teamwork, (2) the role of respect for authority, (3) self-development, (4) group appraisal, (5) nepotism, and (6) long-term employment in the con-

TABLE 3   Japanese Management Ideal Organizations and Management Level

|  | $x^2$ (8df) | LEVEL OF SIGNIFICANCE |
|---|---|---|
| 1. Coöperation | 14.80855 | .0630 |
| 2. Formal authority | 16.64043 | .0341 |
| 3. Written procedures | 8.42324 | .3933 |
| 4. Paternalism | 8.46955 | .3890 |
| 5. Self-development | 7.12708 | .5230 |
| 6. Group appraisal | 9.30957 | .8169 |
| 7. Nepotism | 6.20532 | .6242 |
| 8. Participation indecisions | 7.96811 | .4366 |
| 9. Promotion via seniority | 10.65948 | .0995 |
| 10. Diversified experience | 12.75952 | .1204 |

struction of an ideal organization than their counterparts. But what are the practices where change can be expected?

Five of the variables at the .05 level of significance, and one other variable at the .10 level of significance indicate a difference in congruency between the "way it is" and the "way it should be," which suggests forces for change. The management variables that indicate statistical differences in congruency are teamwork, paternalism, group appraisal, seniority, and diversified experience.

All three groups responded that individuals should work together more rather than to strive for individual recognition, with the two American groups' responses reporting the strongest incongruency between the "way it is" and "should be". On paternalism, the responses of the American samples indicate there should be a greater concern for their subordinates but responses of the Japanese managers project less concern with the personal problems of their employees. The responses of the three groups in terms of group appraisal also varied, with the older Caucasians and younger Japanese supporting a stronger emphasis on group appraisal. Tenure within one's organization — long-term or lifetime employment — has usually been synonymous with Japanese management, but the responses indicate that all three ethnic groups feel tenure should be emphasized less. If the level of significance is increased to .10, the respect for authority variable is also significant for the Japanese, supporting greater respect for authority in their organizations.

## Motivational Profile of the Japanese Manager

Research reported by Borgatta and Bohrnstedt has identified two variables that seem to be important for success in U.S. organizations, the "desire to compete" and the "desire for competition." The 21-item instrument was translated into Japanese, and the translation verified the same way as for the first study. We do not have comparable norms at this point controlling for industry, age, management level, etc., but the comparison with Borgatta and Bohrnstedt's norm encourages further research and explains the connection between the individual Japanese manager's values and "Japanese organization's." U.S. managers with high "competitiveness" scores and low to moderate "security" scores were perceived by their superiors as having more potential. This supervisory perception has been shown by other research to predict success. It is unknown if this sample was one of "successful" or "average" managers but their organizations had seen fit to send them to a seminar 5000 miles away from home in Hawaii which suggests, at least to these authors, relatively successful managers. The median position of the Japanese responses on the "desire to compete" scale was at the 10th

FIGURE 2  Desire to Compete and for Security Scale

TEST

Below is a list of job characteristics. Alongside it is a desirability scale. After each characteristic, circle the number under the heading that best reflects your feeling.

| JOB CONDITIONS | COMPLETELY UNDESIRABLE, WOULD NEVER TAKE JOB | UNDESIRABLE, WOULD AVOID THE JOB | IRRELEVANT, NEUTRAL, OR DO NOT KNOW | DESIRABLE, WOULD FAVOR THE JOB | EXTREMELY DESIRABLE, WOULD FAVOR JOB GREATLY |
|---|---|---|---|---|---|
| 1. Salary increases would be strictly a matter of how much you accomplished for the company. | 0 | 1 | 2 | 3 | 4 |
| 2. The emphasis would be on carrying out clearly outlined company policies. | 0 | 1 | 2 | 3 | 4 |
| 3. The company is known to be involved in heavy competition. | 0 | 1 | 2 | 3 | 4 |
| 4. Seniority is considered very important for promotion. | 0 | 1 | 2 | 3 | 4 |
| 5. Persons are supposed to get the boot if they don't make good and keep making good. | 0 | 1 | 2 | 3 | 4 |
| 6. The job is managing a small group of people doing routine jobs. | 0 | 1 | 2 | 3 | 4 |
| 7. There are opportunities to earn bonuses. | 0 | 1 | 2 | 3 | 4 |
| 8. The work would be routine, but would not be hard to do. | 0 | 1 | 2 | 3 | 4 |

| | | | | | |
|---|---|---|---|---|---|
| 9. Competition would be open and encouraged. | 0 | 1 | 2 | 3 | 4 |
| 10. I would work as a member of a more-or-less permanent group. | 0 | 1 | 2 | 3 | 4 |
| 11. The supervisor might be highly critical. | 0 | 1 | 2 | 3 | 4 |
| 12. The pay is not too high, but the job is secure. | 0 | 1 | 2 | 3 | 4 |
| 13. There is emphasis on the actual production record. | 0 | 1 | 2 | 3 | 4 |
| 14. The work is routine, but the initial salary is high. | 0 | 1 | 2 | 3 | 4 |
| 15. Salary increases would be a matter of how much effort you put in. | 0 | 1 | 2 | 3 | 4 |
| 16. I would be under civil service. | 0 | 1 | 2 | 3 | 4 |
| 17. The rewards could be great, but many people are known to fail or quit. | 0 | 1 | 2 | 3 | 4 |
| 18. Promotions come automatically. | 0 | 1 | 2 | 3 | 4 |
| 19. The work is routine, but highly respected in the community. | 0 | 1 | 2 | 3 | 4 |
| 20. The salary increases are regularly scheduled. | 0 | 1 | 2 | 3 | 4 |
| 21. There would be emphasis on satisfying superiors by carrying out company policy. | 0 | 1 | 2 | 3 | 4 |

percentile of the U.S. distribution and the 65th percentile of the "desire for security" scale. At least for his sample, the Japanese attitude profile was very different than the U.S. profile and more in line with an "organizational man" construct. For example, the Japanese manager's responses were favorable to an environment in which "the emphasis would be on carrying out clearly outlined company policies: "I would work as a member of a more-or-less permanent group" and "the work is routine, but highly respected in the community."

In order to come to any conclusions on these two variables, additional research is required, but the larger difference in the sample distribution does suggest a different motivational pattern. If management style and practices are contingent on the attitudes and values of managers and employees, then it is indicated again that Japanese management is a reflection of their culture.

## CONCLUSIONS

The purpose of the chapter is to look at Japanese and U.S. management attitudes and the role of culture. This is accomplished by (1) a research design planned to isolate culture, specifically the Japanese-American in Hawaii, (2) comparing the "ideal" organization construct and possible changes, (3) looking at Japanese management attitudes in term of age, management level, and other contextual factors, and (4) addressing the question of the motivational profile of the Japanese manager and its role on management practices.

The results of the first study indicate that culture is related to managerial attitudes. The managerial attitudes of Japanese-American managers are a result not only of their present political, educational, and legal environment but also of their culture. Their managerial attitudes are between those of Caucasian American and Japanese managers. A previous study by Kelley and Reeser [11] indicates that Japanese-American managers in Hawaii have managerial attitudes different from Caucasian managers. The present research shows that this difference is in the direction of their culture.

The results of this study support the position of Farmer and Richman on the role of culture in the formation of managerial attitudes and not the position of Negandhi-Prasad, who de-emphasize culture's role. This does not, however, negate the importance Negandhi places on other contextual variables such as organization size, technology, location, and market position. For example, in two research articles by Harari and Zeira ([9], [10]), it is reported that Japanese working in foreign-owned multinational corporations considered clearly defined goals and evaluation to be more desirable than did Japanese employees in Japanese corporations. The results of the Harari and Zeira studies and the contextual factors emphasized by Negandhi's research [16], (size, technology, location, and market) have been shown to be significant in their research, but the present study supports the importance of culture — at least for the Japanese — in the formation of managerial attitudes.

The second study reinforces the position of culture with the Japanese ideal organization more concerned with team effort, respect for authority, self-development, group appraisal, nepotism and long-term employment — the basic elements of what is considered to be "Japanese" management. The research indicates potential changes in Japanese management practices to be (1) less paternalistic attitudes and (2) less emphasis on seniority.

The third study reiterates the notion of the homogeneity of Japanese management attitudes. The impact of age, education, size of organization and management had little impact on managerial attitudes. The last study should only be considered in terms of possible hypotheses for future research, but the differences in the desire to compete and for security are so large that it appears that the Japanese personnel practices are a reflection of motivational profile. A previous study by Kelley, Rollins, and Whatley [13] found this to be true also for Japanese-Americans and Caucasian Americans. In summary, this paper supports the role of culture in the formation of managerial attitudes.

It is felt by the authors that first there are management practices that are culturally free — that is, they are relatively value-less — e.g., practices concerning inventory control. If we compare inventory practices and find that they are the same, however, it doesn't mean that other management practices in the same organizations are more value-related (for example, delegation) are also culture-free. Second, we need to develop a typology of cultures that includes the cultural variables complimentary to industrialization (or different types of industrialization). For example, the following characteristics would seem crucial for industrial organizations: respect for authority, a desire to achieve, an orientation toward the future, materialistic values, coöperative rather than competitive behavior, other-directed behavior, group versus individual orientation, and controlled versus spontaneous behavior. A contingency approach seems to conclude that management practices for a culture with these values would be necessarily different than cultures with different values.

# BIBLIOGRAPHY

[1] Bedeian, Arthur. "A Comparison and Analysis of German and United States Managerial Attitudes toward the Legitimacy of Organizational Influence." *Academy of Management Journal*, 18(4), 1975, p. 897.

[2] Borgatta, E. F. and Bohrnstedt, G. W. "Up." *Psychology Today*, January, 1971, pp. 57–58.

[3] Brown, William. "Japanese Management — The Cultural Background." *Culture and Management: Text and Readings in Comparative Management*, edited by Rose A. Webber. Homewood, Ill.: Irwin, 1969, pp. 428–42.

[4] Child, John, and Kieser, Alfred. "Contrasts in British and West German Management Practice: Are Recipes for Success Culture-bound?" Paper presented at the conference on Cross-cultural Studies on Organizational Functioning, Hawaii, 1977.

[5] Drucker, Peter F. "What We Can Learn from Japanese Management." *Harvard Business Review*. Vol. 49, No. 2, 1971, pp. 110–22.

[6] England, G. W., and Lee, R. "The Relationship between Managerial Values and Managerial Success in the United States, Japan, India, and Australia." *Journal of Applied Psychology*, 59(4), 1974, pp. 411–19.

[7] Farmer, Richard, and Richman, Barry. "A Model for Research in Comparative Management." *California Management Review*, 4(2), 1964, pp. 55–68.

[8] Froomkin, Joseph. "Management and Organization in Japanese Industry." *Academy of Management Journal*, 1964, Vol. 7, pp. 71–76.

[9] Harari, Ehud, and Zeira, Yoram. "Attitudes of Japanese and Non-Japanese Employees: A Cross-national Comparison in Uninational and Multinational Corporations." *International Journal of Comparative Sociology*, Vol. 18(3–4), Sept.–Dec. 1977.

[10] Harari, Ehud, and Zeira, Yoram. "Training Expatriates for Managerial Assignments in Japan." *California Management Review*, Summer 1978.

[11] Kelley, L., and Reeser, C. "The Persistence of Culture as a Determinant of Differentiated Attitudes on the Part of American Managers of Japanese Ancestry." *Academy of Management Journal*, 16(1), 1973, pp. 67–76.

[12] Kelley, L., and Worthley, R. "The Role of Culture in Comparative Management: A Cross-Cultural Perspective." *Academy of Management Journal*, (24)1, 1981, pp. 164–73.

[13] Kelley, L., Whatley, A., and Rollins, B. Socio-Personal Correlates of Competitiveness and Security in the Job Situation. Paper presented at the Western Regional Academy of Management, Las Vegas, April, 1975.

[14] Kerr, C., Dunlop, J., Hazbison, F., and Myers, C. "Industrialism and Industrial Man." Oxford University Press, 1964.

[15] Marsh, R., and Mannari, H. "Lifetime Commitment in Japan: Roles, Norms and Values." *American Journal of Sociology*, pp. 795–812.

[16] Negandhi, Anant R. "Comparative Management and Organizational Theory: A Marriage Needed. *Academy of Management Journal*. 18(2), 1975, pp. 334–44.

[17] Negandhi, Anant R., and Prasad, S. B. *Comparative Management*. Appleton-Century Crofts, 1971.

[18] Noda, Kazuo, and Glazer, Herbert, "Traditional Japanese Management Decision Making," *Management International Review*, Vol. 8, 1968.

[19] Smith, Thomas C. *The Agrarian Origins of Modern Japan*. Stanford, Calif.: Stanford University Press, 1959.

[20] Yamada, T. Japanese Management Practices. *The Conference Board Record*, Vol. VI(II), pp. 22–23.

# 6

# Mindscapes, Workers, and Management: Japan and the U.S.A.

MAGOROH MARUYAMA

## CULTURAL DIFFERENCES

It is often said that it was U.S. theorists who built the conceptual framework for participatory management as well as quality control, and that the Japanese first imported them, subsequently tested and refined them, and are exporting them back to the U.S.A.

Obviously there is always much cross-cultural exchange of ideas and methods. But it is important to realize that many similar-looking management practices may be anchored on very different cultural and epistemological foundations, while an organization converting to a new method on the surface may still be trapped in the same epistemological structure that underlay the old method. It is important to understand the diverse cultural and epistemological bases on which apparently similar or dissimilar forms of management are built. Otherwise, we would be throwing different things into the same bag and the same things into different bags.

I would like to compare the covert cultural and epistemological bases behind various overt forms of management. Furthermore, in order to avoid falling into the usual rut of comparing only two cultures, I would like to discuss four cultures, including Japan and the U.S.A. The two other cultures, as will be seen, help us gain new insights into the differences between

Japan and the U.S.A. They are the Mandenka of West Africa and the Navajos of Arizona and New Mexico.

## MINDSCAPES

To sort things out, it is useful to compare several different epistemological structures predominant in various cultures, and examine management practices based on them. Epistemological, cognitive, cogitative, and perceptual structures, which we call "mindscapes" [10], may vary from individual to individual. In any culture, there are individual mindscape types. However, the percentage distribution of various types varies from culture to culture. Therefore different types are predominant in different cultures. Though there are many types, it is useful for practical purposes to recognize the following four, keeping in mind that there are other types as well as mixtures of types.

| TYPE | CHARACTERISTICS |
| --- | --- |
| H: | Homogenistic, hierarchical, classificational |
| I: | Heterogenistic, individualistic, random |
| S: | Heterogenistic, interactive, homeostatic |
| G: | Heterogenistic, interactive, morphogenetic |

The H-type sees homogeneity as basic, natural, desirable, and even scientific. For them, heterogeneity is due to accidents, errors, abnormalities, deviance, or mere statistical distribution with no advantage. It regards homogeneity as the basis of peace, and heterogeneity as a source of conflict, inconvenience, and inefficiency. The H-type is also hierarchical and classificational. The world is seen as consisting of categories, subcategories, and supercategories, each consisting of homogeneous individuals. In management, workers in one category are supposed to work in the same way, and this is considered to be fair, just, and even scientific. Moreover, the H-type believes that one's gain is someone else's loss (zero-sum game assumption). The management emphasizes competition against other units, and sometimes even encourages competition among the workers within the same unit.

The I-type sees individuals as different, independent, unrelated, and random. The management sees workers as a statistical aggregate of variations. It allows for individual differences, but expects a statistical average over many individuals, in which the differences cancel out. It does NOT make positive use of individual differences, NOR tries to make mutually beneficial combinations among different individuals. In fact, it assumes that individual separation will result in higher productivity (negative-sum assumption).

The S-type and G-type consider heterogeneity as basic, indispensable, and desirable. They regard homogeneity as a source of competition and conflict, and heterogeneity as the basis of mutually beneficial coöperation (positive-sum assumption). They look for and make positive-sum combinations of heterogeneous elements, both inside each unit and between units, as well as toward other firms. The difference between the S-type and the G-type is that the former is stability-oriented, while the latter is change-oriented.

## WHICH MINDSCAPE IS SCIENTIFIC?

Which type is really scientific? The recent advances in biological and social sciences are increasingly making it clear that the basic principle of biological and social processes is increases of heterogeneity and mutually beneficial combinations among heterogeneous elements due to interactive causal loops [7, 8, 9, 10]. Let us take the following examples:

Animals convert oxygen into carbon dioxide by metabolism, and plants do the opposite in their photosynthesis. Animals need oxygen, while plants need carbon dioxide. Animals and plants help each other. There are birds who eat the food debris between the teeth of alligators. The alligators get their teeth cleaned, the birds get food, and the potential predators of the birds are scared away by the alligators.

The advantages of heterogeneity among species within an ecosystem has long been appreciated. The richness of life in a tropical rain forest or on a coral reef is due to heterogeneity of species. If all animals ate the same food, there would be a food shortage, and if all species were not eaten by some other species, there would be an intolerable accumulation of corpses. Even solar energy is used maximally if different organisms use different methods to absorb it, e.g., tall trees, short trees, vines, and algae.

It is a mistake to consider the advantages of heterogeneity only in terms of resource diversification and disaster-risk dispersion, as is done too often. The argument for resource diversification is often based on the zero-sum game assumption of H-type mindscapes, and the concept of disaster-risk dispersion is rooted in the I-type thinking. Both are true and valid, but both overlook another advantage: the advantage of mutually beneficial positive-sum interactions, as we have seen in the example of birds who eat the food debris between the teeth of alligators.

The G-type processes are differentiation-amplifying causal loop processes, which I initially formulated as "The Second Cybernetics" [7, pp. 120–36]. Consider, for example, the development of a city on a fertile plain previously uninhabited by humans. Suppose that groups of migrating pioneers pass through this plain. One group gets stuck in one spot and decides to settle there. The choice of the spot may be accidental, due to factors such as a member becoming too ill to continue migration, or a horse breaking its leg. The group opens farms around the settlement. Other passing migrants join the settlement, and the growth of the settlement attracts more immigrants. The spot has become differentiated from the homogeneity of the plain. Within the village, further heterogenization occurs: shops, factories, schools, and recreational facilities develop, and these heterogeneous elements interact for mutual benefit.

Another example can be taken from biology. The females of fruit flies prefer rare type males for mating [2, 3, 17]. This has the effect of the females preferring males who are mutants or immigrants. The heterogeneity within the species of fruit flies is increased in this process.

## DIFFERENT MINDSCAPES BEHIND SIMILAR-LOOKING PRACTICES

It is important to recognize the mindscape basis of management principles, theories, and even political ideologies. The same principle or ideology may stem from very different mindscapes, and seeming agreement on the surface may stand on undetected mindscape differences. On the other hand, many apparently different principles and ideologies may be based on one common mindscape and share the same fallacies.

For example, take the slogan "Small is Beautiful" or "Decentralization." H-type people can advocate it on the assumption that the whole country is homogeneous and nothing is lost by dividing the country into small parts. I-type people can also support the slogan because they see each community as different, unrelated to others, independent, and self-sufficient. S and G thinkers can endorse it because they see the communities as heterogeneous and interacting for mutual benefit. It makes sense for heterogeneous communities to be administered separately, with the assumption that they interact nonhierarchically. Thus, seemingly the same act of "decentralization" can be based on very different or even opposite mindscapes.

Similarly, "participatory management" and "democracy" can have culturally different mindscape bases beneath the surface. There are even subtypes of democracy within one mindscape type. For example, within the H-type, there are majority rule democracy and consensus democracy. Majority rule is nothing more than domination by quantity, though often implicit and unintentional rather than explicit. But the celebrated statement "the greatest amount of happiness for the greatest number of people" is explicitly quantitative. The alternative *within* the H-type is consensus democracy, which assumes the necessity and desirability of unanimity, often at the cost of coerced and self-coerced unanimity. On the other hand, for the I-type democracy means freedom from interference. But the I-type thinking also contributed to the concept of majority rule by encouraging each person to vote for his/her own interest regardless of others. The white American notion of democracy is a result of a mixture of H-type and I-type ways of thinking: majority rule, individual freedom, self-sufficiency, and independence. When a person has voted for his/her own interest, statistical tabulation will take care of the rest and legitimizes the person as being democratic.

## SOME NON-WESTERN SYSTEMS: NAVAJOS AND MANDENKA

S-type and G-type mindscapes produce notions of democracy very different from those outlined above. Let us take the Navajos as an example. Navajos use a decision-making process quite different from majority rule or white Americans' notion of consensus. Suppose a community must decide whether to build a bridge. In the majority rule system, votes are counted, the decision is implemented, and the matter has been "democratically" settled. On the other hand, Navajos consider the following: If the bridge is built, some persons may suffer. If the bridge is not built, some other persons suffer. Either way, some people suffer. The important point is to give compensations to those who suffer, regardless of which way the decision goes. This is quite different from the majority rule system. But it is also different from the white American's notion of consensus. The main goal of consensus democracy is to give legitimation to the decision by obtaining unanimous agreement, rather than to make compensations to those who would suffer from the decision. But I might add that there are some white American communities that have used Navajo-like methods. The city of Portland, Oregon once contemplated a downtown plan to close every other street to vehicle traffic and convert it to a pedestrian mall. The problem was in choosing which streets to close. Stores facing pedestrian malls would have certain advantages as well as disadvantages compared to stores facing vehicle streets. No matter which streets were chosen, some would benefit and some would suffer. A solution was to modify tax structures to compensate for the differences.

The Mandenka of West Africa [1, pp. 273–84] have another different, very advanced system which we may call "training for poly-ocular vision." The training is accomplished by two methods: (1) job cycling; and (2) joking relations.

During their lives, the Mandenka are made to go through a number of stages: a carefree childhood, several phases of initiation rituals leading to various social roles, an early adulthood with great administrative responsibilities, and a late adulthood with advisory functions. In Mandenka terms,

people "heterogenize themselves" by going through these different activities, and learn to see the same situation from different points of view. Older
persons are admired for having developed more of this ability. The Mandenka are afraid of "Westernization," which locks a person into one job and
makes him/her incapable of seeing a situation from other persons' points of
view.

The other method used for poly-ocular vision training is the joking relations, which also serve the purpose of providing feedback loops. Formally, the Mandenka society has a hierarchical structure. For example, a man
must obey his father, who in turn must obey the former's grandfather. But
the man may be in a joking relationship with his grandfather, and this
would give him an effective feedback channel over his father's head. There
are many other feedback channels as well. A man's joking relations are his
older brothers' wives, his maternal uncles, etc. A woman also has several
sets of joking relations. And for the entire social structure, there are official
clowns who can criticize and ridicule anyone with impunity, including the
kings. Obviously the joking relations are important as feedback channels.
However, the less visible but more crucial function of joking relations is
that they help one's capacity for poly-ocular vision. Persons in joking relations can criticize each other and must take criticisms without getting an-
gry. They are forced to see themselves from others' points of view. During
one of the initiation phases, a person has taken the role of a clown, enjoyed
the role, and thus later can identify with his or her critics, and "internalize"
the criticism. In this way, poly-ocularity becomes "internalized" automatically, instead of remaining as external input to be processed intellectually.
Poly-ocularity is natural and psychologically intrinsic to the Mandenka.
Americans may be trained in the same ability to some extent. But it will remain unnatural, intellectual, and extrinsic to Americans.

## THE JAPANESE, THE MANDENKA,
## AND THE NAVAJOS

Poly-ocular vision is an extension of the concept of binocular vision. Both
can be easily misinterpreted by H-type mindscapes in two ways. First,
H-type thinkers tend to consider the two images in the binocular vision to
be complementary in the sense of supplementing each other's blind spots.
This misses the whole point. What is important in the binocular vision is
that the two eyes see *the same object differently*. The differences between
the two images enable the brain to compute the depth, *which is the dimension neither eye can see*. Second, H-type thinkers tend to attribute disagreements to errors, noises, lack of education, or opposing interest in a zero-sum
game. They often say: "Let us disregard the areas on which we disagree and

stick to the areas on which we agree." The areas of agreement are supposed to be objective and real, while those of disagreements are considered as subjective, political, and immaterial. But if we apply the same reasoning to the binocular vision and discard the parts of the object on which the two images differ, what is left will be only the flat surfaces perpendicular and equidistant to the viewer. The result is far from the reality of the object, and much less real than the monocular vision. In this sense, we can obtain more information from disagreements than from agreements.

In the Japanese, Mandenka, and Navajo cultures, it is taken for granted that different persons have different views of the same situation. Information collection and understanding consist in knowing these differences. In the Japanese culture, the notion of "objectivity" did not exist and is even now unimportant. When the foreign word "objective" had to be translated, the Japanese invented the expression "kyakkanteki" which means "the guest's point of view," while "subjective" became "shukanteki" or "the host's point of view."

Another important cultural difference in the concept of heterogeneity lies in the notion of conflict and peace. H-type thinkers consider sameness as the basis of peace, and differences as sources of conflict. On the other hand, in the G-type culture of Mandenka, it is heterogeneity that enables coöperation, while homogeneity breeds competition and conflict. The Mandenka say: "If you force people to be the same, the only way left for them to be different is to try to get on top of one another. This creates conflicts [1]." They also tell many stories similar to the following one: A sage once passed by the court of a great king. It was teeming with healthy youngsters of the king. The sage exclaimed: "What disastrous ruins we see here!" His disciples were puzzled. The sage explained: "This stupid king has kept his grown-up children around him. They all live in the hope of taking over the same inheritance. When the king dies, the internal conflicts among his children will ruin the kingdom." For a Mandenka, the wisdom consists in orienting his children in different directions before his death because common interests, far from uniting them, often divide them. The testament of Mahan Soudiata, the founder of the medieval empire of Manden, reads [1]:

> The day death reached Maha Sojata
> He called his sons.
> Come! he said to them.
> That each of you tells me what he wants
> That each tells me the place he has in mind to establish himself
> That I bless him.
> If I die leaving you on top of one another
> My efforts will have been wasted.

When one dies leaving his many children on top of one another
It is as if he has left ruins after him.
The oldest son whose name was BA
He came to his father
He brought the hoe and the grain
Father, he said, bless me by the handle of the hoe
I have in mind the land behind the river
The place is Figida
He wanted to go and settle at Figida.
He blessed him.
He went to settle at Figida.
The next son
Fodakaba Keta
He brought the book
With the ink pot
With the reed
With paper
Asked that his father bless him by Koran
Said that he had a vast land in mind after the river
Here at Made.
He said that the place is called Kineboda.
He said that it is at Kineboda that he will settle.
He blessed him by the knowledge
He departed to settle at Kineboda
In the middle of the whole Made.
It was at Kineboda that the first flames of knowledge lit.
The son who was born after him
Was Kulufaba
He brought also the hoe and the grain
Asked that his father bless him by the hoe.
Said that it is the land he has in mind along the chain of mountains,
And that the place is called Kinera
He will leave to settle at Kinera
There, everybody around the mountains comes to buy the grain.
Until today, these people have not known hunger.
Next son
Netewuleba
He brought the gun
With the powder
He said: It is here at Kaaba that I will settle, in your place.
Bless me.
He blessed him by the gun and by the powder.
He became war chief.
The youngest son
He came to ask that his father pray for him to have a long life
And health
And tranquility.

Said that he has a land in mind not far from here
The place is called Degela
It is at Degela that he wants to settle.
Maha Sajata blessed him by the long life
By the health
And by the tranquility.
Even today, if you go to Degela
You will find people with red hair[1]

Harmony is a heterogenistic, interactive concept, while unity is homogenistic. This difference was clearly seen at the World Expo that took place in 1974 in Spokane. Each nation had a pavilion with a slogan. The European and North American pavilions began their slogans with the word "unity," while those of all the Asian pavilions except the Philippines began with "harmony."

## THE JAPANESE AND THE AMERICANS

After having seen the examples from the Navajo culture and the Mandenka culture, we now have a wider comparative perspective. Let us now return to the Japanese management practice and see whether it has an epistemological basis different from the U.S. notion of participatory management.

It is often said that the Japanese management/labor relations are "harmonious," that a labor union exists within each company and identifies itself with the successes and failures of the company, that the employees are guaranteed lifetime employment and take pride in the performance of the company, that the employees receive huge semi-annual bonuses which reflect the profit of the company, etc. These explanations are somewhat mechanistic: they are tangible to outsiders, but they miss a very important point.

For the Americans, management/labor relations are based on the following concepts: (i) labor as something to be purchased; (ii) management as a control mechanism; and (iii) management/labor relations as a contract to be negotiated.

These concepts are quite alien to the Japanese, even though some amount of Americanization may be visible on the surface. For the Japanese, the relationship between the worker and the manager is that of *vertical mutual obligation*. Let me illustrate this with an example. Mr. Y graduated from a university. He had a close friend whom he thought he should help. K, the friend's father, owned a small company. Y entered K's company even though he could have chosen a job with several bigger companies. K could not offer Y a sufficient salary, but promised Y that he would later give Y a part of his large garden to build a house on. A few years later K made a serious business mistake: he purchased expensive manufacturing equipment which would soon become obsolete. The company incurred a heavy loss. K's real estate property became mortgaged against the business debt. He could not give Y the land he had promised. The company sank further. Y could have moved to another company. But he decided to stay on because he had 20 subordinates in his division and did not want them to feel that he was abandoning them. I was a close friend of Y's. K felt so obligated to Y that, when I returned to Japan, K gave my family an extravagant feast at an expensive restaurant that he could not afford.

The Japanese management/labor relations are based on this "sense of vertical mutual obligation." The resulting nonverbal, implicit, nonlegalistic trust has nothing equivalent in U.S. notions of labor as something to be purchased, management as a control mechanism, and management/labor relations as a written contract to be negotiated. Furthermore, the Japanese notion of interpersonal relations and of the individual is based on the concept of continuous and convertible space, in sharp contrast to the American idea of space having boundary and identity, as will be discussed later.

## THE AMERICAN MINDSCAPES: RESULT OF 2,400 YEARS OF DEVELOPMENT THROUGH GREEKS AND EUROPEANS

Many of the assumptions and concepts in the U.S., such as the zero-sum game assumption, are rooted deeply in European traditions, products of the cultural, historical, and philosophical developments of the past 2,400 years. These assumptions, together with the homogenistic, hierarchical concepts of universe and society, were until recently considered "scientific." The architectural and esthetic concepts of spatial identity, separation, opposition, tension and extension also reflect the same assumptions, and have parallels in interpersonal relations.

The homogenistic concepts of the H-type mindscapes correspond to the Newtonian physics. The I-type thinking is congruent with the view that the most natural and probable state of the universe or an isolated system is random distribution of independent events, each having its own probability, and therefore non-random structures tend to decay. This was the cosmology of the nineteenth century thermodynamics. The homeostatic, interactive causal loops of the S-type mindscapes were the basis of the First Cybernetics which developed in the 1940s and 1950s. The pattern-generating interactive causal loops of the G-type mindscapes constitute the basis of the newest direction in biological, social, and physical sciences since the 1960s [7]. And we have seen that the Mandenka of West Africa, among others, have been practicing for centuries the way of thinking that we now associate with the newest way of being scientific.

But our 2,400 years of H-type thinking, along with occasional I-type rebellions against it, cannot be modified overnight. Even most of the avant-garde scientists and artists are still trapped in the same fallacies as the old ways of thinking, against which they rebel. We will discuss this shortly. But in order to appreciate the entrenchedness of the H-type and I-type thinking, let us first look at its history.

The early Greeks were heterogenistic, nonhierarchical and morphogenetic. They had many gods who interacted. But in the sixth century B.C., a Greek scientist Anaximandros conceived the notion of "infinity" as the inexhaustible protosubstance of the universe. As no material knowable by human senses fulfilled his requirements for the infinity-substance, he thought that the substance must be beyond all human experience. Xenophanes applied this concept to religion. Proud of his "discovery" and scornful of the humanlike gods of Greek mythology, he declared that his infinite god was incomparable to humans and was eternal. Here was the origin of our hierarchical and stability-oriented thinking. In the fifth century, B.C., Anaxagoras invented the notion of power-substance that penetrated into things and caused them to move. He thought that the power-substance must be a soul, and must have order and purpose. He ascribed rationality to the power-substance. Thus, European theology had its origin in Greek mathematics and science.

A little later, sophists taught the principle of identity and law of contradiction, i.e., A is A; A is not B. This was the beginning of our categorical and classificational thinking. Plato gave abstract ideas higher reality than concrete things, and advocated that true reality had no materiality. He also formulated the logical subordination of the more particular under the more general. Here was the formalization of our hierarchical thinking. In the fourth century B.C., Aristotle established the logic of deduction of the particular from the general. Circular reasonings became forbidden. Hereafter, Western science mostly ignored the causal loops in natural, biological, and social processes.

The theoretical foundation of a religion with an absolute God, one-way flow of authority, dichotomy between good and evil, and disdain of "material things" was firmly established 300 years before the arrival of Christ. When Christ arrived, European tradition was ready to advocate his "universal" validity. Missionary work based on the assumption of the superiority of one's own religion began. Inspired by Christian theology, Mohammedanism was born six centuries later, and became more hierarchical and homogenistic than the Christian religion.

Europeans recognized other hierarchical and homogenistic monotheistic systems, such as Mohammedanism and Hinduism, and "religions," often with the misinterpretation that all religions worshipped the same god by different names. They considered harmonistic and heterogenistic belief systems, either with many gods or without god, to be "animisms" or superstitions. Furthermore, their homogenistic and hierarchical reasoning led them to the view that all cultures followed the same path of evolution, and that if two cultures were different, one must be more advanced than the other. The same view persisted in the business sector. It was often assumed that other countries ought to learn our way of doing business.

But not all Europeans were homogenists. Rebellions against homogenistic thinking did occur from time to time, but usually took the forms of predominantly I-type mindscapes rather than S-type or G-type, even though the degree of mixtures varied from individual to individual. The medieval nominalist were strongly of the I-type. The existentialists of the nineteenth and twentieth centuries were more varied. Søren Kierkegaard's existentialism was that of extreme individual isolation and impossibility of communication. The only possible communication between two individuals was through God. The main orientation of his philosophy was of an I-type mindscape, but his notion of an omnipotent god gave his philosophy a flavor of H-type thinking. Jean-Paul Sartre [14] stressed the individual's responsibility and freedom to choose without any possibility of excuse to put a blame on others in making the decision. His mindscape was strongly of an I-type. But his notion of the responsibility toward others makes his philosophy non-isolationistic. Furthermore, he put an emphasis on visualizing new alternatives that do not yet exist, and on becoming different from what one is at the present. He had a G-flavor. Martin Heidegger [4] was even more preoccupied with an individual's care and concern for others. Psychologically he was dependency-oriented. He was of an I-type with an S-shade. But by and large, H-type philosophers such as Descartes, Kant, Hegel, and Fichte dominated European thoughts. A new, G-type trend is brewing in the works of philosopher Edgar Morin [11], and around the theories of biologists Henri Laborit, Henri Atlan, Ruper Riedl [13], chemist Ilya Prigogine [12] and others. But some of them — Prigogine, for example — are partially trapped in H-type and I-type thinking [10]: they could go much further if they could get out of the trap. Needless to say, ordinary scientists and thinkers are still immersed in H-type and occasionally I-type thinking.

In many fields of art the situation is similar. In trying to do something new, modern music composers in Europe and in North America resort to the use of randomness combined with the traditional principles of composition which are highly hierarchical, repetitious, and sequentially predictable. European architects also talk about combining variety with sameness. As we have seen, H-type and I-type are two sides of the same coin. On the other hand, the S-type and G-type are based on causal loop interactions, which are shared neither by H nor I types. S and G are NOT located between H and I. Clear examples of design principles based on S-type and G-type mindscapes are given in the following section.

## THE JAPANESE MINDSCAPES: 2,300 YEARS
## OF DEVELOPMENT THROUGH JOMON,
## YAYOI, AND YAMATO CULTURES

If the development of the European patterns of thinking has a 2,400-year history, the origins of the Japanese mindscapes can be traced back to about the same antiquity. There are three main origins of the Japanese culture: the oldest, somewhat morphogenetic Jomon culture that began 9,000 years ago, the homeostatic yayoi culture that began 2,300 years ago, and the hierarchical Yamato culture that arrived via Korea about 1,500 years ago.

The Japanese people expressed their philosophy more readily in various art forms and design principles than in verbal discourse. Much philosophical thinking particularly went into designs of gardens, architecture, and flower arrangement. It is from archaeological and anthropological studies of such designs that we gain an understanding of the development of the Japanese thought patterns.

I often conduct public lectures and seminars with slide projections of designs from various cultures based on different esthetic principles. I sometimes ask my American audience to identify the principles used in the designs. The way my listeners respond tells me much about their mindscapes. I show, for example, a Gothic cathedral or a palace, and ask my audience: "What are the principles of this design?" The usual response is "Symmetry." This indicates their preoccupation with symmetry. Then I say that there are other more basic principles, and ask them to find these. Usually no one responds to this question. These principles are so much taken for granted that the audience has never become conscious of them. The basic principles are: (i) unity by repetition and similarity; (ii) hierarchy; and (iii) reflection of the main theme in the subthemes. These principles were also used in much of the eighteenth- and nineteenth-century European music composition. Then I show a slide of a Japanese garden, and ask my audience what the design principles are, and how they differ from those of the traditional Italian or French gardens such as the one in Versailles. The most usual answer is "asymmetry," which does not explain anything about the Japanese garden, but indicates again their preoccupation with symmetry. Another frequent answer is "natural." When I ask further what they mean by "natural," they usually say that it means "random." It does not occur to them that nature had patterns. For them, there is only one kind of pattern: symmetry. Anything that is not symmetrical is perceived to be random or chaotic.[2]

Some of the basic principles of the Japanese garden design and flower arrangement are: (i) avoidance of repetition; (ii) harmony of *dissimilar* elements; (iii) interrelationship between *heterogeneous* elements. The Japanese designers themselves are often not conscious of these principles, because they take these for granted and never verbalize them. They almost automatically, "without thinking," use these principles. But beyond these basic principles, detailed principles are quite specific and verbally spelled out. There are more than 2,000 different "schools" of flower arrangements in Japan. Each of them has its own rules of design, clearly specified, to which the students must adhere strictly.

Let us now compare the Japanese architectural principles with those of Europe. Some basic European principles are: (i) opposition; (ii) tension; and (iii) extension. The mass of the building protrudes into space and opposes space. Space is defined as something between masses. Space itself is a transparent mass, and has a volume, identity, boundary, specialized function, and immutability. The house is intended to separate the humans from the environment. Curves are contours of an actual physical mass. Straight extension of lines and surfaces of a building can generate streets, spaces, and other masses, and tension between points causes something to be built in-between.

Compare these principles to the ones used in traditional Japanese houses: (i) boundarilessness; (ii) outside-in principle; (iii) black hole principle; (iv) convertibility and connectability; and (v) imaginary curves and flows. For example, the garden penetrates into the house like a deep recess and as a sort of room. Outer shells of a house can be removed, which creates an instant outdoors. Eaves can extend over the stepping stones in the garden, and floors can extend beyond the cover of the roof. A house can appear inconspicuous and dark — almost camouflaged — when seen from outside. But it is bright inside because it sucks in the outdoors like the black hole in astronomy. The same black hole principle enabled the Japanese to absorb European and American technology in the past. Furniture is stored away when not in use, and the same room can be used for many different purposes depending on the time of the day. The partitions between rooms can be removed, and with furniture stored away, the entire house can become a free space continuing from the outdoors. The concept of individual is related to the concept of space. The individuals in a company are continuous and have no boundary between them. They are convertible to one another. Job rotation is a very natural concept in Japan.

Interdepartmental temporary transfer of workers or job rotation of managers is very natural to the Japanese. The worker in most of the large factories in Japan is rotated among many types of jobs [5, 6], learns many skills, and understands the entire process in his or her factory. The workers can step into one another's thoughts, not just shoes. When a worker finds a defect in a product caused by someone else's error, he feels obligated to correct it, and has the know-how to do so. Many top executives prefer to share their offices with colleagues rather than having an office of their own. New managerial employees first learn the jobs on the factory floor, and later spend much of their time in factories with workers. These principles of convertibility and connectedness among the individuals are highly related to the Japanese concept of space.

How has such a philosophy developed, as reflected in their concept of space? For the answer, we must look into the prehistory. The earliest conceptualization of space is related to the concept of Mononoke [15], which may go back in time to as early as the late Jomon period or early Yayoi period. Each locality has a Mononoke which, like the "mana" of the Polynesians, permeated the locality. At the beginning, the Mononoke was quite undifferentiated and undefined, but later it was considered to condense into rocks, not very large in size, often less than a foot. Rocks came to represent the special *quality* of the Mononoke of the locality. Hence, a rock *represented* the space instead of opposing it. The rock was the quality of the space, not mass. This concept was incorporated into the Japanese garden design and architecture. Therefore, there is *no* opposition between space and matter.

With the cultivation of rice, the concept of land as property occurred. Land was marked with stakes, ropes, or pebble carpets, not by physical mass or walls. Such space still had continuity to the outside. The concept of a space enclosed by fences or walls arose with the arrival of the hierarchical Yamato culture via Korea, which took place fifteen hundred years ago. This hierarchical culture had a considerable influence on the Japanese, especially among the ruling class. When the middle class expanded in the nineteenth century, it embraced much of the ethics of the ruling class. However, all the three cultural streams are fused in every modern Japanese, with individual variations as to their relative preponderance.

What distinguishes the Japanese way of thinking most from the American way are the homeostatic and morphogenetic components in the former, and I would like to elaborate a little on the distinct way in which these components have developed in Japan.

The Jomon culture produced many potteries but also many figurines. The Yayoi culture also left many clay figures. The facial expression and body proportions of the Jomon figures are often called "demonic," "vital," etc., while the Yayoi expressions are lyrical, peaceful, and even passive. From this and other data, we can infer that the life was harsh and difficult during the Jomon period, while the Yayoi people felt that nature was kind to them. The harvest was abundant, and thanksgiving festivities seem to have been held around the grain storage houses, giving rise to a shrine architecture. Even after the arrival of Yamato culture, a lyrical approach to nature survived in architecture and literature, especially among the leisured noble class. The climate in Japan is mild. The nobles could sit on a boat on a lake in a garden and play poetry games all day, sit in a house, smelling the outdoor flowers and wet soil after the rain, watching the leaves change their color, and hearing insects sing, autumn wind rattle the leaves, and snow lumps fall off tree branches. The famous Katsura Palace [16] was designed by an aristocrat to recreate the scenes from the Tales of Genji. Such a lyrical attitude toward nature is still quite alive in every Japanese of today, and is extended to the interpersonal relations as well. On the other hand, the inspirations from the older Jomon culture have always provided the Japanese with vitality, change-orientedness, and bold innovative spirit. Management/labor relations, business/government relations and industry/ environment relations in Japan must be understood in terms of such influences.

## THE AMERICAN SOLUTION SHOULD NOT BE A COPY OF THE JAPANESE MANAGEMENT

Now that we have examined the epistemological, cultural, and historical differences between the U.S.A. and Japan, the following should have become clear to us: (1) The Japanese way of management has an epistemological basis different from what is called "participatory management" in the U.S.A.; (2) The future principles of the U.S. management should be NEITHER an imitation of the Japanese way, NOR traditionally American. Some of the important principles are: (a) recognition of heterogeneity as an asset, not liability; (b) combination of heterogeneous individuals into mutually beneficial interaction patterns, which may be called "morphogenetic management."

Both heterogenistic principles and morphogenetic principles are scientifically more correct and viable than homogenistic principles. Moreover, they have become a social and psychological necessity. In the past, the workers were to perform standardized works, and were rewarded for their capacity to be standardized. But two recent developments have changed this situation: one is technological, and the other psychological.

First, a new type of production efficiency is achieved by tailor-making the products with direct input of specifications from the customer to the factory via computers. This eliminates both excess inventory and stockouts, as well as the costly pre-production market research and post-production advertisement to make the customer buy what has already been manufactured. This is true in such industries as garment and automobile, in which in the past efficiency was attained by mass production of standardized products. But it is even more true for the growing technology-intensive, capital-intensive, and research-intensive industries such as aircraft manufacturing and computer manufacturing. Not only human workers but also robots are adjusting to this new situation. Until now, the main advantage of robots was thought to consist in their ability to do the dirty or monotonous work that human workers did not want. However, the new generation of robots can do much more. The same robot can be programmed to do different jobs with changes in instructions. Production in small batches as well as customized production can be increasingly robotized.

The second reason that necessitates heterogenistic principles and morphogenetic principles is psychological. The new generation of workers want not only participation in decision making but also the right to be human beings and individuals. They want to adapt the work to the individual, not the individual to the work.

In the traditional homogenistic way of thinking, such individualization would have been a disruption. However, in the new heterogenistic and morphogenetic ways, the individual differences are an asset and an advantage. What we need are methods to combine heterogeneous elements in such a way as to generate mutual benefit. But how? Let us begin with simple examples. There are old people who love to take care of children, as well as families needing babysitters. They will make mutually beneficial combinations. But there are also old people who do not want to have children around. They should not be combined with children.

Suppose there are three individuals, P, Q, and R, in one neighborhood. P wants to do some physical exercise and has two choices: mowing lawns or playing frisbee. Q wants to relax and has three choices: blow a trumpet, go to the university gymnasium, or play frisbee. He has no car. On the other hand, R wants to study quietly and has two places to do so: at home or at the university library. He has a car. Since P has 2 choices, Q has 3, and R has 2, there are altogether 2 times 3 times 2 equal 12 different combinations. Some of these combinations are positive sum; others are negative-sum or zero-sum. If there are several hundred people in a business firm and each has several choices, the number of possible combinations is astronomical. Not even large computer programs can handle all combinations. Even if they could, human programmers must instruct the computers what to look for and what to combine together. We must first develop some theoretical frameworks and the methodology to study such combinations. Such a science might be called "morphogenetics" [9], but has not yet been developed.

One very important difference between the natural ecological processes and the social processes is that in the former the negative-sum relations eventually die off, while in the social processes we do not want to wait until many people die as a result of negative-sum relations. We must devise ways to avoid combinations of elements which would result in negative-sum relations, and invent new positive-sum networks to relocate them into.

The problem has become particularly acute due to accelerated culture change; large influx and mixing of professional, skilled, and unskilled immigrants from many cultures into countries such as Saudi Arabia; Cuban refugees and officially illegal but economically often welcome Mexican labor force permeation into U.S.A.; and the new phenomenon of foreign manufacturing facilities in North America with U.S. or Canadian workers under Japanese or European management.

But again this new type of heterogeneity can be regarded as an asset if we can meet the challenge of inventing the methods to generate mutually beneficial combinations with them.

While the participatory management based on the traditional homogenistic epistemology still seeks consensus and agreement, the morphogenetic management generates symbiotization of diversity without homogenization. It goes into a new dimension, yet to be explored.

## FOOTNOTES

[1]Among the Mandenka, it is not white or grey hair that is the sign of old age. The hair of extremely old people turns red after having been grey.

[2]An exception is Yehuda Yannay, who composes music based on patterns found in nature, such as insects' movements.

## BIBLIOGRAPHY

[1] Camara, Sory. "The Concept of Heterogeneity and Change among the Mandenka." *Technol. Forecasting and Soc. Change*, Vol. 7, 1975.
[2] Ehrman, L. "Rare Male Advantages and Sexual Isolation in Drosophila Immigrants." *Beh. Gen.*, Vol. 2, pp. 79–83, 1972.
[3] Ehrman, L., and Probber, J. "Rare Drosophila Males." *Amer. Sci.* Vol. 66, pp. 216–22, 1978.
[4] Heidegger, Martin. *Sein and Zeit*, 1927.
[5] Koike, Kazuo. "Japanese Workers in Large Firms." *Keizai Kagaku*, Vol. 26, pp. 1–37, 1978.
[6] Koike, Kazuo. "Japan's Industrial Relations: Characteristics and Problems." *Japanese Economic Studies*, Vol. 7, pp. 42–90, 1978.
[7] Maruyama, M. "The Second Cybernetics: Deviation-amplifying Mutual Causal Processes." *Amer. Sci.*, Vol. 51, pp. 164–79, and 250–56, 1963.
[8] Maruyama, M. "Heterogenistics: an Epistemological Restructuring of Biological and Social Sciences." *Acta Biotheoretica*, Vol. 26, 1977.
[9] Maruyama, M. "Heterogenistics and Morphogenetics." *Theor. Soc.*, Vol. 5, pp. 75–96, 1978.
[10] Maruyama, M. "Mindscapes and Science Theories." *Cur. Anthro.*, Vol. 21, pp. 589–608, 1980.
[11] Morin, Edgar. *La Méthode*, (Paris: Seuil, 1976).
[12] Prigogine, I. and Nicolis, G. *Self-Organization in Non-Equilibrium Systems*. (New York: Wiley, 1977).

[13] Riedl, Rupert. *Strategie der Genesis*. (München: Piper, 1976).

[14] Sartre, J.-P. *L'Être et le Néant*. (Paris: Gallimard, 1943).

[15] Tange, Kenzo and Kawazoe, N. *Ise*. (Cambridge, Mass: MIT Press, 1965).

[16] Tange, Kenzo. *Katsura*. (New Haven, Conn.: Yale University Press, 1972).

[17] Watanabe, T. and Kawanishi, M. "Mating Preferences and Direction of Evolution in Drosophila," *Science*, Vol. 205, pp. 906–907, 1979.

# 7

# Japanese Values and Management Processes

DAVID M. FLYNN

## INTRODUCTION[1]

Japan is a culture characterized by both traditional and modern values. It retains the values of a traditional, family-oriented culture while continuing to reëvaluate its other institutions in pursuit of the most effective methods. Vogel [32, p. 5] notes " . . . no country is more experienced in evaluating the effectiveness of existing institutions and in creating or reshaping institutions by rational planning to meet future needs." Perhaps what stands out most in Japanese history, as well as in current Japanese managerial behavior, is the capacity for making 180° turns [6, p. 111].

The flexibility of the Japanese individual is limited, however, seemingly due to the relative constraints of the traditional family system; this family is, indeed, the nucleus of Japanese society [21], [30], [32].

Within the family hierarchy, self-discipline and goal aspirations are taught, naturally affecting future supervisor-subordinate relationships [10], [11], [21], [32]. The deemphasis of the ego and self-centered needs contributes to the high level of success of the work group within Japanese organizations [11], [32].

The focus of this paper is the hypothesized expression of Japanese cultural values upon managerial processes within Japanese organizations.

# VALUES, CULTURE, AND BEHAVIOR

## Values and Behavior

Personal values are constructs observable through behavior reflecting an individual's standards of what is right and just. Nowak [26, p. 45] defines values of a person as " . . . the standards that define for him how people should behave, what actions or events merit approval or condemnation, what patterns of relations should prevail among people, groups, and institutions. By comparison with such standards the person makes evaluations and holds things to be good or bad, just or unjust, proper or improper, desirable or undesirable". Hofstede [14, p. 19] succinctly defines a value as " . . . a broad tendency to prefer certain states of affairs over others".

Values influence behavior and may motivate action when a situation arises that is perceived as inconsistent with one's norms or standards. The amount of action taken is dependent on some expectation of success in bringing a situation or object closer to one's value standards [5], [26].

## Values and Culture

Culture is the active and often subtle vehicle in the teaching of values to its members. It is the collective programming of the mind that distinguishes the members of one human group from another [14, p. 13]. A more traditional culture is less flexible in accepting change or alteration in its institutions as agents of value teaching and reinforcement.

Japan, as noted earlier, is characterized as both traditional and modern in its values. Japanese business organizations are successful in quite diverse cultural environments. This success indicates a flexible or a situation-specific mode of behavior operating with traditional Japanese familial values. Education and age, however, have been found to lessen the importance of these traditional values [2], [29].

## Japanese Managerial Value Studies

While value studies may vary in sample size, they often utilize at least two sub-samples to ensure the researcher's ability to compare and contrast between cultures. Haire, Ghiselli, and Porter [12] included a sub-sample of 165 Japanese managers in their study of 3,600 managers in 14 countries. In a more recent study, England [7], [8] studied 2,500 managers in Australia, Japan, Korea, India, and the United States. The Japanese sample consisted of 374 managers from a variety of industries. The results characterize the Japanese managers as follows [8, p. 41]:

(1) Very high element of pragmatism
(2) Value magnitude very highly (size and growth)
(3) Place high value on competence and achievement
(4) Have the most homogenous managerial value system of the countries studied.

England also detected a high degree of value change occurring among the younger managers. This was evident in the humanistic and egalitarian measures that may indicate a fundamental change in the value system of younger Japanese managers — a question presently under investigation by the author.

While England studied the values of Japanese managers in Japan, Kelley and Reeser [16] investigated the attitudes of managers of Japanese ancestry in Hawaii. Their findings suggest a high degree of similarity with Japanese managers in Japan versus management of Caucasian descent in Hawaii. Those of Japanese descent felt more strongly about the importance of a long-term employment commitment to one company, indicated a greater respect for formal authority vested in a position, and inclined more to being "team workers" and less to striving for outstanding individual performance. A higher degree of paternalism toward subordinates was also exhibited.

A more recent study by Kelley and Worthley [17], supports the results of Kelley and Reeser [16] and suggests the importance of both national and cultural differences in determining managerial attitudes. The results support the Farmer and Richman [9] model which emphasizes the importance of culture in the formation of values not the position of the Negandhi-Prasad [24]. Negandhi and Prasad argue that managerial attitudes are independent of the cultural environment in which it operates.

Both England [7], [8] and Austin [2] have noted a degree of change occurring among the traditional values held by the Japanese people. Reichel and Flynn [29] attempted to determine whether value changes are occurring among Japanese managers of Japanese citizenry working in the United States. The results support England's and Austin's conclusions and also point to a group of values that may be entrenched in the Japanese culture in general and in its managerial behavior in particular, regardless of external influences (i.e., location of work setting). The 162 Japanese upper managers responding to the questionnaire placed high importance on security, group success, coöperation, authority and off-the-job problems. Even when broken down by age, size of U.S. subsidiary, size of Japanese parent firm, and years in the U.S., there were no statistically significant differences, apart from authority. Thus, no matter whether the Japanese managers have just arrived in the U.S. or have spent more than ten years here, they still place high importance on security, group success, coöperation and off-the-job problems.

Contrary to these core values, there exists a set of values that may be considered as flexible in different cultural environments. These are identified by the importance placed on the following variables: conformity, acceptance by subordinates, compromise, hierarchy, experience in one firm, age of thirty, personal problems, obedience, autonomy, seniority and universalism.

# JAPANESE MANAGEMENT

## Introduction

The presence of tradition in Japan is perceived to be especially prevalent within its management system. The Japanese have developed distinct approaches to the concerns of top management. These concerns include: (1) making effective desisions; (2) harmonizing employment security with other needs such as productivity, flexibility in labor costs, and acceptance of change in the company; and (3) developing young professional managers [6].

## Management Systems

As previously mentioned, the sense of belonging and commitment to the group, as well as the organization, is an aspect of Japan's inherent family ties. This cultural value is evident in the Japanese practice of management. Yang [33] has distinguished between the U.S. objective-performance linked system and the Japanese organic equivalent. The organic type of management emphasizes that:

> . . . the sense of belonging to an organization is far more important than the function one performs within the organization. Therefore, human relations rather than professional capabilities of the employees form the core of a business organization. An organization is considered a collective entity. Any member within an organization, even if he is a professional, can only identify himself with the company rather than with his profession. The results are the organic pattern of management, with a strong emphasis on human relations, the seniority system, life-time employment, low rate of employee turnover, and practically no contractual agreements. The role of top management is to maintain harmony in the company and to create a favorable climate for it to operate in the society [33, p. 25].

This sense of belonging to the organization and the tendency to behave as a group is one of the most striking characteristics of the organic system. Marengo [20] believes that Japanese industrial "groupism" implies loyalty not only of employee to employer, but also responsibility by the employer towards the total well-being of the employee.

The objective-performance linked system type, on the other hand, " . . . focuses on relationships between sub-systems as well as system entities through centralization, yet operations within the organization are systematized to achieve the integrated objects, subject to a set of external and policy constraints" [33, p. 24]. According to Yang, the principle roles of top management under the American system type are to design an efficient system of operation, set corporate goals and objectives, and map strategic plans, as well as make policies. (See Table 1).

Yang believes that each model fits different situational configurations. For example, Japan required management that could foster group strength in order to deal with internal and external adversaries. However, as Japan moved up to assume a position of technological leadership, the situation required management to be innovative and inclined to risk taking, and to demonstrate greater flexibility in adapting to change. Yang concludes, as opposed to Drucker [6], that recent developments in the U.S. and Japan have finally brought about the meeting of the East and the West, at least in the terms of managerial philosophies.

In addition to contrasting the system and organic models, it has been suggested that the Japanese distinguish between the Western notion of the *organization* and their notion of the *company*. According to Pascale [28], the Japanese view the term organization as referring only to the system. The concept of company, however, includes its underlying character, that which describes " . . . a shared sense of values long held by members and enforced by group norms. . . . The company may accomplish the same tasks as an organization does, but it occupies more space, moves with more weight, and reflects a commitment to larger ends than just the ac-

TABLE 1   Characteristics of Top Management: A Comparison*

| SYSTEM TYPE (U.S.) | ORGANIC TYPE (JAPAN) |
| --- | --- |
| Decision maker | Facilitator |
| Professional | Social leader |
| Individual initiative and creativity | Group strength |
| Emphasis on functional relationships | Emphasis on human relations |
| Management by objectives | Management by consensus |
| Decentralization | Centralization |
| System adapts to changes | Leader adapts to changes |

*Source: (33, p. 25) Reprinted with permission from the *Columbia Journal of World Business*, (Fall 1977), p. 25.

complishment of a mission" [28, p. 161]. Thus the emphasis is not only on efficiency, but also on dealing with the idiosyncratic requirements of human nature."

## Decision-Making Process: The Ringi System

Japanese decision-making style, known as the *Ringi* system, has been the focus of numerous studies. Drucker [6] calls it decision making by consensus. Fox [10] described it as consensual understanding. Vogel [32] views the *ringi* process as actually root binding that leads to the high level of commitment necessary for implementation of decisions by lower echelons of the organization. Litterer [19] considers it to be diffuse decision making. But no matter how one defines it, the *ringi* system is characterized by the great amount of effort placed on discussing the need for a decision and the definition of the problem before any decision is actually made [6], [15], [19].

In a thorough examination of decision-making processes in a Japanese corporation, Hattori [13] described the *ringi* system as a confirmation-authorization process of decision making. When there is a need to make a decision or to find a solution to a problem, a proposal is written by a staff member. After examination by the manager of the division, the document is circulated to related departments for review and confirmation, then to top management for final authorization. Hattori maintains that this process is not a method for analyzing problems or finding alternatives, but rather confirms that all elements of disagreement have been eliminated, the responsible section or person can be assured of coöperation from other sections, and the proposal can be turned into an administrative assignment. While this process is time-consuming, it significantly increases the likelihood of commitment to implementing the decision.

Litterer [19] points out, however, that there are both advantages and disadvantages to the *ringi* system. It permits initiative by lower-level managers, gives them responsibility for carrying out action, gives higher management control, and provides a method of integrating effort. Additionally, he maintains that, given the rigid hierarchical nature of Japanese organizations and the fact that promotion based on seniority may not always put the most competent people in superior positions, the *ringi* system provides a way for competent persons to exercise their abilities.

As for drawbacks, first, the lower managers may not have enough knowledge about the overall condition of the company. Thus, decisions are made on a piecemeal basis and any coherence becomes a matter of chance. Second, the document seldom contains enough information for any subsequent rigorous decision to be made. Third, the system encourages complacency and apathy among managers. Similarly, Fox [10] argues that, for the rank and file, the *ringi* system helps to obscure individual responsibility for the quality or effects of a plan of action and therefore helps to "deindividualize" the exercise of power.

It should be noted, however, that some authors of Japanese management studies reject the notion of consensual decision-making process as a means to "deindividualize" or to escape personal responsibility. For example, Noda [25] argues that the consensual features of the decision-making process are accentuated by the institution of Harakiri: the voluntary assumption of responsibility with or without fault. Thus the *ringi* system entails both decision making by consensus *and* responsibility.

Marengo [20] has observed that some studies of the Japanese decision-making process maintain that the consensual features are kept in simply because they allow the actual decision maker to preserve a degree of convenient ambiguity. This is regarded by Pascale [28] as a managerial tool. He maintains that "ambiguity has two important connotations for management. First, it is a useful concept in thinking about how we deal with others, orally, and in writing. Second, it provides a way of legitimizing the loose rein that a manager permits in certain organizational situations where further insight is needed before conclusive action can be taken."

Furthermore, Pascale believes that although ambiguity in reference to sensitivity and feelings is alleged in the Western world to be "female," one should consider their adoption in Western management. But Marengo [20] argues that Pascale does not explain Japanese ambiguity from a truly Japanese perspective, but rather from a Western one, as a tactic that affords the decision maker to buy time for maneuvers in order to defeat the opposition.

Kono [18] found the *ringi* system is applicable to operational or short-term decisions. However, the process of strategic decision making tends to be more formal and originate at the upper management level due to the accelerated rate of change in the competitive environment. This variation within the *ringi* system is evidence of Japanese management assessing the need for change within an established managerial practice and making change for greater effectiveness.

## The *Nenko* System

One of the aspects of Japanese management that has been widely examined is the permanent employment system known as *Nenko* [1], [3], [4], [22], [23], [31], [34]. Although seldom operative in any but the larger Japanese firms and applied to a minority of Japanese workers, it has been suggested that some of its principles be applied in the U.S. [6].

According to Oh [27], the *Nenko* system gives employees job security and promotes strong corporate loyalty and group effectiveness while maintaining the flexibility to meet fluctuations in demand for labor and new developments in technology. An individual joins a firm and has a job for life. This involves a high degree of commitment between the individual and the organization. The person who joins the firm not only has a job but also many of the employee's and family needs are taken care of by management.

As noted by Litterer [19], the *Nenko* system has several disadvantages. It locks the firm into a set of employees that they will have for a long time, even though the needs of the firm may change and individual talents or capacities may become obsolete. From the viewpoint of the employee, they are locked into one employer, denied opportunities elsewhere, and have no employment outlet when they find themselves no longer as useful as they once were. The employee who leaves a firm is looked upon as either a disloyal employee who has abandoned his obligations or one that absolutely had to be terminated.

## CONCLUSION

The Japanese management culture, as the research indicates, distinguishes between the traditional family-based values and behaviors and an external (nontraditional) flexible set. Perhaps a finer distinction can be drawn to indicate the existence of a "core" and a "peripheral" group [29]. More specifically, one could identify two sets of factors characterizing the existence of this duality.

The core set would include the family system, the group orientation, a high degree of organizational loyalty, the lifetime employment system, and the "consensus" or "root binding" decision-making process (*ringi*). These factors are associated with the traditional non-changing aspects of the Japanese culture.

Conversely, the peripheral set would identify a high degree of flexibility, constant reëvaluation and change of its institutions to fit the "best" model, a high degree of pragmatism, achievement orientation and the continuous educational process.

During the 1980s, Japan is expected to become the most powerful industrialized nation. This calls for further investigations into the delicate balance of pragmatism and modernism vs. the core of traditional values, attitudes, and behaviors. The question is whether increasing industrialization will be associated with a radical transition away from traditional values, or will there be a tendency to adhere to past inheritance? Observations, case studies and surveys in Japan can be most useful in detecting shifts in management culture and practice.

In addition, it is suggested to further explore the concept of core vs. peripheral values and behavior by examining native Japanese managers working outside of Japan.

The expectation of further research would be to further appreciate, understand, and learn from a most successful nation. These lessons could serve as directives for managerial behaviors rather than as blueprints of a culture distinctive from most.

## FOOTNOTE

[1] I thank Arie Reichel for his assistance in an earlier draft of this manuscript.

## BIBLIOGRAPHY

[1] Abeggelen, J. C. *Management and Worker: The Japanese Solution.* Tokyo: Sophia University, 1973.

[2] Austin, L. "The Political Culture of Two Generations: Evolution and Divergence in Japanese and American Values," in L. Austin, ed., *Japan: The Paradox of Progress.* New Haven: Yale University Press, 1976, pp. 231–54.

[3] Bairy, M. "The Motivational Forces in Japanese Life," in Robert J. Ballon, ed., *The Japanese Employee*, Chapter 6. Tokyo: Sophia University, 1969.

[4] Ballon, R. J. "Lifelong Remuneration System," in Robert J. Ballon, ed., *The Japanese Employee*, Chapter 6. Tokyo: Sophia University, 1969.

[5] Brown, M. "Values — A Necessary but Neglected Ingredient of Motivation on the Job." *Academy of Management Review* (1:15), October 1976, pp. 15–23.

[6] Drucker, P. F. "What We Can Learn From Japanese Management," *Harvard Business Review*, Vol. 49, No. 2 (1971).

[7] England, G. W. *The Manager and His Values: An International Perspective from the United States, Japan, Korea, India, and Australia.* Cambridge, Mass., Ballinger Publishing Co., 1975.

[8] England, G. "Managers and Their Value Systems: A Five Country Comparative Study," *Columbia Journal of World Business*, (Summer, 1978) pp. 35–44.

[9] Farmer, R., and B. B. Richman. *Comparative Management and Economic Progress.* Homewood, Illinois: Richard D. Irwin, Inc., 1965.

[10] Fox, W. M. "Japanese Management: Tradition Under Strain," *Business Horizon* (August, 1977).

[11] Frager, R., and R. Rohlen. "The Future of a Tradition: Japanese Spirit in the 1980's," in *Japan: The Paradox of Progress.* New Haven: Yale University Press, 1976, pp. 255–78.

[12] Haire, M., E. Ghiselli, and L. Porter. *Managerial Thinking: An International Study.* New York: Wiley, 1966.

[13] Hattori, I. "A Proposition on Efficient Decision-Making in the Japanese Corporation," *Columbia Journal of World Business*, (Summer, 1978) pp. 7–15.

[14] Hofstede, G. *Cultures Consequences*. Beverly Hills: Sage Publishers, 1980.

[15] Kabayashi, S. "The Creative Organization—A Japanese Experiment." *Personnel*, Vol. 47, No. 6, (November–December 1970) pp. 8–17.

[16] Kelley, L., and C. Reeser. "The Persistence of Culture as a Determinant of Differential Attitudes on the Part of American Managers of Japanese Ancestry," *Management International Review* (March, 1973), Vol. 16, No. 1, pp. 67–76.

[17] Kelley, L., and R. Worthley. "The Role of Culture in Comparative Management: A Cross-Cultural Perspective." *Academy of Management Journal*, Vol. 14, No. 1, pp. 164–73.

[18] Kono, T. "Long-Range Planning—Japan—USA—A Comparative Study," *Long Range Planning*, October 1976, pp. 61–71.

[19] Litterer, J. F. *An Introduction to Management*. Santa Barbara: John Wiley and Sons, 1978.

[20] Marengo, F. D. "Learning from the Japanese: What or How?" *Management International Review*, Vol. 19, (April, 1979) pp. 39–46.

[21] Moos, F. "Accumulations and Cultural Change: Reflections on Japanese Social Structure," in Fodilla, Gianni, ed., *Social Structures and Economic Dynamics in Japan up to 1980*, Vol. 1. Italy: Universita Bocconi–Milano, 1975.

[22] Nakane, C. *Japanese Society*. Berkeley: University of California Press, 1970.

[23] Nakayama, S. "Management by Participation in Japan," *Management Japan*, Vol. 6, No. 4, and Vol. 7, No. 1 (1973).

[24] Negandhi, A. R., and S. B. Prasad. *Comparative Management*. New York: Appleton-Century Crofts, 1971.

[25] Noda, K. "Big Business Organization" in Ezra F. Vogel, ed., *Modern Japanese Organization and Decision Making*. Berkeley: The University of California Press, 1975.

[26] Nowak, S. "Values and Attitudes of the Polish People." *Scientific American*, Vol. 245, No. 1, July 1981, pp. 45–53.

[27] Oh, T. K. "Japanese Management—A Critical Review," *Academy of Management Journal*, Vol. 1, No. 1 (January, 1976) pp. 14–26.

[28] Pascale, R. T. "Zen and the Art of Management," *Harvard Business Review* (March/April, 1978).

[29] Reichel, A., and D. M. Flynn. "Core and Peripheral Values of Japanese Managers in the United States." Presented at the National Meeting of the *Academy of International Business*, New Orleans, October, 1980.

[30] Reischauer, E. O. *The Japanese*. Cambridge, Mass.: Harvard University Press, 1979.

[31] Shuichi, K. "Reconstruction of the Japanese Group," *Japan Quarterly*. Vol. 21 (Jan.–March, 1974).

[32] Vogel, E. F. *Japan as Number One: Lessons for America*. Cambridge, Mass.: Harvard University Press, 1979.

[33] Yang, C. Y. "Management Style: American vis-à-vis Japanese," *Columbia Journal of World Business*. (Fall 1977) pp. 23–31.

[34] Yoshino, M. Y. *Japan's Managerial System: Tradition and Innovation*. Cambridge, Mass.: MIT Press, 1968.

# 8

# Individualism in the Japanese Management System

C. S. CHANG

## INTRODUCTION

Great attention has been recently focused on the Japanese management system in the United States to uncover possible reasons for the great success in economic growth in Japan during the post-war period. Japan is now one of the most industrialized countries in the world, and many attribute such an achievement to the unique management system in Japan.

It is agreed that group-oriented management is the most important feature in Japan. Traditionally, the Japanese society has emphasized the group rather than individual [4, p. 30]. In other words, Japan is a rather peculiar country where the consciousness of self is underdeveloped and the group consciousness overdeveloped [4, p. 30]. This group-oriented behavior is a decisively contributing factor to high productivity and effective management in Japan.

When a management system is a function of purely group-oriented behavior, there seems to be no room for individualism in the system since it has been ignored or buried in society. Is there truly no concept of individualism in the Japanese management system? Nobody can conceive how individualism could not exist in a society. Individualism in management must also exist in Japan.

The purpose of this chapter is to locate the role of individualism in Japan. The relationship between group-oriented behavior and individualism will be also examined.

## UNIQUENESS OF THE JAPANESE MANAGEMENT SYSTEM

If one agrees that a management system is the product of an environment, then the Japanese management system is the product of the Japanese culture. Its culture is different from the Western culture in many aspects, and there are many unique features in the Japanese management system [1, p. 107]. (See Table 1.)

A close relationship exists between government and business in which the latter clearly understands government policies and the former provides every support to business in achieving its goals, which are in line with overall government policies. Such coöperation is a contributing factor to an effective management system in Japan.

It is also a well-known fact that the Japanese workers are well educated and well disciplined. There can hardly be any questions of their high productivity.

If the Japanese management is very effective, it is the result of the combination of this uniqueness in management and environmental variables. If one investigates the uniqueness of management in Japan closely, he can identify that the core concept of Japanese management is group-oriented behavior among managers and employees.

As mentioned before, team spirit or group consciousness is very strong in Japan. Japanese managers do not behave like an individual being, but as

TABLE 1    Uniqueness of the Japanese Management System

| MANAGEMENT CONCEPTS | JAPANESE IMPLEMENTATION |
| --- | --- |
| Goals/objectives | Emphasis on long-term perspectives |
| Decision making | Ringi system or consensus |
| Leadership style | Paternalistic leadership and personal approach |
| Loyalty to company | Very strong |
| Employment pattern | Lifetime employment |
| Seniority | Strictly observed |
| Team spirit or group consciousness | Very strong |

members of groups or sub-groups. The linking-pin concept of Rensis Likert applies literally to organizations in Japan. A manager is both a member of a sub-group and a leader of a sub-group below. All the members of this sub-group move together as a single entity. There must be no deviation by members against the standards or norms of the group. To be a good group member is an absolute requirement in Japanese organizations. One of the paths to success in the organization is to melt themselves into the group atmosphere by becoming loyal company men [3, p. 40].

Leadership style in Japan coincides with this group orientation. A manager acts like a father to his subordinates and they are required to show their strong loyalty. All of these processes aim to transform each subordinate into a group or company man. This process is facilitated by lifetime employment in Japan. If one is guaranteed his job until he retires, it will be much easier to show his loyalty to the organization and his group.

In decision-making processes, group consciousness functions more intensively [5, pp. 37–39]. No individual member of the organization can make decisions by himself. No decision can be reached until all the members involved agree on it. Decision making by consensus means a process of depersonalization.

In summary, the virtues of becoming a group-man have been emphasized in the Japanese management system as a result of the country's traditional cultural pattern. Group behavior has produced an effective system for Japanese management. It is not certain whether such group-mindedness can be effective in other management systems with different cultural bases.

## PERCEPTION ON INDIVIDUALISM

If any management is the product of its environment, then the group consciousness in the management system is closely linked to its culture. In the context of the Japanese culture, the people have no distinctive consciousness of their individual selves; in fact, the Japanese language does not provide a clear concept of the individual self [2, p. 56]. Individualistic attitudes take on distasteful connotations of egoism and arrogance in Japan.

Does individualism have a role in this context? It is the assumption of this writer that individualism cannot be completely destroyed in any society, even though it may be overshadowed by group life. A society suffocates if individualism has no room to function.

Individualism does play a role in the management system of Japan, although few studies in the Japanese management literature have introduced it. There is a word in Japan, *risshin-shuse*, which can be translated as establishing oneself in a successful career. For many ambitious Japanese, this word has become the motto for their self-actualization. The individual Japanese in an organization is concerned with his own promotion and success and is constantly striving to achieve them [4, p. 41]. This means that competition among individual Japanese is very vigorous. Competition virtually starts at the nursery school level and continues until the latter part of life. Ambitious and capable Japanese must be admitted to Tokyo University or to one of the few other prestigious universities in the country for a successful career later. If one does not graduate from one of these universities, he has a very slim chance to lead a good career life. Since competition among high school graduates for these universities is so intense, it has produced the so-called "examination hell." Students must fervidly prepare for college entrance examinations. Those high school graduates who fail to enter one of these universities would try again every year until they are finally successful. They care called *ronin*, [4, p. 43] literally an unsettled and wandering warrior. Some of them have committed suicide out of disgrace and hopelessness. In order to be admitted by a prestigious university, one must attend a good high school. Again, competition is very keen for admission to these high schools. And one must attend a good junior high school, elementary school, and even kindergarten. So competition for a successful career starts at nursery school.

In this respect, Japanese society is not basically different from other societies that emphasize individual competition. Aspiration for excellence and individual glory is a common phenomenon in Japan. Sumo wrestling is a good example. It has a purely Japanese origin. The ultimate goal of every sumo wrestler is to become the champion, which brings great recognition as a folk hero and a huge reward. Even though group consciousness may work in sumo wrestling, individual aspiration and talent determines the status of each wrestler.

All athletes in boxing, tennis, swimming, gymnastics, and track, to name a few, aspired to one thing: to be an individual champion. Even in team games such as baseball, basketball, and soccer, each individual player tries to distinguish himself in various ways. This indicates that individualism plays a crucial role in sports in Japan just as in other countries. This individualism is applied in other fields such as art, music, literature, and motion pictures.

Of course, this individualism also plays an important role in Japanese management. The concept of promotion is a good example of this. Promotion to a higher position in an organization is due to personal desire in most cases. Aspiration for promotion is as common a phenomenon in Japan as it is in other societies. This aspiration elicits fierce competition within the organization. In a society where the seniority system is dominant, competition for promotion is limited to a significant extent. In Japan, the seniority system has an almost absolute importance. However, it is a very dangerous assumption that competition for promotion in Japan is unusual. On the contrary, competition is a very vital phenomenon in the Japanese management, since promotions continually occur on the basis of the best candidates.

Competition in Japan is different in one sense from that of other societies, for it is often engaged in under cover. If one desires to be promoted, he must first show his strong loyalty toward his superiors and the organization. In other words, the Japanese must seek "self-expression or individualism through the group," [4, p. 50]. Thus, individualism does exist in Japan as in other societies, but one cannot pursue it openly. It must be sought within the framework of the group.

However, there is no guarantee that individual aspirations and goals will always be in accordance with group goals. Therefore, the potential conflict between individualism and group consciousness has developed in Japanese management. This potential becomes greater still through interaction with U.S. and Western management systems, where individualism plays an explicitly crucial role.

## MANAGEMENT OF CONFLICTS IN JAPAN

The conflict between ego interests and the group interests exists in Japan as in other societies even though the former is overpowered by group consciousness. The way the Japanese settle such conflicts, however, differs from the methods used in other countries.

In the United States, for example, individualism is taken for granted and high individual aspiration, motivation, and creativity are strongly encouraged to achieve organizational effectiveness. Personal growth is everyone's utmost concern and group consciousness or team spirit is not emphasized extensively. The management of conflict in this situation focuses its attention on how to introduce the virtues of group-oriented behavior in the management system. This is one of the reasons why the American managers have begun to pay attention to the Japanese management system where group behavior has been instrumental in achieving great productivity and efficiency.

Japanese conflict management has a unique dimension. Its main focus is on how to balance individual aspirations and goals to group and organizational goals. Japanese managers can survive and succeed only when they demonstrate their skills to balance these two goals, which conflict with each other in many cases. An extreme solution to this problem is to become a perfect company man, believing that one's interest completely coincides with that of the group and organization. Many Japanese managers fit this description. The opposite extreme is to pursue one's own interests vigorously by ignoring the goals of his group and organization. Between these two extremes, various degrees of combination exist. The Japanese managers have been leaning toward the zone of extreme conformity. Many of the Japanese managers try to believe that they can achieve their personal goals and interests by pursuing organizational goals aggressively.

However, a clear sign indicates that many Japanese managers at middle and lower levels in the organization do not content themselves with this approach. They claim that individual interests can not entirely be cut off under any circumstances. A growing discontent has developed among many young Japanese toward the more traditional, conforming approach. They try to enhance the sense of their own being or identity. They speak of individual freedom from their families and communities, and criticize the existing system of denying individual identity. They insist that this practice must be modified accordingly. However, they are also aware of the fact that they cannot change their culture and the system overnight, and that they must eventually conform to their society. Here again they experience conflict.

The Japanese managers have developed an original way of solving or mitigating their conflicts. This may be called the Japanese-style management of conflict. After a day's work is over, Japanese managers usually do not go home directly. Instead, they go to bars by groups to eat and drink with each other. Under this relaxed atmosphere, they chat and laugh. But the main topics are related to company matters, and they discuss them informally. Usually the subordinates of these socializing groups speak out or express their complaints to their superiors. These subordinates are very reluctant to raise their complaints to superiors during office hours. In their rigid and structured workday environment, they remain men of conformity. However, socialization at bars and other places after work changes this rigid attitude to a significant degree. Under the influence of a relaxing drink, each subordinate freely speaks his mind. Superiors listen attentively and respond positively. Through this process of dialogue, there develops a good human relation. In many cases, superiors encourage their subordinates to present their complaints and other opinions later to them and their company. Subordinates are thus consoled by this informal process of dialogue, although they are not always completely satisfied. Such occasions function as a safety valve in the Japanese management system. Subordinates try to improve relations with superiors through these occasions for personal benefit.

During these informal gatherings, managers and subordinates try to restore respective self-interests and individual aspirations that may have become overlooked during regular work hours. In this atmosphere, such self-interests and aspirations emerge as a formidable driving force. It is interesting to note that the wives of these managers and subordinates are very tolerant of their husbands' coming home so late at night because they know it is indispensible to their careers.

Japanese managers thus balance their conflicting interests or goals in two different atmospheres — at work and the bar. During official work hours, they conform to group norms and company goals, but they try to develop their self-interests and personal goals during informal talks at bars and other places.

## CONCLUSION

Group-oriented behavior is one of the most important features of Japanese management, and a strong correlation seems to exist between this group consciousness and productivity and effectiveness. Individualism in Japan has been overshadowed by this group-oriented behavior. Many managers are reluctant to speak out for individualism in the management system. It would be understood as to threaten the system itself.

However, individualism exists in Japan as in other societies, and many managers and workers try hard to achieve their self-interests and goals. They understand well that they cannot pursue them openly in the system, so they try to accomplish them in a more implicit way. This has created conflicts in the management system and caused discontent among middle- and lower-level managers who are keenly interested in pursuing their individual goals.

These managers try to solve this conflict through informal gatherings at bars and other places during frank talks with their superiors and colleagues in a more relaxed atmosphere. This method has operated rather well in the Japanese management system, although it has never provided complete satisfaction to Japanese managers.

## BIBLIOGRAPHY

[1] Chang, C. S. "How Is The Japanese Management System Different?" in D. F. Ray, and T. B. Green, eds., *Management In An Age Of Complexity And Change.* Mississippi State: Southern Management Association, 1977.

[2] Kahn, Herman. *The Emerging Japanese Superstate: Challenge And Response.* Englewood Cliffs: Prentice-Hall, Inc., 1971.

[3] Maccoby, Michael. *The Gamesman.* Des Plaines, Ill.: Bantam Books, Inc., 1977.

[4] Ike, Nobutaka. *Japan, The New Superstate.* San Francisco: W. H. Freeman and Company, 1974.

[5] Yoshino, M. Y. *Japan's Managerial System.* Cambridge, Mass.: The MIT Press, 1968, and Chang, C. S. "The Decision-making Process In Japanese Corporations," in D. F. Ray, and T. B. Green, eds., *Management Perspectives On Organizational Effectiveness.* Mississippi State: Southern Management Association, 1975.

# 9

# The Japanese Business Value System

MOTOFUSA MURAYAMA

## INTRODUCTION

Business ethics should be a "way of business" in a broad sense and normally deviate from both social ethics (a "way of society") and religious ethics (a "way of religion"). Of course, neither does social ethics function as religious ethics. In fact, the three value systems (business ethics, social ethics, and religious ethics) do not coincide but tend, rather, to diverge greatly unless some kind of continuing effort is made to ensure their flexibility. For example, the collection of interest on business loans was once considered to be sinful or criminal by religious authorities. But this idea was gradually altered by a changing social consensus. Today, no one questions the validity of interest revenue earned from contracted loan agreements. Such transactions have become commonplace; to engage in them, socially acceptable and legally authorized behavior.

In Japanese business, it is extremely difficult to distinguish among the three aforesaid ethical standards. The Christian standards of the West, such as Protestant ethics[1] are not analogous to the Buddhism and Shintoism in the Japanese way of business life, because Shintoism comprises more than religious tenets. Its function includes defining "the entity of Japan" on the basis of comparative studies between the Shinto doctrines and those of religion with foreign origins, particularly transplanted Buddhism and Confucianism or Chinese Taoism.

Shintoism has contributed to the development of business ethics by teaching unquestioning devotion to the national entity, which generally furthers the value of group communication amongst Japanese people. Moreover, in terms of the Japanese managerial system, Shintoism can be viewed as the preconditional energy for refinement of business ethics. Prior to the development of business ethics per se, the Japanese manager has already learned the importance of affection held with respect to such groups as the family, the regional unit and the nation. Therefore, Shintoism provides the spiritual background for a "feeling of loyalty" to the Japanese business practice and company organizational unit if it is applied properly.

In the meantime, Buddhism has been treated more as a philosophical subject than as a source of religious ethics by Japanese intellectuals. Thus, in contemporary Japanese society, Buddhism is concerned with funeral affairs and ceremonial events, and likely to be discussed in the Oriental philosophy course at the university level for development of humanity and thinking. But one form of Buddhism still exists. A few new sects such as "Rissho-Kosei-Kai" or "Sokagakkai" operate under the reformation concept of traditional Buddhism, which usually attracts those who have unsatisfactory social and income status or suffer from insecure environment or mental anguish.

In the view of many Japanese managers, contemporary Buddhism and similar religious movements have been successful in helping to solve management problems where business ethics has failed. These include disputes about human nature and management concerning, for example, mental stability and concentration during work, self-fulfillment, assimilation of the individual by the group, etc. The essential doctrine of Buddhism involves, of course, the promotion of goodness and punishment of crime (kanzen choaku). This underlying religious ethic has been merged in Japanese society with non-Buddhist ethical conventions. In consequence, the Japanese way of conducting business has been influenced by its disciplines, especially Kanzen choaku, which views human behavior in light of its long-term effects.

"Confucianism" is hard to categorize as religion or philosophy, but still forms the basis of tacit rules in the way that social conventions do in the West. These efforts may be defined as the so-called "Japanization of the foreign culture" to make it suitable to the Japanese environment (social and management climate).

This chapter constitutes an attempt to characterize Japanese business ethics. Unfortunately, no exact analytical method exists to distinguish business ethics from social and religious ethics in Japan. Business ethics is an integrated doctrine and, vertically as well as horizontally, has mixed value premises. Sometimes, business ethics is a cause factor, but most of the time it has been regarded as an effect factor in the matrix of Japanese value systems. This can be inferred from the dominance of situational law over universal law in the Japanese business community.

In subsequent chapters, the Japanese way of doing business is defined in terms of this business ethics dimension and the input-output relationship in four areas: group value, individual value, behavioral value, and philosophical value. There are many disputes over the way Japanese business is conducted. For example, the Matsushita (National) Electric Co., Ltd., presents many faces to the world: it is a shrewd exploiter to the subcontracters, a severe banker to the divisional plant managers, a free publicity-driven efficiency man to the advertising specialists, a morale trainer to the new college graduates, and a social worker to the readers of its publication, the PHP (Peace, Health through Prosperity).

Matsushita is a typical example in that it represents business' identification with social goals and unspoken religious values in the cause of ambitious hidden profit motives. Mr. Konosuke Matsushita announced, "Production is social production and work in the plant leads to prosperity for the society as a result." In his comments, we find business ethics co-mingled with social ethics, while the pursuit of individual goals is identified with the general attainment of the goals of both business and society. This situation presents some questions from the international management standard (theories and practice viewpoint). Dr. Robert N. Bellar of Harvard University has concluded that Japanese society is motivated by "performance" and "particularism" while the United States is sociologically structured by the concepts of "performance" (achievement) and "universalism," referring to socio-analytical theories presented in the book by Parsons and Shils, *Toward a General Theory of Action*.[2]

The same business goal is attained by American universalism and Japanese particularism on the world stage. The philosophy and behavior of General Electric is based upon "contract philosophy" and "guilt culture." On the contrary, Matsushita Electric is heavily influenced by "family relationship type philosophy" and "shame culture," if we extend the theory from Ruth Benedict's book *The Chrysanthemum and the Sword* to management. Universalism is a determinant factor in the U.S. management as far as it is used in business conventions, contract arrangements, social rules, and majority-supported agreements.

The character of the U.S. universalism is such that business ethics is rather easily identified with socially accepted rules that are explainable by the concepts of rationalism, individualism, materialism, functionalism, and welfarism.

But the many sides of Japanese business ethics can sometimes be obscured by the often confusing warehouse of cultural influences — religious and pragmatic, opportunistic yet conservative of tradition — in which they are rooted. This problem will be discussed further in the following sections.

## GENERAL CONCEPTS OF JAPANESE
## BUSINESS ETHICS

During the decade of the 1970s, Japanese business became a major determinant of the country's way of life. Ethics per se is generalized as "the premise for one's fundamental value system that provides one with guidelines in the living of one's life." But this definition is ambiguous and oversimplified because such ethical values have difficulty maintaining their primary position under the law of nature. "Horizontal" influences often take precedence over "vertical" authority. Influences become "inputs" to the unknown true ethical value and thus the author views the dynamic value of ethics in light of the empirical facts that one's value judgment drifts from the law of nature to the law of situation. Thus, accepted situational truth is the primary underlying origin of business ethics just as flexibility is symbolized as an asset to businessmen.

Given this general definition, can we arrive at an accurate concept of business ethics? Let us first say that business ethics is the behavior of a business entity. A business entity has two facets: (1) The business organization as the system group concept and (2) The businessman as the nonsystem individual concept. After all, the former is treated as the company-goal motivated group, the latter as the personal happiness-attainment motivated individual. The business entity as an organizational system cannot separate a profitability goal from a social goal. This implies that the concept of rationalism traditional to business organization has been extended to accept the dominating political value system and thus the central ethical system of Japanese society. For example, pollution in the air, rivers, or seas generated by the chemical, steel, petroleum, and electric industries in Yokkaichi, Keihin, and Keiyo districts are currently the most discussed industrial issues in Japan. Pollution is not just the companys' problem, but a governmental and social problem as well, attracting the attention of academicians, scientists and other industrial groups, for the basic issue is considered to be the health and survival of the whole society.

The component of the business entity is the businessman, who must cope with the unstable Japanese mixture of humanity and profit achievement. He always wonders whether or not he should sacrifice himself, his family, and friendships, all of which are considered to be "private and individual," to "public and group" goals: business functions, moneymaking, production, and sales competition. As a result, the businessman is perplexed by a tangle of value considerations: ethics from Japan and other countries, and from the west, progressive rationalism with its emphasis on modernization, industrialization, technological innovation, and internalization.

Turning back to the definition of business ethics as the "way of a business entity" (*Keieijittai no arikata*), let us now attempt to define the conceptual framework for that "way." Here "way" (*arikata*) means "as it is valued" (*rashiku*) rather than the result of numerous discussions over its characteristics. However, "way" can be understood by taking either a philosophical or a behavioral approach. The philosophical approach to a "way" of business focuses upon the "inner" aspects of a business entity (*keiei jittai no naimensei*) such as spirit (*seishin*), emotion (*kimochi*), consideration (*omoiyari*), loyalty (*giri* or *chuseishin*), and affection (*ninjyo* or *itsukushi-mi*). The process involved is analogous to centripetal force in dynamics, since these separate aspects tend to be pulled into the central core of a business entity and generally defined as management philosophy in actual business practice. In a more narrow sense, this "inner" movement has often been presented in terms of "qualities" and subjective targets in management.

In the behavioral approach to understanding the "way" of a business entity, on the other hand, its activities are measured, hypothesized, or evaluated by conditional quantitative models, forms, monetary values, ratios, and other objective standards. This can be expressed as sales quota achievement, production budget attainment, planned profit goal-seeking, principles of scientific management efficiency motivation, etc. which all rationally relate to maximization of available resources, including investment, labor, and technologies.

Figure 1 illustrates the aforesaid conceptual framework of business ethics: the double sets of vertical and horizontal relationships assure that the "unknown" true core of business ethics will substantially reflect the values of the society as a whole.

The relationships depicted in Figure 1 are exemplified by the attitude of the Shin Nihon Steel Co., Ltd., and its chairman, Mr. Shigeo Nagano, when the People's Republic of China attempted to compel it to cease all business with Formosa and South Korea, threatening that 30% of the company's total export to China would otherwise be curtailed. In answer Mr. Nagano declared that "consistency of business attitude is what the nature of business demands." This expresses "loyalty to dignified business ethics" in terms of devotion, indulgence, justice, and equality. He quoted the words of mutual benefits (*gokei*) and the philosophy of equality (*byodo*), both of which can be traced back to the ancient Chinese Confucianism.

Mr. Nagano (an individual), who is identified with the company group goal from the managerial system viewpoint, is known as one of the most prominent company and industrial community leaders. His individual value standards are usually reflected by his individual philosophy while the group organizational value system of Shin Nihon Steel Co., Ltd. is more influenced by the rationally driven behavioral value system. To illustrate further, Mr. Nagano's individual value judgment must lead or be led by the company's or society's expectation which is based upon the acceptance and support of the majority. If he perceives that his justice is not comprehended

FIGURE 1    Conceptual Framework of Japanese Business Ethics

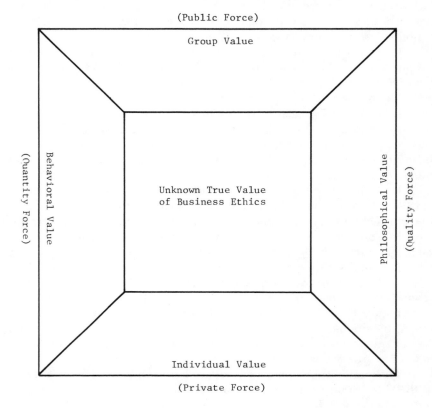

due to the immaturity of business realism, he may try to convince others, and the total system, not purely by management organization theory, but by political and psychological theories adapted to management. In this case, he continued his quest for a "common value" so that his individual personality could be depersonalized and completely unified with the company and the society as a whole, and thus function through the media of an influential, key leaders' coalition.

This ability on the part of the manager to achieve a synthesis of individual and group values is essential until the type of decision made becomes part of socially accepted business ethics. Therefore, the absolute confidence in personal ties and mutual trust plays a more critical role in management decision making than ambiguous management theories narrowly applied.

The behavioral and philosophical value systems of Mr. Nagano of Shin

Nihon Steel Co., Ltd., should be considered as one. To sell steel products at the Koshyo Koekikai market of Red China will benefit the company operation as well as the national gross income. The control mechanism of Mr. Nagano's philosophical values functions like an alarm clock as if to sell to China contradicts the inner, unspoken spiritual standards.

Under the refining process of modern capitalistic society we can anticipate that business ethics, even though fundamentally ambiguous, may be seen as a balance between quality (loyalty in the case of Shin Nihon Steel Co., Ltd.) and quantity (sales promotion) — an attempt to reach an equilibrium of these two forces without distortion. Such an ideal balance, of course, can occur only in theory, and in Japan it seems that situational law determines business ethics prior to the application of universal law. Therefore, the four value systems (individual, group, behavioral, and philosophical) shown in Figure 1 receive input *from* each other and contribute output *to* each other according to situational variations. Generally speaking, however, group values and philosophical values take precedence on the surface under an assumption that the Japanese business firm or the individual in a Japanese society is incessantly devoted to the assimilation of an "individual statics" with group dynamism, and of rational discomfort with sophisticated managerial philosophies.

## QUALITATIVE ANALYSIS OF THE INDIVIDUAL IN JAPANESE MANAGEMENT

A person viewed as a "freeman" in a social system, is designated as "personnel" in a managerial system of business administration. If a social system is genuinely identical to a business system, "freeman" and "personnel" can be conceptualized in the same definition. In actuality, a social system is motivated more by irrational "humanities" with multilateral purposes while a business system is oriented more toward thoughts of "efficiency" supported by conventional rules of both humanity and productivity.

Characteristics of an individual in a business organization are found in his relationships with (1) the workplace (a business system) and (2) the social system outside the work place (3) his own individual interest of goal attainment. Modern management theories have been constantly aiming at the integration of the three areas of goal attainment (company goals, society goals, and individual goals).

To implement the aforesaid integration process, the business executive (a business individual) needs a management philosophy. The following quotation is provided from Professor Ralph C. Davis's article "Management Philosophy and a Business Executive.[3]

The problem of greatest importance in the field of management is and probably will continue to be the further development of the philosophy of management. A philosophy is system of thought. It is based on some orderly, logical statements of objectives, principles, policies, and general methods of approach to the solution of some set problems. A managerial philosophy cannot supply a basis of effective thinking for the solution of business problems if it is satisfactory only to owners and employees. A managerial philosophy that is necessary, therefore, for unity of thought and action is the accomplishment of economic objectives. We cannot have an effective industrial economy without effective industrial leadership. We cannot have an effective leadership without a sound managerial philosophy. Industrial leaders without such a philosophy are business mechanics rather than professional executives.

This concept of the goal of an economy, as described by Professor Ralph C. Davis, can be extended to the goals of industrial societies in the 1980s, and his ideas of identifying employees' goals with management's

FIGURE 2    Dynamics of Goal Relationships

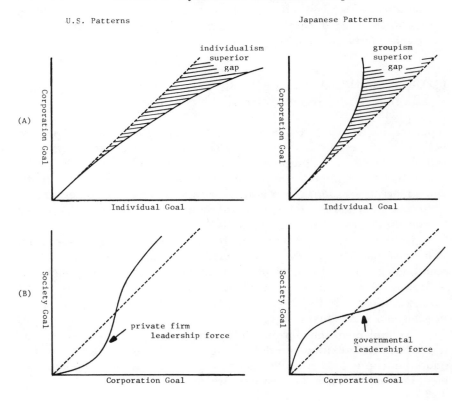

goals, management's goals with the industrial society's goals, provide a distinctive method by which to define the role of business executives. This will be discussed further below.

Up to now, the author has described a "business individual" on the basis of the Western management infrastructure. Hereafter, the focus will be on Japan. As the first step in an analysis of the three above mentioned business relationships, the values inherent to each area should be expressed in some way. These values can be made explicit as (1) "personal satisfaction variables," which can be measured by a number of factors, including job satisfaction and material satisfaction related to the attainment of an individual goal; (2) company goals such as "strength of organization and potential for continued expansion," gauged according to qualitative and quantitative variables such as sales, productivity, profit ratio, technological innovation, staff education, etc.; and finally (3) social goals such as "a humane industrial system," computed on the basis of provisional variables reflecting universal concepts in the humanities such as love, trust, justice, etc.

In Figure 2, a comparison of Japanese and American values in these

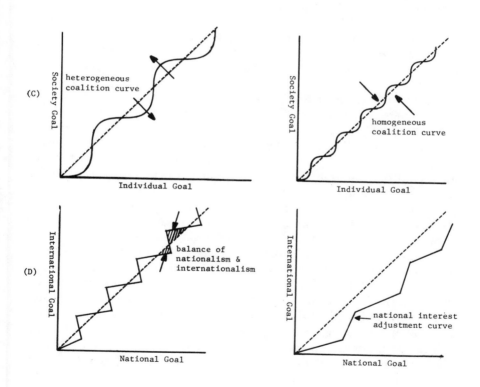

areas, as well as in a fourth area — that of international matters — is made. Illustrating a concept of "equilibrium of different goal values," also defined as "optimum identification of goal attainment variables," the broken central lines in (A), (B), (C), and (D) represent an optimum point where individual, corporate, social (national), and international goals are equalized under an assumption of a "most desirable" world managerial system.

## Group Goal Management

The first chart in Figure 2 shows "groupism particularity" in Japanese management. An individual is basically oriented by unavoidable traditional value standards such as self-denial for the group (corporation). A person is more willing to identify himself with Toyota Motors Co., Ltd., per se rather than with a specific job in Toyota, such as that of engineer, accountant, or sales manager. This man stands on the group's prestige, and his pride and independence in society originate from his sense of belonging to the Toyota Group. Moreover, his personal satisfaction is measured by the degree to which he can assimilate himself into the group motivated activities.

In many instances, corporate goals cannot be justified by the standards of an individual. Any conflict between the group value and individual value standards is usually secondary due to the historical pattern of private individual (watakushigoto) goal negation and public or group (company) goal affirmation.

This placement of group goals above individual goals in business makes a person highly dependent, but is strategically advantageous to the Japanese managerial system since the individual is afraid to be cut off from the group pride or lose face if he is not loyal to the group goal statement. (The dominance of the group in management can be traced back to the Japanese cultural philosophy, especially Confucianism in the Edo Period, and will be discussed in subsequent chapters.)

The lifetime employment convention prevailing in a Japanese managerial system can be considered to support this groupism. For example, in a previous research project conducted in 1968, 500 engineers, specialists, and management staff selected from the Chiyoda Chemicals and Industrials Company Ltd. were questioned as to their interest in more job opportunities. Only five of the questionnaires returned indicated any desire to change employment. In a further investigation of these five persons, they were found to be individuals who could not overcome rumors of failure in job and human relations generated within the corporation. If Chiyoda Chemicals can be presumed representative of Japanese companies, we would conclude that in Japan there is but one corporation called Japan Company Ltd., united by group goals. This is statistically reflected by the fact that the gross national income of Japan in 1969 reached second place in the international ranking in the amount of 166 billion dollars, while the personal income per capita was sixteenth, amounting to 1,290 dollars yearly.

## Public Leadership Management

In common usage of the words, "public" (ko) and "private" (shi), as they are applied in describing an individual, a corporate organization, and a government, we found serious discrepancy between the American and Japanese. These findings are illustrated in Table 1. In Japan, the company is recognized as a public factor clearly separated from private individual matters, but without a clear disassociation from the government.

As indicated in Table 1, an individual in a Japanese Corporation (example: Matsushita Electric Co., Ltd.) presumably believes that his working environment is synonymous to the social and public environments. This illusion is completed by the belief that Matsushita and the Japanese society (government) are unified to achieve the same goals, since he obviously sees the government entity through the eyes of Matsushita Electric, which means everything to his life and family in conjunction with the aforesaid lifetime employment system, which in turn has been accepted as a rule of society. Consequently, the corporation goal is liable to take full advantage of this illusion if there is no governmental injunction to the contrary. In the meantime, if Matsushita Electric has a weak position relative to foreign competitors in the international markets, then the Japanese government would automatically guide the firm with a candid recognition of the firm's "immaturity" and admission of protectionism due to the Japanese business amateurism, because Matsushita Electric is part of a Japan Company Ltd. as a whole, quasi-family unit.

TABLE 1   Public and Private (Ko and Shi) Differentiation Chart

| SOCIAL UNITS | AMERICAN CONCEPT | | JAPANESE CONCEPT |
|---|---|---|---|
| Individual ⟶ | Private (big) | = | Private |
| | ‖ | | × |
| Corporation ⟶ | Private (small) | × | Public (small) |
| | × | | ‖ |
| Government ⟶ | Public | = | Public (big) |

Legend:    = agreement
           × disagreement
           ( ) relative description

Returning to Figure 1(B), the corporate goal is strongly led by the society's goals (public, governmental, cultural, political, and other nonbusiness goals, mixed). Especially, governmental leadership force functions as a business innovator in the beginning and, later on, as buffer and adjuster for the driving factors of corporate development. For example, the original units of the present major leading corporations in Japan including Mitsubishi Group, Mitsui Group, Shin Nihon Steel Group, etc., were founded by the Japanese government and given away to them practically free or at minor cost under the national policies of (1) nation wealth, (2) strength of military force, (3) industrialization, and (4) culture and civilization (in Japanese terms, Fukoki, Kyohei, Shokusan Kogyo, and Bunmeikaika) during the Meiji Reformation Era (1868).

The U.S. and Japan have similar attitudes toward the relationship of corporate goals and social goals. It is conceivable that ultimately their two systems of implementation could also become very much alike. Both managerial systems are aiming at the same answers, but the solution process is differently called "privately motivated industrial democracy" and "governmentally motivated industrial democracy." Of course, the Japanese government does not always deal with each corporation. The same line of industries are guided by the government to organize associations such as Japan Steel Industries Association (Tetsukoren), Japan Electric Power Association (Denryoku Renmei), Japan Petroleum and Chemical Industries Association (Sekiyu Kagaku Renmei), Japan Textile Industries Association (Seni Renmei). The government's and private firms' penchant for organizing such horizontally structured business groups leads to the development of semi-government or quasi-private corporate entities with competition eliminated to the extent that the society and company goals coincide with the government intention. This may be described in terms of the "rational Japanese way of doing business." Thus, in the Japanese management environment of big firms, the roles of (1) the government, (2) the associations of similar industries or executives, and (3) the individual executive in a firm may be likened to those of (1) a dignified and strict grandfather, (2) an understanding father, and (3) an obedient child.

## Homogeneity Management

In Figure 2(C), the vertical line indicates the society's goals as determined by the general attitudes of political and governmental leaders. The goals of individuals in a business enterprise are represented along the horizontal line. An individual who belongs to a Japanese company does not have independence of mind from the company group behavior because he knows that if he did he would become a misfit in the lifetime employment system. However, we can still look for an individual personality and human quality in business, which have become acceptable both in society and the work environment.

The relationship between individual and social goals should be dealt with from several viewpoints considering that here measurable factors such as wealth or national income are entangled with unmeasurable factors such as peace or happiness in the course of their achievement. But we can infer a link between society and individual factors in the cultural heritage or cultural and sociological background of the management environment. We postulate that the Japanese cultural determinant of behavor is "shame" or "face saving" and sociological patterns under the "shame culture" of individual behavior are "other-directed" (to borrow the term from David Reisman's *The Lonely Crowd*). The cause of the "shame culture" and "other-directed" behavior can be seen in the homogeneity of Japanese national and social units.

Homogeneous particularism in Japan covers the areas of race, language, education, neighborhood relationships, national feeling, and so forth, which are observed in vertical and horizontal line association. Homogeneity solves premanagement problem areas and becomes the basis for mutual trust and deeper comprehension of unspoken feelings in Japanese management. Moreover, homogeneity functions in the Japanese way of life as if it were an automatic feedback control mechanism in a computer operation.

This means that any errors made by individuals and society will be automatically corrected or adjusted without serious deviation from a presumably shared value. Referring back to Figure 2(C) one may see that the direction of the individual and society by "shame" and the "other person's emotion," and the homogeneous nature of Japanese management, creates the "quasi-village"-minded structure and philosophy of Japanese management particularism.

## Nationalistic (Egoism and Conservatism) Management

Through their "closed-society consciousness," the Japanese people have discovered beauty in nature, value, discipline, and peace. Using the analytical methods of cultural anthropology, Professor Chie Nakane of Tokyo University defines the Japanese social structure as a "vertical line system society" in her book, *Human Relations in a Vertical Society (Tateshakai no Ningen Kankei)*.[4]

An individual who lives in a vertical line society is extremely fearful of the revision of existing vertical line relationships and the expansion of horizontal associations. Matters of international interest are regarded as horizontal aspects in the development of a national entity. A businessman from Japan, holding rigid loyalty (vertical) to the parent company in Japan, is still puzzled as to how the Japanese national entity can identify itself with international goals, since international interests are more geared to the horizontal line relationships attending such goals as economic coöperation among countries, protection of human rights and world peace and prosperity.

Note, however, that regarding the immaturity of thinking among the average Japanese as to international goal seeking, as well as conservative behavior favoring the continuation of vertical associations, Figure 2(D) shows a gradual movement in the direction of the optimum intersection of national and international goals.

## JAPANIZATION THEORY I: CULTURAL HERITAGE OF JAPANESE EXECUTIVES

### General Theory of Foreign Culture Japanization

The previous section described the "core character" of individual and organizational units in a Japanese firm using a comparative, or "horizontal," approach.

In this section the author will conduct a vertical analysis of a Japanese business entity, in which Japanese management philosophy must be viewed from an historical and cultural standpoint. Whenever we attempt to define "Japanese management concepts," we must first develop a theoretical framework in which the traditional values of Japanese culture can be elucidated in terms of "premanagerial values." These traditional values, found in the vertical relationship of personnel in the Japanese managerial system and defined as latent value, are a mix of spirituality, prejudice, kinship, territorialism, tribalism, and so forth.

Japanese business ethics can be analyzed in terms of Japanese "core character" and "cultural values." Japanese culture itself can be discussed: (1) an external (foreigner's) evaluation, (2) in terms of the historical influence of Chinese culture and civilization, (3) in terms of the influence of Western culture and civilization after the Meiji Reformation, and finally (4) in terms of its own particular environment with reference to comparative studies, including (1), (2), and (3).

Definitely, Japanese culture has been influenced by foreign-based philosophies, especially from northern Asia, China, India, southern Asia, Europe, and America. In spite of the fact that racial distribution in Japan is homogeneous, Japanese culture is heterogeneously mixed so as to result in the improvement of the Japanese core character. Professor Shuichi Kato defines, in the book, *Theory of Japanese Culture (Nihon Bunkaron)*,[5] that the culture of Japan is "miscellaneously-rooted" (Zatshu Bunka) and that a healthy mixture results in a happier creature. Also, Professor Konan Naito (1866–1934) concluded that the character of Japanese culture must be "bittern culture" (Nigari no Bunka). Bittern is an essential ingredient to make bean curd (Tofu). Bean curd is gradually solidified by a certain quantity of bittern added. In the same way, foreign culture has been absorbed into Japanese culture through the passing of time, geographical distance, and quantity-input control. This is identical to the situation analysis in which the foreign influences of Buddhism, Confucianism, and capitalism gradually blended into Japanese soil to reappear in a new form within the natural framework of the Japanese climate (Nihon Fudo) and cultural framework (Nihon Bunka). This pattern can be called the "aboriginality movement" (Dochakuka), of Japanization (Nipponka), converting foreign and heterogeneous but suggestive ideas into homogeneous Japanese ideas.

For further illustration, the aforementioned is visualized in simple form in Figure 3. The upper horizontal line of boxes shows the foreign cultural factors that contributed in a major way to the Japanese-originated core culture found in the books of *Kojiki* (712) and *Nihonshoki* (681). The lower horizontal line of boxes indicates the Japanization process. In the center the transformers of culture, "go-betweens" whose revolutionary efforts helped get rid of the static character of Japanese culture, are circled.

Professor Saburo Ienaga identifies two specific characteristics of the Japanese core culture as (1) continuity of a world view and (2) positiveness of a life view. The first means that the present world is completely identified (even geographically connected) with Takamagahara (the land of gods and goddesses). In other words, there is no clear distinction between individuals and gods. They are considered to be united in some universal sense. Therefore, the people believe that the place where gods function must be within walking distance. This belief is called "continuity of a world view." And this idea is expressed as "Ashiharano Nakatsunokuni" (the province of Yamato believed as heaven).

"Positiveness of a life view" is the doctrine of "sin denial." All mankind is positively accepted and purified, while existence of crime is denied in this view of life on the basis of the understood world-view. In cases where a sinful act is committed, the authority of Norito (ritual prayer) can clear the mistake.

FIGURE 3   Culture Japanization Process

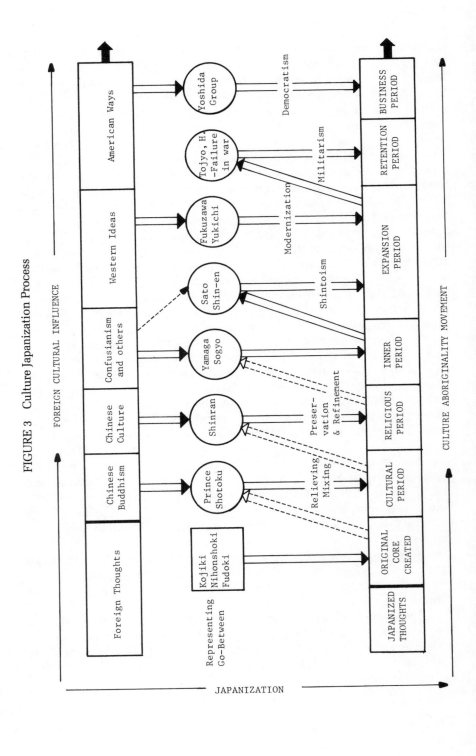

104

# Traditional Ethics of Japanese Business Executives

Traditional business ethics are still very much alive in Japanese management decision making. Traditional business ethics can be described by the following criteria:

1. Residual value in empirical evidence.
2. Immutable value in the candid recognition of durability (survival) and majority support.
3. Inner value in the liberation from fear, uncertainty, and disunion from affinitive community.
4. Unspoken value in the informal reflection of society's rules and hidden religious precepts.
5. Inherent are the oriental values emphasizing spiritualism, emotionalism, and scientific logic, with indirect rationalism suppressing direct rational behavior.

How have traditional business ethics been cultivated? This query will be supplemented with material research on Japanese management history conducted by Professor Takao Tsuchiya of Takushoku University.[6] Business ethics in Japan were preconditioned by the advent of a primitive system of capitalism in the Edo. In this period, the Tokugawa Shogunate government was stabilized and marketing channels for products distribution as well as a monetary economic system were solidly established on a nationwide scale. From this time, commercially based business was given consistent government support for approximately three centuries, and we can recognize here the beginnings of a uniform concept of group-accumulated value of "goodwill" (noren), in which a store, a family, and/or employees were all united into one single unit, reputation, and creditability.

Thus, the origin of business ethics can be traced back to the Edo period because economic-man's spirit was formed in a parallel course with the primitive economic system. Some scholars, however, take the position that the capitalist's spirit differs from capitalistic system in the same way the Christian spirit is not entirely represented by the church system. In other words, merchants of Edo era were owner-oriented managers or nominal representatives supported by loyal key staff using the contemporary management definition. Nevertheless, their management doctrines were composed in conformity to the feudal society framework and the leading philosophies of that era. Therefore, hereafter the term "Edo management spirit" should be understood in this sense. The social philosophy that formed the basis of the Edo management spirit will be analyzed in a following chapter from two viewpoints. These are: (1) the feudalistic social stratification (warriors, farmers, craftmen, and merchants); and (2) the merchant family (store) system and the loyal and affectionate relationship between owner and workers.

Links between the Edo management spirit and contemporary business ethics are summarized in Figure 4. Three major influences have helped form traditional business ethics in Japan: (1) latent Confucianism-vertical authority, (2) constant input of new thoughts from the Western hemisphere for reformation of historical business ethics-horizontal push power, and finally (3) intuitive survival rules under the law of situation (i.e., "Japanese ways," in most instances of business behavior and decision making).

FIGURE 4    Historical Trend of Traditional Business Ethics in Japan after the Edo Period

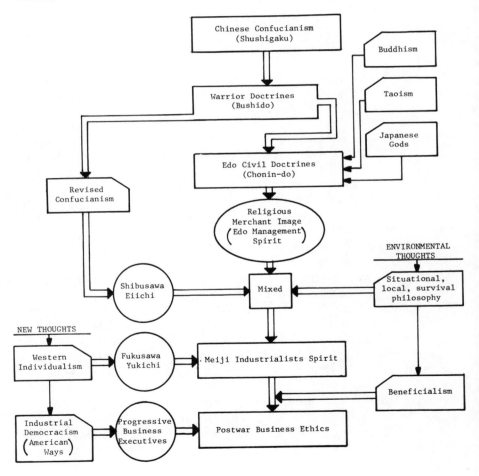

# JAPANIZATION THEORY II: SCHOOLS OF JAPANESE MANAGEMENT PHILOSOPHY

Two types of analysis have been used to explain Japanese management philosophy. The first method is elucidation through historical study, present existence traced from the past events. For example, the "history of economic thought" studies the economic doctrines of our predecessors, and economic history involves historical studies on the development of economic systems.

The second method can be tentatively defined as sociological, in which the past is reviewed from the perspective of the present. Using sociological approach, the author will attempt to develop a trial theory of Japanese management philosophy by seeking to identify the present decision-making mechanisms of Japanese business executives with the historical sources of four schools of management in Japan.

These four schools are the following:

1. Confucian Management School (Jyukyo Chuyo Keieiha)
2. Western Management School (Seiyo Kakushin Keieiha)
3. Religious Management School (Shukyo Seishin Keieiha)
4. Unclassified Management School (Kongo Rinen Keieiha)

For further discussion, more intensive analogies of the above four basic management philosophies must be pursued to the extent that the heterogeniety of the present Japanese business doctrines can be hypothetically systematized.

## Confucian Management School (Jyukyo Chuyo Keieiha)

Precisely speaking, the Confucian Management School is management philosophy based upon Confucianism — the virtue of constant mean (the Doctrine of Mean). The doctrine of Confucianism will be explained in terms of business management in spite of the fact that Confucianism itself was originally developed for the political leadership in China as well as in Japan.

The essential nature of Confucian doctrines can be discussed through a comparison of the terms "public" (ko) and "private" (shi). In a previous discussion, the company in Japan was shown to have an "implied public" nature, with a prevailing vague differentiation between the affairs of the society (public) and those of the company. With this in mind, the doctrine of Confucianism is summarized in Table 2.

TABLE 2    Confucian Viewpoint toward Public-Private Relationships

| COMPARATIVE STANDARD | PUBLIC (KO) CONCEPT | PRIVATE (SHI) CONCEPT |
| --- | --- | --- |
| Social unit | A group | An individual |
| Importance degree | Superiority | Inferiority |
| Attitudes | Straight (kochoku) Fair (kohei) | Irregularities (shikyoku) Emotional (shijyo) |
| Origin | Man-made doctrine: 1. Loyalty 2. Justice, etc. | Natural doctrine: 1. Humanity 2. Personality (character), etc. |
| Direction | External progress | Inner progress |
| Learning methods | To be taught: 1. Loyalty for master 2. Generosity for father 3. Filial piety for children 4. Faith for husband 5. Subordinance for wife, etc. | To be experienced: 1. Love 2. Hatred 3. Desire (greed), etc. |
| Value system | Universal truth Universal order Harmony creature No god (gods) accepted | Being ignored (No value given, if compared to group justice) |

From the Confucianism Management School, we are able to conclude that:

1. A group comes first and an individual is willing to sacrifice or deny himself for group doctrines.
2. Group doctrines are always superior to individual doctrines; therefore, an individual who creates group support, regardless of right or wrong, generally gains victory in business competition, and individual justice or universal justice is liable to be rejected by situational, specific, and artificial considerations of group justice in many instances.
3. Emotion and attitude regarding group behavior are expressed in such hard touch but soft content words such as "straight" and "fair." On the contrary, individualistic behavior has been termed as "irregularity," "corrupt practice" and "unfair dealing."
4. Public group doctrines are said to be universal and supposed to govern unstable emotionalism (individual feelings). Private emotionalism is based upon the law of nature and has the character of uncontrollability that can be manifested through, "love," "hatred,"

or "desire" (greed). However, group universalism originates from recognition of the "way of universal truth" (tendo) beyond ordinary human knowledge. And the enlightenment of individuals comes with one's grasp of this "way of universal truth." Unfortunately, this is not easily accomplished, and usually the spoken group universalism replaces the unspoken enlightenment of "tendo."

5. The doctrines of Confucianism function like the spirit of God as the result of the way that both should be taught and recognized. But emotionalism or private affairs can be experienced without proper education.

6. From the viewpoint of decision making, harmony (chowa) is a first choice and the virtue of the constant mean must be sought. Universalism is another expression of harmony. The author believes that group behavior appears to be a substitute for real universalism in the quest for universal order, because genuine universalism is quite rare and not accessible to everybody.

The concept of public (ko) as clarified above is termed as the "way of warriors" (Bushido). Bushido and Confucianism have had a close relationship because Confucianism could provide solutions to political problems for the Tokugawa Shogunate government after the factional wars were ended, whereby the nonproductive warriors group could be disciplined in a spirit of harmony, eliminating the feeling of materialism, and promoting a high spirituality (self-denial and self-respect).

Sogyo Yamaga (1622–1685), in his theory of the warrior class (shidoron) searched for the reason for the high social status of the warrior class even though it had little value to the then social system from the viewpoint of economic productivity, while other groups of people — farmers, craftmen, and merchants who were concerned with economic behavior and economic system operations — were of lower status. Only a small portion of the warrior group (Bushi) actively represented the Edo government; the majority of warriors did not have work opportunities in this politically peaceful period. Still, the Tokugawa Shogunate government had to maintain these warriors in order to control the nation. This caused the development of a Confucianism-based warrior spirit that also provided moral patterns for the general public, putting loyalty to the federal authorities above materialistic interest. In such a life doctrine for warriors, and the society, harmony with the static organization was the essential concept, and a philosophy that would not upset the existing social system was adhered to. Consequently, justice was regarded as situational and provisional because of the priority of the preservation mechanism of the federalists system. This state of affairs developed the specific mental structure of warriors (zonshin no kufu, kokorogamae).

Tsunetomo Yamanoto in Edo era defined Bushido as the way of death in his book, *Hagakure*. Tranquil strength of will power by self-sacrifice was recognized and practiced as the unavoidable code of the warriors. This implies that the way of death in war time was converted to the discipline of absolute loyalty, the peace time equivalent of death.

Bushido was influential in forming the merchants' moral background in the Edo Era. After the Meiji Reformation, it helped create the basis for the Meiji Business Doctrines, which can be summarized by the terms of shikon shosai (samurai spirit with merchant talents). The purpose of the shikon shosai was to comingle the spirit of the warriors with the working abilities and attitudes of merchants and mechanics, changing the traditional attitudes in which warriors disregarded business operations. During the Edo Period the warrior group disdained the commercial activities of the merchant group because Confucianism and Bushido denied the profit motivated business behavior, in accordance with the Analects of Confucius (Rongo).[7]

However, Eiichi Shibusawa (circa 1840), the most outstanding propounder of both the modern capitalist spirit and the framework of capitalism in the Japanese way successfully modeled a new interpretation of Bushido and Confucianism. Professor Buzan (Akira) Taba, Chiba University, studied this well-known conversion from Edo Bushido Confucianism to the Meiji business spiritual system as promulgated by Shibusawa. Shibusawa's business philosophies are represented by Giri Ryozensetsu (Theory of Both Faith and Profit justified in Equilibrium) or Rongo-Soroban Setsu (Theory of the Analects of Confucius with merchant-minded practice) or Keizai Dotoku Ichi Setsu (Economy and Moral Matching Theory). Mr. Shigeo Nagano, Chairman of Shin Nihon Steel Co., Ltd., is one of the typical examples of this Confucian Management School. His undisturbed will power and belief in vertical line relationships are expressions of his Confucian management philosophy. In other words, his attitudes represent the traditional business value system and the normal acceptance of majority business and governmental support. To summarize the Confucian Management School, its central value system lies in the inner efforts of preserving vertical-line practices such as seniority, superiority of personnel relationships within the company, and father-type presidential leadership. Even though Western management practices have been thoroughly studied by him and his staff, the aforementioned type of organization remains.

A more intensive analysis of the remaining three management schools as listed above will be reserved for other chapters. However, a summary table showing socio-management analysis of the four schools is presented in Table 3.

A business executive varies himself from School 4 to School 1 and so forth in accordance with the progress of his business or the sophistication of his career. To be more specific, individual management philosophies can be said to vary in terms of the following indicators:

TABLE 3  Summary of the Japanese Management Schools of Thought

| SCHOOLS | CENTRAL VALUE | ORIGINAL THOUGHTS (IN EDO ERA) | FOUNDERS | TYPICAL FOLLOWER AT PRESENT |
|---|---|---|---|---|
| (1) Confucian Management Schools | (1.) Political value system (2.) Personnel relationship | Confucianism Bushido Buddhism Japanese ways | Eiichi Shibusawa (1840–1931) Meizen Kinpara (1832–1927) Teiichi Sakuma (1841–1918) Tsuneta Yano (1865–1951) Tanji Kosuge (1882–1961) | Taizo Ishizaka (1886– ) Shigeo Nagano (1900– ) |
| (2) Western Management School | (1.) Economic value system (2.) Functional relationship | Rationalism Beneficianism Competition Materialism Individualism Christianity | Yukichi Fukuzawa (1685–1744) | Kazutaka Kikawada (1898– ) |
| (3) Religious Management School | (1.) Religious belief and society moral value system (2.) Spiritual relationship | Sekimon Shigaku Kansai Business Practice Ways of Merchants Life Contemporary Religion | Baigan Ishida (1685–1744) | Konosuke Matsushita (1894– ) |
| (4) Unclassified Management School | (1.) "Survival of the fittest" value system (2.) Business egoistic relationship | Commercialism in pure sense | Small businessman | |

1. Degree of profits retained
2. Degree of availability of cash assets liquidity
3. Growth rate of number of workers and staff
4. Amount of executive experience
5. Corporation history
6. Degree of market exposure show
7. Degree of technological proficiency
8. Degree of planned goal attainment
9. Degree of management quality and training

Japanese executives align themselves along the aforementioned philosophical continuum in response to the influence of the said determinants. Usually, an executive intends to encompass the vertical line thoughts (traditional value premise by Confucian Management Approach) with horizontal line concepts (scientific reasoning and innovative organizational behavior, i.e., a mix of hard core Western management ideas with Confucian-derived or religiously expressed management ideas).

## SUMMARY

It is difficult to measure the business value system on an empirical basis due to its inherently vague nature. This article has focused on the unmeasurable "ethical characterization," as the expected business moral standards that every Japanese can accept as "good" individual and institutional behavior. This vagueness stems from the fact that concepts of business ethics in Japan derive in most instances from the conflict between collectivism (groupism) and economic individualism. Direct expression of economic individualism can not win social acceptance, but if economic individualism is skillfully covered by sophisticated spiritualism and the emotionalism of collective (group) acceptance, we often find its social acceptance (and thus of the dynamic value of business behavior) within the Japanese psychological framework, represented by the term, naniwabushi-cho. Therefore, universalism in the true business value-finding process cannot be essential to the individual. On the contrary, a rational factor as well as a material factor in determination of business value should be presumed as a reliable quantitative and scientific standard for measurement of business value in Japan. For this purpose the successful achievement of goals can be expressed in dollar figures and ratios (for example, accumulation of profits, increase of sales amounts). In other words, the degree of business value is equally paralleled with the degree of quantitative goal attainment or performance level. This indicates that the business value is determined in relation to the quantitative approach of money-motivated materialism and nonhumanistically orientated rationalism. The author cannot deny this actual trend in the contemporary Japanese business system.

However, the quantitative, rational determinants of business value, including time, space, money, and other objective standards, are quite different in the Japanese way of business, than in the west. In the West, business value based on a quantitative approach still generally reflects an essential acceptance of both the individual and a collective organization. And of course the Western concept of business ethics (the qualitative approach) universally postulates the importance of the individual as well as the organizational group.

The Japanese way of doing business, both ethically and quantitatively speaking, takes a one-sided view, stressing the group, rather than attempting to achieve equilibrium between individual and organizational goal attainment.

Since group values tend to be less universally recognizable than individuals' values and more prone to be determined by the particular situation, Japanese business values are more difficult to define. Due to the specific management environment in Japan, therefore, group particularism has not acquired a standard business value system beyond the law of situation combined with the laws of nature and a traditional value consciousness. This implies that it must be joined with emotionalism (nonrational feelings) against rational individualism for the creation of harmonious and continuing management environments.

Through our scrutiny of Japanese business values we may recognize an immaturity in the Japanese managerial system. The developed and modern management system is preconditioned by the normal ethical expectation to increment both the desires of an individual in an organization and the group goal. In Japan, the management environment is not identically matured to the level of the developed Western standards (especially U.S. standard) or patterns because the business value system still retains the federalistic cultural heritage and an independence from the Western conceptual framework.

The model for this description of the Japanese business value system is based on today's system. But influential thoughts from more developed foreign competitors will undoubtedly force the present management system of group amateurism to change toward either professional group management or amateur individual management. The former pattern of progress will strengthen and refine the present system, but the latter will lead to the deterioration and confusion of the Japanese managerial system. If the Western pattern of management is presumed as individual responsibility-based professionalism, the Japanese (Oriental) pattern is supposed to intersect the Western management ideas with the future group responsibility-based professionalism. This is another way of defining the Japanese business value system using the empirical approach. Empirical definition leads to the concepts of hard core traditional, vertical line thoughts, in contrast to the more mobile Western, horizontal line thoughts that are serviceful for adjustments, remodeling, and innovation.

From its post-war education, Japan has received Western conceptual fluency and flexibilities. Therefore, there is still a great confusion between the traditional group particularism and the newcomer, individual universalism. Also, Western educational influences have brought quantitative methods of materialism and rationalism. This has challenged the traditionally firm belief in group priority and its attendant requirements of modesty and obedience in the individual. In the short run, the Japanese business value system will be radically redirected towards individualistic and materialistic rational management. But from the long-term viewpoint, there will be an adjustment in the educational system, and the sophistication of the business value system will be pursued as a result of technological innovation and international competition; that is, the Japanese way of rational management will strengthen the group dynamism of business value thoughts. Therefore, social system, business system, and human nature will be further integrated to generalize the ethical and quantitative aspects of the business value system in Japan.

## FOOTNOTES

[1]Walter Goldschmidt, "Ethics and the Structure of Society: An Ethnological Contribution to the Sociology of Knowledge", in *Management and Society*, Lynn H. Peters ed., (Belmont, Calif.: Dickenson, 1968) pp. 102–118.

[2]Talcott Parsons, and Edward A. Shils, *Toward a General Theory of Action*, (Boston: Harvard University Press, 1954).

[3]"Research in Management During the '50s" in *Research Needs in Business during the '50s*, Indiana Business Reports, Report No. 13 (Bloomington, Indiana: The School of Business, Indiana University, 1959), p. 32.

[4]Chie Nakane, *Tateshakai no Ningen Kankei*, (Tokyo: Kodansha, 1967), pp. 70–112.

[5]Shuichi Kato, *Nihon Bunkaron* (Theory of Japanese Culture) (Tokyo: Tokuma, 1966).

[6]Takao Tsuchiya, *Nihon Keiei Rinenshi* (History of Japanese Management Philosophies) (Tokyo: Nihon Keizai Shinbun, 1970).

[7]Chie Nakane, *Tateshakai no Ningen Kankei* (Tokyo: Kodansha, 1967), pp. 70–112.

## BIBLIOGRAPHY

[1] Adams, T. S. M., ed. *World of Japanese Business*. Tokyo: Kodansha International, 1968.
[2] Ballon, Robert J., ed. *Doing Business in Japan*. Tokyo: Tuttle, 1968.

[3] Ballon, Robert J., ed. *Joint Venture in Japan*. Tokyo: Tuttle, 1968.

[4] Hazama, Hiroshi. *Bunka Kozo to Keiei Shi*. Keieishigaku I (1), 1966–6.5.

[5] Hazama, Hiroshi. *Keieishigakukai*. Tokyo, 1966, pp. 13–25.

[6] Iinuma, Akio. *Nagano Shigeo—Shin Nihon Steel, Daiwa*. Tokyo, 1970.

[7] Ishikawa, Ken, *Ishida Baigan to Tohimondo* (Ishida Baigan and His Book Tohimondo) Yuwanami, Tokyo, 1968.

[8] Ishizaka, Taizo. *Yuukiaru Kotoba* (Brave Words). Tokyo: Yomiuri Shimbun, 1970.

[9] Kaizuka, Shigeki. *Koshi* (Confucius), Tokyo: Yuwanami, 1969.

[10] Kamei, Tatsuo. *Nihon no Keiei, Nihon no Keieigaku* (Japanese Management and Japanese Management Science), Shogaku Shushi Vol. 35 (4), 1966–2. Tokyo: Nihon Daigaku Keizaigaku Kenkyukai, 1966.

[11] Kamiyoshi, Sadakazu. *Keieino Nakano Nihon Hadden* (Find Japan in Management). Tokyo: Diamond, 1966.

[12] Nakamura, Hisao. *Matsushita, Konosuke no Sekai* (The World of Matsushita Konosuke). Tokyo: Bunken Shuppan, 1968.

[13] Nomura, Kentaro. *Fukuzawa, Yukichi—Hito to Sono Shiso* (Fukuzawa Yukichi's Personality and his Philosophy). Tokyo: Keio Tsushin, 1965.

[14] Ono, Shizuo. *Bukkyo Shakai to Keizaigaku no Kenkyu* (Study of Buddhism Society and Economic Theory). Tokyo: Yuhikaku, 1965.

[15] Sakata, Yoshio. *Shikon Shosai* (Samuri Spirit and Manuever). Tokyo: Miraisha.

[16] Sato, Takeshi. *Businessman's Japan: A Survey of Japan's Divine Wind Economy in the 1960s*. London: Michael Joseph, 1964.

[17] Sekiguchi, Misao. *Nihon no Keieishakai (1)—Sono Soshiki to Mibunsei*, (Japanese Management Society—Organization Structure and Social Status System), Mita Shogaku Kenkyu, Vol. 91 (1), 1966–4. Tokyo: Keio University, 1966, pp. 94–116.

[18] Shibusawa, Eiichi. *Keiei Rongo* (Management Confucianism). Tokyo: Tokumo, 1960.

[19] Tada, Akira. *Keizai Shisoshi ni Okeru Shosan*, (Suzuki, Shosan in Japanese Economic History), Kenkyu Hokoku, Vol. A-2. Chiba: Chiba University, 1969, pp. 3–21.

[20] Tada, Akira. *Shibusawa Eiichi, Rongo, Sadanobu*, (Logical Relationship-Shibusawa Eiichi, Confucianism, Matsudaira Sadanobu), Bunka Kagaku Kiyo, Vol. 10 (1968–3), Chiba: Chiba University, 1968, pp. 71–96.

[21] Taguchi, Kenichi. *Keiei Nihon Shugi—Dokutokuna Idemitsu Shoho*. Tokyo: Shinchosha, 1966.

[22] Takamiya, Susumu. *Nihon Keiei no Tokushitsu to Saikin no Doko* (Japanese Management Characteristics and Current Trend), Sosiki Kagaku, Vol. 4-1, Soshikigakkai-Maruzen. Tokyo, 1970, pp. 4–18.

[23] Takamiya, Susumu. *Nihon no Keiei*, (Japanese Management), Soshiki Kagaku, Vol. 3-3, Soshiki Kagaku, Vol. 3-3. Tokyo: Shoshiki Gakkai—Maruzen, 1969.

[24] Takamiya, Susumu. *Nihon no Keiei Tokushu* (Special Edition for Japanese Management), Soshiki Kagaku, Vol. 3-4. Tokyo: Soshiki Gakkai—Maruzen, 1969.

[25] Takeuchi, Yoshio. *Rongo no Kenkyu* (Study of Confucianism). Tokyo: Yuwanami.

[26] Tasugi, K. *Keiei Rinen no Ruijisei to Soi*, (International Comparison of Business Philosophy — Similarities and Differences), Keizai Ronshu, Vol. 99(6), 1969-6. Kyoto: Kyoto University, 1967, pp. 19-41.

[27] Tsuchiya, Takao. *Nihon no Keiei Rinenshi* (History of Japanese Management Ethics). Tokyo: Nihon Keizai Shimbun, 1967.

[28] Tsuchiya, Takao. *Zoku Nihon no Keiei Rinenshi*, (History of Japanese Management Ethics, cont'd.). Tokyo: Nihon Keizai Shimbunsha, 1967.

[29] Uchida, Yukio. *Nihonteki Keiei no Tokushoku*, (Characteristics in Japanese Management), Soshiki Kagaku, Vol. 3-1, Tokyo: Soshiki Gakkai- Maruzen, 1969, pp. 61-65.

[30] Wakamori, Taro, ed. *Nihon no Rinri Shisoshi*, (Historical Thoughts of Japanese Ethics). Tokyo: Gakugei Shoho.

[31] Yoshino, Yotaro. *Japan's Managerial System — Tradition and Innovation*, Boston: MIT Press, 1968.

[32] Yoshiya, Yoshishige. *Keiei Rinri*, (Management Ethics). Tokyo: Shinjyusho, 1966.

[33] Yui Tsunehiko. *Meiji Nihon no Kigyosha Seishin Nitsuite* (Japanese Entrepreneur Spirit in Meiji Era), Keieishigaku I(2), 1966-9, Tokyo: Keieishigaku-kai, 1966, pp. 88-106.

# 10

# Participative Management as a Reflection of Cultural Contingencies: A Need to Reevaluate Our Ethic

ROBERT LANGE

## INTRODUCTION

When dealing with macro topics (in this case cross-cultural issues), one must remember that the tendency, out of necessity, is to make generalizations concerning behavior and motivations. Generalizations, if analyzed under a microscopic eye, will always prove to be faulty and, to a degree, even contradictory. However, an understanding of tradition or cultural history is necessary in order to comprehend the complex phenomena that various human groups create, reflect, and absorb. Identity, both cultural and individual, does not exist in the vacuum of the absolute present but is a product of historical contingencies as well as present reactions and future expectations.

In this chapter I will look at the notion of participation in management as a product, in part, of cultural contingencies. I will examine the social, economic, political, and religious traditions of northern Europe, America, and Japan, contrasting these traditions in order to understand what cultural criteria make for more successful participation in organizations. Having done this, I will look at the possibilities of applying successful techniques indigenous to the cultures of northern Europe and Japan to the United States, for it is in America that the crisis in management is becoming most dramatic and threatening.

First, however, it is necessary to support the notion that participation is, in great part, a cultural variable. A global rationale would suggest that all behavior, group or individual, is predicated upon some sort of cultural conditioning (Skinner). Expectancy theory, like that of operant conditioning, states that people will move toward goals that promise to be reinforced by rewards equivalent to the value of the desired behavior. Consistency in reinforcement produces "learning," i.e., identification with the value. Thus, culture can be seen in Hofstede's terms as "The collective mental programming of the people in an environment; . . . it encompasses a number of people who were conditioned by the same education and life experience" [5]. In conjunction with this definition, culture may also be defined as a group of people within a bounded environment who are faced with similar problems and solve those problems in similar fashion. The similarity of problem-solving techniques is determined by appropriate and successful "collective mental programming." (It should be noted that the term "programming" does not necessarily define this process as dehumanizing or leading to mindless collectivism for, as we shall see, individuality, as a cultural phenomenon, may be a conditioned response.) Thus the propensity toward or against participation as normative behavior has a basis, partially, if not totally, in proscribed cultural imperatives. But what are these imperatives?

As a general overview, I propose that the tendency toward participation in organizational life is greater in Japan and northern Europe than in America. However, the reasons for the former two cultures adopting such a pattern of behavior are quite dissimilar. European tradition has, as part of its history, rejected feudalism and replaced it with a moral and philosophic social consciousness akin to the ideals of Marxian socialism. In this case participation takes the form of works councils. Japan, on the other hand, has accepted and identified with many of the basic principles of feudalism. Here participation is not only allowed but encouraged, for this form of management is not seen as threatening by those in the top positions of the hierarchy due to the cultural imperative of loyalty to authority.

America finds itself neither accepting nor rejecting the feudal system. Rather, it seems to be caught in the precarious position of contradicting itself. On the one hand, it prides itself as a nation of rugged individualists. As Peter Drucker points out, our national heroes take the form of Horatio Alger or John Wayne [1]. Individualism, as a rejection of authoritarianism, is a far cry from socialism and, as a product of the Protestant ethic, does not have its roots in philosophic but rather economic criteria. I will examine Weber's thesis as it applied to United States management techniques in greater detail later in this paper but for the moment I would like to suggest that this American ethic reinforces the "ideals" of the hierarchy, competition and the differentiation of power. These "ideals" are seen by management as not only economically propitious but morally just.

However, America has another ethic, that of equality. This idea connotes collectivism and society's demand for conformity. As people become more equal, they share in the common good of the state. This is a contradiction to individualism. Thus, American democracy is somewhat schizophrenic. Double messages always elicit feelings of ambiguity and, consequently, of anxiety, a rather diffuse sense of discomfort most often expressed behaviorally as alienation. Work, as a social function, is only one place in American life where alienation and anxiety are highly identifiable. Marriage and family life is another, as seen in the increasing rate of divorce and domestic violence. As social rather than individual phenomena, these are symptoms of a culture's inability to cope successfully with the needs of its people and with the environment in which it exists. Traditional values no longer work. A feeling of emptiness exists, for the values are no longer human. In Japan and Europe, work is a source of human value. In America, work is something to be avoided, or at least it is not the place where we find humanistic or spiritual fulfillment. Note the American obsession with leisure.

These, of course, are large generalizations. Let me support them by looking at the three different cultural traditions.

## EUROPEAN CULTURAL TRADITION

One of the first significant studies that compared European and American attitudes on participation was the Coch and French study (1948) of the Norwegian factory. There were two significant findings. One was that participation seemed to work in the Norwegian setting because there was a greater cultural emphasis on group standards as opposed to the United States where emphasis was on productivity. The other finding was that participation was most successful when it was seen as legitimate, i.e., philosophically ethical and organizationally meaningful. In both cases we see the manifestation of socialistic philosophy.

According to a recent NBC White Paper Report (1981), West German socialism is clearly manifested in their National Training Programs. In this instance one sees a nation investing in labor as part of its national economy and as a primary resource. Under this system workers receive substantial pay benefits (80 percent of original salary for a long as three years) if they train for new skills after they have been laid off. Workers in ailing industries can enter training programs before they are laid off and are encouraged to do so. Training programs, including aptitude testing, are paid for by the government. Although expensive, the West Germans feel it is to their advantage to invest in labor rather than be combative with it. In reference to both the West German and Norwegian situations, where do these ideas come from?

One place to begin an analysis is the guild system prevalent during the Middle Ages. Guild members were craftsmen who identified themselves highly with their product, which was often artistic and bore the unique imprint of its maker. Centuries later Marx referred to this system as it contrasted to the fragmentation and alienation of work in the industrial revolution. But perhaps more important was the belief on the part of the guilds that they were responsible for the training of new craftsmen, thus ensuring that their craft be preserved in its finest form. Thus, a high value was placed upon group responsibility.

The Enlightenment valued rationalism and it was this rationalism that passionately rejected feudalism and the monarchy. The English utopianism of Locke and Hume combined with the rationalism of Voltaire and Descartes and the Romantic politics of Jean Jacques Rousseau to produce, among other things, the French Revolution. And though the revolution deteriorated into the mockery of social and political virtue known as the Reign of Terror, it was founded on the ideals of "Liberty, Equality, Fraternity," which again suggest the ideals of democratic socialism.

By the early 1880s, while a few radical poets in England and Europe were waging a revolution of their own known as Romanticism, the common working person was embroiled in the mixed blessings of the Industrial Revolution; for while society was marching forward, humanity was becoming dehumanized. Literature became a vehicle for social criticism as writers from Paris (Balzac), St. Petersburg (Dostoëvski), and London (Dickens) spoke of urban blight, the suffering humanity, and the false and supercilious values of the wealthy. While they were preaching reform, Karl Marx was preaching revolution. The problem of worker alienation became one of his major themes and again addressed the notion of ownership of the task if not the ownership of the organization. For Marx, worker participation (though radically idealistic in his theories) and ownership of the task were antidotes for problems of alienation that were not only present in the work place, but in society in general. Emile Durkheim's study of suicide defined the socio-psychological state of "anomie" or normlessness as a motivator of self-destruction. Normlessness is a product of ambiguity and fragmentation in the life experience. (I refer you back to earlier comments on America.)

By the end of the nineteenth century, the influence of Victorianism was beginning to wane. The bourgeoisie came under attack from the intellectuals. Matthew Arnold criticized what he called "the Philistines" for their emptiness, lack of understanding of truly significant human concerns, and false values. Oscar Wilde satirized the upper classes as being devoid of any substance or purpose. Perhaps the most notorious attack was made by the Frenchman Alfred Jarry whose theatrical character King Ubu insulted audiences with vile speech and odious examples of immorality but was meant to exemplify, although in exaggeration, the true spirit and values of the audience he horrified.

So by 1900 a moral crisis had struck Europe. Man was no longer made in God's image but was the brother of an ape (Darwin). God was dead (Nietzsche), and man's true spirit was no more than a cacophony of hedonistic sexual and aggressive urges (Freud). And as if to prove that all of this was true, World War I proceeded to decimate an entire generation of European men and shatter any false sense of security the Europeans might still have had. Later, in 1929, Freud would write in *Civilization and Its Discontents* that if man were to destroy himself it would be due to a cultural nervous breakdown due to his alienation from a society he could no longer control.

Europe, in its need to reëstablish control, looked to socialistic ideals as an alternative. Whether it was socialism of the right (Fascism), socialism of the left (Communism), a socialism of the center (democratic socialism), the emphasis was on group responsibility. Crisis had produced a need for survival, cohesiveness, and a nationalistic sense of the greatest good for the greatest numbers.

One might say this is a mature attitude reached through a long history of struggle and defeat, as well as triumph. America, on the other hand, has never had that long a history nor the experience of defeat to temper its egoism into a mature perspective. In all its ambiguity, America may be seen as going through an adolescent identity crisis.

## AMERICAN CULTURAL TRADITION

It seems to me that the dominant ideal upon which the American culture is based is the Protestant Ethic. It was in fact some Puritan colonists, escaping persecution in Europe, who founded many of the New England colonies. The insecurity felt by Protestants during the reformation was translated into religious and secular codes of behavior that were severely strict, and thereby provided a sense of security for its membership. The emphasis on structure vis-à-vis hierarchical positions of grace begat competition as a means of defining individuality and identity within the system.

The prime directive of the Protestant sects was the notion of duty. Work was seen not as a means to an end but rather as an end in itself. It was not associated with pleasure, for happiness led to complacency, which was considered the devil's tool. Leisure was a waste of time and a sin. One's work, on the other hand, was a matter of a calling which Weber defined as "the fulfillment of obligation (to God's will) imposed upon the individual by his position within the society" [13, p. 80]. Hence, work as a moral obligation became an ascetic activity, marked by cold determination and hard frugality. Profit, as a manifestation of success, likewise was a means of determining one's state of grace. If one accepts the idea of predestination, as did the Calvinists, the important earthly question becomes, "How do I know where I am fated to end up?" The Protestants interpreted worldly success in the social and economic hierarchy as a sign of future success in terms of the eternal hierarchy. This concept further strengthened a social and organizational structure based upon vertical differentiation by associating the worldly bureaucracy with heavenly states of grace. "Seest a man diligent in his business? He shall stand before Kings" (Proverbs XXII, 29). Thus did work become a means of attaining salvation (God helps those who help themselves). It is not difficult to assess the impact of such an ethic upon the possibilities of participation within organizational life. Weber himself pointed out that, just as feudalism protected the pleasure seekers from the rising middle-class morality in the Middle Ages, capitalism protects those who identify with the Protestant Ethic against the class morality of the proletariat and anti-authoritarian trade unions [13, p. 167].

The American identification with this ethic became translated into a host of American euphemisms, all of which had as their basis economic rather than social concerns. Protestant terminology colored such expressions of "Manifest Destiny" and American ingenuity. Economic rationalism was and still is the driving ethic of American business and politics. Historically, the American Civil War is often interpreted as a battle over states' rights and human rights, but was also a struggle between this same economic rationalism of the North vs. the agrarian romanticism of the South. At its end, as Margaret Mitchell said, a land of cavaliers was brought into the modern world and lost forever.

Perhaps the greatest euphemism is the American Dream. Like the Protestant Ethic, recognizable status was associated with wealth, power, and materialism. Millions of immigrants came to the United States seeking freedom, individuality, and the Horatio Alger myth. For the majority, then and today, the American Dream remains just that—a dream. The Protestant Ethic and the bureaucratic system has become an imperative value of American organizational life. Top management not only shares in but is also controlled by these values. But top management can afford to identify with the ethic because they have attained their individuality and the associated state of grace vis-à-vis their corporate success. But because of pyramidal structure of bureaucracies, very few attain these goals. The great majority are not destined to "succeed" yet are expected to acquiesce to and identify with those same values.

But the American worker did identify with these values. At least for a time. But very few things remain static. With greater education and media stimulation, American workers are beginning to see the discrepancy that exists between the cultural ideal and the social realities. The wider the gulf and the greater the awareness of this disparity, the greater becomes the frustration, alienation, and rebellion (Merton).

Thus ethics and imperatives must be redefined. But to what extent and under what conditions will redefinition work? Some answers might be provided by taking a look at Japanese management practices. Japanese labor under the notion that what is good for the individual comes from the organization. The Japanese realize that this applies only if the organization has the interests of the worker in mind. Subservience to an organization is beneficial only if the organization is consistently benevolent. As our Weberian analysis has suggested, benevolence is not part of U.S. corporate philosophy. It is in Japan. But before one can analyze Japanese management practices, one must understand, as in the two previous examples, the cultural imperatives that have led to such a practice.

## JAPANESE CULTURAL HERITAGE

Japan is a country that has imported many of its cultural ideas, as well as its economic ideas, from other places. It first imported Confucianism and Buddhism from China. These philosophies stressed the concepts of integration or, as the Germans call it, *gestalt*. Value and virtue are seen in observing the similarities among various phenomena and synthesizing them into a unified whole. Thus the individual's goal is to become integrated into the much larger environment, be it social, religious, or organizational. In contrast, Western culture is based upon the ideas of Greek Apollonian logic, which focuses upon analysis via differentiation and segmentation of reality as a way of discovering truth or meaning (the Greek term "logos" is translated to mean "meaning"). Thus European and American bureaucracies exemplify differentiation and individualism as virtuous while Japanese culture values integration and conformity.

These oriental values were more than religious beliefs, however. The emperor was supposed to be seen by his subjects as a god-king, an authoritarian figure who was worthy of homage. The political realities were such that by approximately A.D. 1000 the emperors had proved to be sufficiently weak that there emerged the feudal warlord known as Shogun. The feudal system that developed in Japan was quite similar to that in Europe, although each evolved independently. The Shogun surrounded himself with warrior-guards known as Samurai, who adopted a code of honor known as Bushido. This was much like the European oaths of submission. This code did not allow the Samurai to recognize any authority or obligation other than his

Shogun. In a country whose clan structures were strong and cohesive, Bushido superseded even the customs of filial or parental love and responsibility. An example of Bushido was seen in the act of Junshi, in which a Samurai would kill himself at the death of his lord so that he could be with him in the afterworld [2, p. 847].

By 1700, these severe ideals of group responsibility and loyalty to authority were directed toward the family unit. It became customary for an entire family to be held responsible for the behavior of each member. Thus if a man were to be condemned to death for a treasonous act, his older sons would be executed also while his younger sons were banished and wife and daughters sold into slavery. Thus group reinforcement, cohesiveness, and accountability became matters of necessity, not choice. Under this system, parental autocracy flourished. Due to a weak central government that provided little in the way of economic or social support, the extended family became the primary social and economic unit. It is interesting to note that, in contrast, Western governments had a tendency to be fairly strong and stable, thereby allowing for the development of individualism [2, p. 860]. Individualism could be seen under these conditions as a social luxury, something that both U.S. management and labor have taken for granted.

Thus identification with the early cultural traditions of the Samurai mentality and Bushido attitudes coupled with cohesive clan orientation and patriarchal domination reinforce the integrative and conformist philosophies manifested in Japanese religious theology. All of this, to a great degree, accounts for the high level of loyalty to authority (in this case the organization) that provides for and protects the individual. It also accounts for the propensity to find value in participative, group efforts.

Feudal discipline allowed Japan to move into the twentieth century with amazing speed and success. With the coming of Admiral Perry in 1853 and again a year later, Japan became open to Western influence. A politically dominant faction in Japan saw the necessity of bringing the medieval country into the modern world. These people had watched China being torn apart because of its inability to unite its feudal states, which both Western and Eastern imperialist powers easily dominated one by one. By 1868, this faction had dismantled the Shogunate and had restored the emperor to "real" power. Of course, the emperor was a puppet of this group, and they immediately began to import what they felt were the most advantageous qualities of various Western cultures, always modifying them to suit their needs and traditions. They brought in English engineers to build the railways, French lawyers to codify the laws, American educators to create a national education system, Italian artists and German medical technicians [2, p. 916]. When they had gotten what they needed for modernization, they dismissed their foreign guests and began to build an industrial power so strong that by 1904 it successfully went to war against

Russia, then considered to be one of the most formidable powers in the world.

The bloodless revolution of 1868, aside from being one of the few peaceful transitions from the medieval to the modern industrial state, also brought into power a new class of people. These were the merchants, financiers and manufacturers, formerly artisans, who had previously been at the bottom of the Japanese social ladder but who would now forge the destiny of modern Japan.

The reparations paid to Japan after the war with Russia financed her industrialization for the next thirty years and allowed Japan to begin her movement into the modern world with two important advantages: new machinery and a feudal sense of discipline and loyalty. (It is interesting to note that the same thing was going on in Germany at approximately the same time.)

Of course there were other advantages that graced Japan's success. Labor was cheap and a history of submissiveness did not allow, at least at the beginning, for much talk of labor reform or unionization. Furthermore, government subsidies to industry were substantial. By 1918 the number of factories in Japan had doubled from that of just a decade before, and it doubled again by 1924. While the West was suffering with the depression of the 1930s, Japan's industrial strength grew another 50 percent by 1931.

By this time, though, the individual worker was becoming aware of his plight. Daily wages averaged about $.50 for women and $1.20 for men. The urban environment was deteriorating as slums spread. Strikes became more common and communistic rhetoric began to appeal to the ears of workers. So, in 1931, the government cleverly turned the nation's eyes away from its internal problems and focused on Manchuria. Patriotism was ignited as was a return to the old virtues of loyalty and conformity, which always seem to prevail in a time of crisis.

It was such a response to crisis that allowed Japan to resurrect itself after its defeat in World War II. Out of necessity it had to re-industrialize itself and thus today, while the victorious Americans struggle with outdated industrial equipment, Japan (and Germany) flourish with relatively new technology.

Aside from the cultural internalization of the feudal mentality and the propitious events of history, Japan's success can be seen as a product of foresight and the willingness to modify tradition so that necessary change could be achieved. Modern Japan sees no advantage in entrenching itself in tradition for tradition's sake. Neither does it wait for the crisis to occur before it is spurred into action. Yet the traditionalism of the bureaucratic method and crisis management seem to be the basis for American managerial style. What alternatives does Japan present?

# JAPANESE MANAGEMENT PERSPECTIVES

While America traditionally and romantically holds on to the virtues of individualism, Japan prefers the advantages of teamwork. While participation by workers in American organizations is generally limited to the adversarial posture of collective bargaining, participation as manifested by coöperative decision making flourishes in Japanese organizational life. While Western heritage seeks to differentiate work and human values by way of bureaucratic structure, Japanese tradition demands an integration of work and human values.

Like West Germany, Japan sees labor not merely as a human resource but also as the most important industrial resource. To this end, Japanese managers attempt to "adapt the organization to the people because you can't adapt the people to the organization" [4, p. 19]. This quotation by a Japanese manager not only supports the thesis of the importance of predefined and internalized cultural imperatives but also contradicts the American business practice of force fitting an employee into a job that may not be appropriate. How does this system work?

First, a great deal of time and money is spent on articulating and promulgating a humanistic philosophy that all levels of the organization support. An example of this is offered by Hatvany and Pucik [4] as they quote from a Japanese-owned company in California:

### Management Philosophy

Our goal is to strive toward both the material and spiritual fulfillment of all employees in the company, and through this successful fulfillment, serve mankind in its progress and prosperity.

### Management Policy

. . . Our purpose is to satisfy the needs of our customers and in turn gain a just profit for ourselves. We are a family united in common bonds and singular goals. One of these bonds is the respect and support we feel for our fellow family co-workers.

Second, hiring procedures try to select those applicants who have the same values as the organization. Personality appraisals rather than productivity box scores are important here. The Japanese feel that the "average" worker who feels comfortable in the work environment will produce more in the long run than the high output "star" who feels alienated from it. American personnel departments traditionally look for the up and coming individual rather than the one whose personality is congruent with the organization.

Third, a well-planned policy of job rotation (suggesting job enrichment), helps integrate employees into all areas of company life. Under this system employees come to appreciate the problems and skills associated with various departments. Not only do employees get a holistic view of the organizational functioning but such a process helps to produce future managers whose skills include an awareness of the integrated functioning of the organization. In America, by contrast, workers rarely come to see or appreciate functions of the organization other than their own. This produces a feeling of separation, identification with one's own work group at the expense of identification with the organization as a whole. Distrust among work groups is common, and the resulting conflict is almost always dysfunctional socially and productively. Furthermore, the Japanese value the flexibility of the generalist rather than the rigidity of the specialist. This proves to be particularly helpful when dealing with a dynamic environment.

Fourth, work is structured so that it fits into the culturally accepted norms of group activity. Group behavior in the Japanese organization not only takes the form of production units (product orientation) but also may be a self-contained management system (process orientation) as in the example of the quality circle. In this case, a group of workers meet to determine and solve their own production problems. Increased identity and esteem among group members leads to increased productivity. There are two reasons for this. To begin with, there is greater ownership of the problem and the solution, and then group identification, in itself, is a very powerful intrinsic reward for the Japanese. Rewards are motivators toward goal attainment as long as those rewards are valued. In this case they are.

Again, this may be contrasted to the position of American workers who are, more often than not, isolated from the decision-making process and, as a result, experience alienation rather than identification and gratification.

Fifth, the Japanese structure their work areas and work attitudes around an open system of communications that allows both for a great deal of vertical information flow from the bottom up and a significant amount of horizontal communication. This is accentuated by the implementation of job rotation. In the traditional American organization, information flows, if it flows at all, from the top down. It is the assumption here that upper-level managers have better knowledge and therefore are better qualified to make decisions, regardless of their unfamiliarity with the specific problems or area of production. The idea that collective wisdom creates the best decision is not part of the American work ethic. This is probably because shared information means shared power. In the bureaucracy, power is the reward one receives from having made it to the top. Once attained, power is internalized. One's identity in the organization is defined with power as its axis. Thus to give it away would be an act of self-denial. The problem with this perception is that power is seen as quantifiably finite rather than a potentially infinite resource [7]. This concept leads us to the next criterion.

Sixth, the Japanese employ a system of consultive decision making. Under this system, if a problem crops up, the "appropriate people" (those directly involved with the various dimensions of the problem) get together to determine 1) the nature and extent of the problem (*i.e.*, the extent of change necessary to solve the problem), and 2) possible solutions. The Japanese, consistent with their cultural philosophy, spend as much time in defining the problem as they do in discussing solutions. They feel that if the problem is stated correctly, the solution becomes self-evident. The American technique is to jump into a discussion of solutions without having clearly understood the problem. The consequences of such impetuousness are either short-lived solutions or misdirection.

The Japanese system of consensus as a participative device confuses Westerners. As William Ouchi explains, "To the Westerner, it means endless meetings, argumentation and ultimate indecision. Such is the case where "Individualism" is prized, where value is given to quick decision making, where slow process of choice is equated with inefficiency and where interpersonal skills are not well developed (or are avoided altogether as cumbersome) [11, p. 66].

To the Japanese, however, consensus elicits initiative from below where the understanding of the problem may be more clearly formed. Consensus does not involve adversarial squabbling between special interest factions who identify only with their egocentric viewpoints. It is interpreted by the Japanese as meaning that each member of the group feels that he or she has been fairly heard and is willing to go along with the prominent idea, even support it, even if he or she may disagree. Ouchi feels that this is one of the most important managerial techniques for success since, through the participative system, those relevant to the problem "own" the solution, which makes implementation easy, unlike in the United States where a great deal of time is spent "selling" the idea. Consensus also asks for different points of view with the idea that more information will lead to better and more permanent solutions.

Seventh, many large Japanese corporations use a system of long-term employment and social benefits known as Nenko. Under this system, young people are brought into the organization upon completion of college, high school, or even junior high school. What is unique about the system is that it provides lifelong employment security. The corporation, in its benevolent paternalism, also provides welfare benefits that range from housing facilities to vacation trips and low-interest loans. Movement up the corporate ladder is slow and generally based on seniority rather than productivity.

This allows the worker to achieve competence without the fear that time or the competition is passing him or her by. In Japan technical skill is associated with time on the job. And if a worker fails to develop technical skill in one area, he or she can be shifted to another area where competence may be manifested. As one Japanese personnel director said, "The secret to Japanese management . . . is to make everybody feel, as long as possible, that he is slated for a top position in the firm, thereby increasing his motivation during the most productive period of his employment." As Hatvany and Pucik point out:

> The public identification of "losers," who of course outnumber "winners" in any hierarchical organization, is postponed in the belief that the increased output of the losers, who are striving hard to do well still hoping to beat the odds, more than compensates for any lags in motivation of the impatient winners. By contrast, top management in many American organizations is preoccupied with identifying rising stars as soon as possible and is less concerned about the impact of the loser's morale. [4, p. 13]

These provisions for security and the care and nurturing of all employees, not just the top 10 percent, promotes strong corporate loyalty, increased motivation, and group effectiveness while allowing the organization to maintain the flexibility needed to meet the functional demands of a highly dynamic environment [10, p. 14].

A specific example of this nurturing process is manifested in the use of the "godfather" system. Managers who have been with the firm for a long time and who see that they will not be promoted take on the responsibility of becoming "mentors" to newly recruited members of the organization. Their counselling does not only concern corporate life but the social graces as well, for the ability to socialize "successfully" is an important part of corporate success in Japan. Godfathers will also honestly evaluate the progress of their charges and report their opinions to promotion and job rotation committees. As veterans of the system, the godfathers are highly respected by younger employees and are seen as personifications of the paternal benevolence of the organization as a whole. Thus each employee feels that there is personal interest taken in him.

The Nenko system is expensive and this accounts for the fact that only 30 percent of Japan's nonagricultural workers are engaged in such a system. However, both government and industry see the necessity of investing in labor and labor's needs as part of an overall program of industrial success.

Ouchi (1981) stresses that equity in Japanese organizational life is perhaps the single most important issue. He defines an organization as "any stable, patterned set of transactions among a set of individuals or units.

This pattern of transactions will remain stable without defections, only as long as each party to the transaction is satisfied that he of she is receiving an equitable share of the rewards" [11, p. 41]. Therefore, there must be equity between the trading partners within the organization, that is, between labor and management. If this idea is accepted, its consequences are a reduction of the bureaucratic hierarchy, compartmentalization of employees, closed communication networks, etc. In other words, the organization will become more organic.

## THEORY Z AND BEYOND

All of this sounds nice, but the major question is, given the cultural imperatives inherent in American organizational life, is it possible to transfer such a system into so dichotomous a culture? Ouchi says that we can and have been doing so.

Having come to this point in the paper, it would be contradictory for me to say that the imposition of organizational methods that are so integrally tied into the traditions and psychology of a specific culture could easily be transplanted into a different culture with a different ethic. But one can always modify the methods and still retain the spirit of those methods. Ouchi has contrasted the Japanese method to the American method and formulated a modification which may be applicable to the United States. The Theory Z organization, as he calls it, retains the Japanese commitments to long-term employment, consensual decision making, a holistic concern for the employee, etc., but adapts itself to the American Ethic by employing monetary incentives as the primary reward structure, greater individual rather than total group responsibility, and moderately specialized rather than generalized careers (see Table 1). Ouchi points to companies that have incorporated Theory Z, such as Eli Lilly, as major success stories.

Needless to say, the ideas suggested in this paper are not the only perspectives. While I have posed a rather pessimistic and critical view of American organizational life, not only in terms of values but also in terms of diminishing productivity, others do not see a similar crisis, or if they do, they rationalize it away. Williams, Whyte, and Greene imply that all things are relative; in their article, "Do Cultural Differences Affect Worker Attitude?" (1966), they compared workers in Peru with those in America. They hypothesize that "individuals who are high in interpersonal trust will expect and appreciate a leader-group climate that is democratic and participative as contrasted to those who are very low in interpersonal trust, who will anticipate a more authoritarian and nonparticipative climate and therefore will be satisfied with supervisors as long as they can provide the

TABLE 1  Application of Japanese Management Practices in the United States

| JAPANESE MANAGERIAL STYLE | AMERICAN MANAGERIAL STYLE |
|---|---|
| 1. Long-term employment and security<br>2. Slow evaluation and promotion<br>3. Nonspecialized and flexible careers via job rotation and training<br>4. Consensual decision making<br>5. Group responsibility<br>6. Implicit, informal control<br>7. Holistic concern for the employee<br>8. Open communications and reduction of hierarchical structure<br>9. Group reinforcement as motivator | 1. Employment insecurity and mobility (U.S. = 24%/yr.; W. Europe = 12%/yr.; Japan = 4%/yr.)<br>2. Necessity to move quickly up hierarchial ladder<br>3. Specialization of job<br>4. Decision making by individuals<br>5. Individual responsibility<br>6. Explicit and formal control<br>7. Concern for individual is secondary after productivity<br>8. Closed communications (vertical)<br>9. Monetary incentives as motivators |

| INTERPRETATION OF THEORY Z ORGANIZATIONS | |
|---|---|
| 1. Long-term employment<br>2. Slow evaluation and promotion<br><br>4. Consensual decision making<br><br>6. Implicit, informal control<br>7. Holistic concern for individual<br>8. Open communication | <br><br>3. Moderately specialized careers<br><br>5. Individual responsibility<br>6. But with explicit measures<br><br>9. Monetary incentives |

structure in which work can be done" [14, p. 112]. They see America, with its principles of democracy, encouraging the de-emphasis of authority structures and the "direct thrashing out of differences between supervisors and the work group" [14, p. 116]. Several points can be made here. First, the principles of democracy, as we have seen, make up only one side of the ethical coin in America, and it is debatable which side of the coin prevails most frequently and consistently. Second, in comparing America to Peru, whose cultural history contains a succession of authoritarian and dictatorial regimes, the virtues of the American Ethic will be most noticeable. But when we make a similar comparison between the United States and Japan, America comes out second best. Third, the "thrashing out of differences between supervisors and the work group" does not take place informally, as the authors suggest, but formally, as collective bargaining. It is highly debatable whether this form of participation is beneficial to organizational life or even worker goals. The traditional adversarial position of labor and management serves to reinforce the segmentation and differentiation between the two sides rather than allowing for integration and coöperative ventures. Goals are almost always defined in economic rather than humanistic terms. Unlike European trade unions, who organized themselves as a power-balancing technique for the purposes of class struggle (Marxist orientation), the American labor movement is job-conscious, focusing on the specific situation rather than on the larger political or economic issues. Thus, participation as a coöperative venture enhanced by mutual respect is often sabotaged as both sides bicker over petty issues and lose sight of larger concerns.

Finally, the world is not the same place today as it was in 1966. Fifteen years ago we were not worried about double digit inflation, usurious interest rates, dependence on foreign oil, and a level of competition from abroad that threatened the well-being of some of America's largest industries. This is not to mention our military and moral defeat in Vietnam, which split the country and caused us to question the validity of our ethics. It has been said that twenty years of prosperity has made America self-indulgent and overly secure while the rest of the world has been engaged in organizational activities that are now beginning to surpass ours. If the work ethic in America has been dormant, will the present situation provide enough of a crisis incentive to awaken it? And will this rejuvenation be too little too late?

It seems to me that the American work ethic needs not only to be awakened, if it has been asleep at all, but redefined. Perhaps this is already happening as Ouchi suggests. In 1971, Alvin Toffler stated that the days of the bureaucracy were numbered and that future organizations would evolve into what he called the adhocracy, characterized by decision making by expert groups, task forces, etc. Toffler echoed Bennis's notion that bureaucracy may be dysfunctional as the competition and differentiation inherent in such a structure create stress, alienation, and eventually either "burn out" or apathy. Both consequences, among other things, result in decreased productivity. We can also apply Woodward's idea that in environments that are dynamic, organizations must become more "organic" and flexible if they are to maximize their potential. So it is not merely a matter of reënlisting the old overworked ideas that may have served us well in the past, but of modifying those ideas.

What will cause this redefinition? Must we react only in times of crisis or can we be as foresightful as our competitors have proved to be? Whatever the answer, I suggest that what is needed within the American labor-management relationship is a coöperative spirit rather than an adversarial and competitive one. Management must begin to value labor like West Germany and Japan do, as both a critical human and organizational resource. It can no longer afford, ethically or economically, to define the role of the worker in Machiavellian terms as simply a means to an end, for labor, as an integral part of life, is both the means and the end. Likewise, labor must be willing to look beyond its often momentary and selfish perspectives to become truly humanistic as well as productive as a movement. Perhaps then work can be integrated into life's values as opposed to being separated from those values. The most recent statistics show that Americans spend $288 billion (one out of every eight dollars spent) escaping from work by engaging in leisure activities. This movement away from work may prove to be most disastrous to an economy that is already faltering. We must therefore make work valuable again not simply by creating jobs but by redefining what they mean.

Value comes from identification. When one "owns" the decision and therefore feels that he or she has control over the situation, security rather than anxiety, ambivalence, and alienation is produced. We all know how highly security is valued, not only in terms of itself, but also as a motivator. It is the participative process that allows one to own and control. It also stands to reason that direct forms of participation, rather than indirect (representative) forms will allow ownership and control among more people. Furthermore, the greater the scope (range of managerial functioning), the degree (to which power is shared) and the extent (how widespread in the organization) of worker participation, the greater the identification and value.

This does not mean the demise of the role of the manager but redefinition of that role. Under this type of management perspective, managers must become leaders, not just proprietors of the status quo. Their principle task should be (as was true of the medieval guilds) to develop new managerial skills and talents in others. They must also become brokers of information rather than dispensers of it.

Cultural ideals change slowly and it would be unrealistic to believe that all of this can be done at once. What will be needed to move this process along are educational programs dedicated to consciousness-raising. Evaluation of the organizational climate as an indicator of the firm's readiness to accept such modification is requisite. Training programs must be instituted to help develop new managerial skills. Constant evaluation of the process and its effects are necessary so that it can be determined whether things are progressing at the proper pace. There must also be reward systems that are consistent and meaningful so that participation does not become a matter of tokenism.

No doubt more criteria can be added to this list. But the point is that unless we in America become foresightful and create new organizational structures that fit the changing nature of our economic and social environment, we will be doomed to the fate of the dinosaur. The structures that we create must not only reflect economic creativity but also human value, for without our humanity there is little else to value.

# BIBLIOGRAPHY

[1] Drucker, Peter. "What Can We Learn from Japanese Management?" *Harvard Business Review*, Vol. 49, No. 2 (1971).
[2] Durant, Will. *Our Oriental Heritage*. New York: Simon and Schuster, 1954, pp. 826–933.
[3] French, J. R. P., and Israel, J. "An Experiment on Participation in a Norwegian Factory." *Human Relations*, 1960, 13, pp. 3–19.
[4] Hatvany, N. and Pucik, V. "Japanese Management Practices and Productivity." *Organizational Dynamics*, Spring, 1981.
[5] Hofstede, G. "Motivation, Leadership and Organization: Do American Theories Apply Abroad?" *Organizational Dynamics*, Summer, 1980.
[6] Johnson, R., and Ouchi, W. "Made in America (Under Japanese Management)." *Harvard Business Review*, Vol. 52, No. 5, 1974, pp. 61–69.
[7] Kraus, William A. *Collaboration in Organizations: An End to Hierarchy*. New York: Human Sciences Press, 1980.
[8] Lehnner, U. "Comparing Japan and America's Master Managers." *Wall Street Journal*, June, 1981.
[9] Levine, S. "The White-Collar, Blue-Collar Alliance in Japan." *Industrial Relations*, 1966.
[10] Oh, T. K. "Japanese Management — A Critical Review." *Academy of Management Review*, January, 1976.
[11] Ouchi, W. "Organizational Paradigms: A Commentary on Japanese Management and Theory Z Organizations." *Organizational Dynamics*, Spring, 1981.
[12] Toffler, A. *Future Shock*. New York: Bantam Books, Inc., 1971, pp. 124–51.
[13] Weber, Max. *The Protestant Ethic and Spirit of Capitalism*. New York: Charles Scribner's Sons, 1958.
[14] Williams, L., Whyte, W., and Green, C. "Do Cultural Differences Affect Worker Attitude?" *Industrial Relations*, No. 5, 1966, pp. 110–17.

# Part III

# THE JAPANESE MANAGEMENT ENVIRONMENT

In this part, we attempt to explore various environmental factors important in the success of Japanese management. In "Japanese Management: Reasons for Success," Joseph W. Leonard and John Thanopoulos analyze 56 recently published works about Japanese business success, and show that it can be tied to 17 basic "reasons." They classify those reasons under three categories—*employees, management,* and *environment*—and proceed to build a conceptual framework for further research and analysis.

Anson Seers, in "Japanese Management Success: Implications for the Field of Organizational Development," suggests that U.S. business might benefit by incorporating Japanese experience. His paper reviews the growth of OD, the recent increase in articles attempting to explain the success of Japanese business, and the development of the business trends that will characterize the 1980s. He concludes that Japanese business success is best understood as the result of a combination of cultural, legal, political, and organizational factors.

In "Competition, Cooperation, and Technological Innovation in Japan," Leonard H. Lynn looks at the way the Japanese manage relationships between businesses, and between business and government, focusing on the interaction of steel makers, vendors, and government as it affects the introduction of a major new technology. In this study, the Japanese users of the new technology are shown to be more aggressive in finding out about it independently than their American counterparts, who rely more on vendors to bring them information. Japanese steel makers also rely more on coöperation with vendors to improve technology, while the Americans depend more on competition between vendors. Moreover, the government in Japan constrains competition between the steel makers, forcing them to share technology.

In "*Kazokushugi* and *Shudanshugi* Management Approaches: Source of Concept Variance in Japanese Business Settings," Motofusa Murayama explores the role of "kazoku" not only as a kinship unit but also as a functional management unit. Preceding from this concept, the author analyzes "shudanshugi," or group ideology, and its impact on Japanese management.

Allan S. Baillie in "Education, the Foundation of the Japanese Productive System?", suggests that Japanese firmly believe that their country's most important resource is its people and that the educational system is the key to productivity. This chapter attempts to relate that system to the country's phenomenal success in business management.

In "Differences in Japanese and American Corporate Tax Incentives and Their Investment Implications," Steven B. Johnson examines the investment implications of two corporate tax incentives available to Japanese firms, but not to their U.S. counterparts, during the period 1967–1980. The incentives studied are: (1) a tax credit for increasing research and development expenditures; and (2) a special percentage of sales deduction for the development and collection of revenues from overseas markets. Although only circumstantial evidence is examined, the preliminary findings support the hypothesis that these tax incentives may have contributed to certain differences in Japanese and U.S. investment strategies during this period.

So much has been written about the "unique" style of Japanese management that many believe Japan will enjoy a permanent advantage in the world market. The purported uniqueness obscures the fact that Japan has evolved in much the same way as other industrialized nations. In "Toward Consumption in Mercantilist Japan," Howard W. Barnes and Clayne L. Pope suggest that Japan is moving gradually, but steadily, from a production-oriented economy to a consumer society, with the inevitable consequence that its resources will be increasingly diverted from investment to consumption.

Toshiyuki Tamura and Sohtaro Kanihisa, in "Education, Transport Capital, and Productivity Change: The Case for Japan's Experience Since the Meiji Era," examine the effects of education and transport capital on productivity during the course of industrialization of Japan since the Meiji Restoration. They first give a brief historical sketch of the industrialization process and confirm that the demand for, and investment in, educational and transport facilities have almost paralleled the steady increase in industrial output. Then, the authors construct a simple macroeconometric model for 1885–1975, and create an ex-post simulation in order to demonstrate that it is education and transport capital that have contributed to industrialization, and not vice versa.

It is generally acknowledge among corporate strategists that, as domestic opportunities continue to deteriorate, growth opportunities in the international sector must be constantly monitored and cultivated. However, as the international competition for new market opportunities intensifies, U.S. multinationals must become more sophisticated in managing their foreign operations. Unfortunately, as has been the case on numerous occasions, American firms have committed blunders of monumental proportions due to an incomplete environmental analysis of the host country. In "An Examination of the Japanese Direct Investment Environment," Garland Keesling attempts to explore in part several major environmental factors germane to direct investment in the country of Japan.

Accounting and computers relate well to one another. Auditing and accounting are also related. However, when computers and auditing are combined, certain problems arise. To determine how Japanese audit corporations and U.S. certified public accounting firms operating in Japan handle such problems is the main thrust of Richard S. Savich's "Computer Auditing in Japan: Lessons and Constraints." Interviews were conducted with personnel in twelve such organizations and the results of these interviews are discussed. Historical, cultural, educational, and professional background material is presented to explain the current state of computer auditing in Japan.

# 11

# Japanese Management: Reasons for Success

JOSEPH W. LEONARD and JOHN THANOPOULOS

---

## INTRODUCTION AND CONCEPTUAL MODEL

"Reasons for Success" is a truly misleading phrase. What is the meaning of "success"? By whose standards? By what priorities? When? Where? Under what conditions? What is the meaning of "reason"? Is it a "raison d'etre" proposition? Is reason a success factor? Is reason a latent variable?

Without hoping to completely escape this quandry of definition, we did our best to reduce it. We investigated what others have thought and expressed in recent literature. We tried to systematize *their* reasoning, hoping that eventually this would lead to a methodological frame of reference, or at least to a useful bibliography.

The paper has the following parts: 1) the introductory section, which also develops the model used to classify the sources cited; 2) the 17 different reasons for success that the literature most often cites, followed by a contingency table that cross-presents the "reason" with the authors; 3) the concluding remarks; and 4) the listed references.

Several of the contingency, cluster, and system type elaborations attempted failed to offer a working classification model. Subsequently, we decided to adopt a modification of the following standard categories: environment, management, and employees.

Under each of these categories we classified the seventeen most-often mentioned reasons as follows:

- Employees (creativity; effective labor unions; lifetime employment; training and development);
- Management (concern for the employees; creativity; face-to-face communications; decision-making process; planning; quality, inventory, and financial controls); and
- Cultural and Environmental (adaptability; business-government relations; "godfather" guidance; group loyalty; harmonious, homogeneous, paternalistic people; shared purpose).

Obviously, the above listing can not claim to be an all-encompassing analysis. However, in a basic sense, the employees (and therefore the reasons that make them happier and eventually more productive) are the "core" of the model, for they are the element that makes things happen, they are the builders and the workers. The management interfaces with them and also (by applying the classical entrepreneurial attributes — risk-taking, innovation, and so on) with the environment. Therefore, in some ways the management dimension must be more flexible than that of the employees. Finally, the cultural and environmental dimension includes the traditional reasons that made the Japanese successful both as warriors and businessmen. It seems, however, that these reasons are even more flexible than those in the previous two categories, for they must continually adapt to changing outside circumstances.

In Figure 1, the classification system is illustrated as a series of concentric cycles. A represents the core — the employees, the working force. The Japanese management system depends for its success on this "seed." It communicates in a two-way manner with B (management). Changes in A

FIGURE 1   Conceptual Model

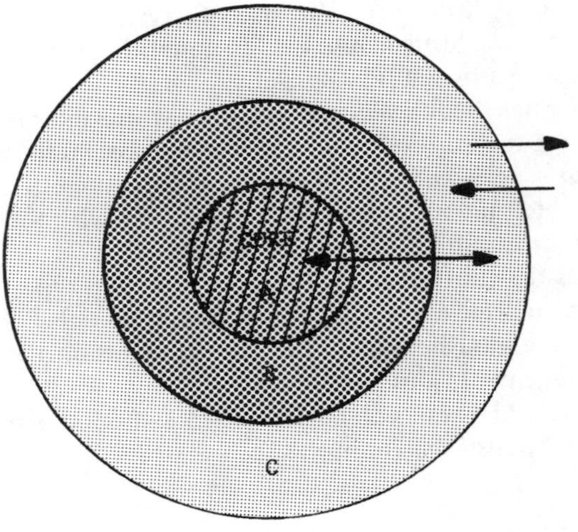

tend to be slower than those in B because B must adapt to the rapidly changing external environment, C. At the same time, B operates as a protecting cell for A. A second level of protection is C. However, C is even more liquid at its perimeter than B. It adapts continuously to pressures, and this is achieved primarily through the success factors described under "cultural and environmental." Finally, these concentric areas are hierarchically overlapping (C contains both B and A, and B contains A), and vertically interdependent (in Figure 1, this is shown by the shadowed areas).

## REASONS FOR SUCCESS

A more extensive presentation of the three categories follows. Specific references for the "reasons" cited are to be found in Table 1 on p. 142.

### Employees

A. *Creativity.* As discussed in the following section on management, creativity applies as a desired characteristic and a concern all the way down to the lowest-level workers.

B. *Labor unions.* Relatively harmonious relations exist between organized labor and business management. For the most part, the Japanese unions are more localized than their U.S. counterparts, and this allows for more effective communications.

C. *Lifetime employment.* This personnel factor has several implications: (1) employees do not fear layoffs (permanent or temporary); (2) long-term work groups can be maintained; and (3) personnel administration is able to spend either less time in recruiting and selection, or have more time per employee in recruiting and selection than in the United States.

D. *Training and development.* Employee training and development are viewed as continuous projects. It is suggested that the Japanese view of long-term job rotation is a positive motivational factor. Also, when lifetime employment is coupled with the phenomenon of increasing technological change, such comprehensive training appears even more critical to success.

### Management

A. *Communications.* The Japanese management group does a good job in direct, face-to-face communications. The Japanese system of management uses more direct verbal dialog and relies less on written instruc-

TABLE 1   Japan's Reasons for Success: A Matrix Summary

| MAJOR CATEGORY/ REASON FOR SUCCESS | AUTHORS |
| --- | --- |
| *Cultural and Environmental* | |
| Adaptability | [4], [9], [38] |
| Business-government relation- ships | [18], [22], [28], [41], [47], [54] |
| "Godfather" guidance | [9], [10], [32] |
| Group loyalty | [3], [14], [17], [25], [34], [48] |
| Harmonious, homogeneous, paternalistic people | [11], [13], [15], [22], [27], [32], [39], [46], [52], [55] |
| Shared purpose | [1], [3], [32] |
| *Management* | |
| Communications | [32], [52] |
| Concern for employees | [6], [17], [21], [32], [34], [39], [53], [56] |
| Creativity | [20], [39] |
| Decision-making process | [3], [4], [9], [13], [14], [16], [17], [19], [21], [22], [25], [32], [34], [36], [37], [39], [40], [41], [43], [49] |
| Financial controls | [44], [51] |
| Inventory controls | [13], [45] |
| Planning | [4], [5], [12], [18], [29], [35] |
| Quality controls | [4], [6], [7], [23], [26], [31], [33], [40], [42], [47], [51] |
| *Employees* | |
| Creativity | [20], [39], [50] |
| Labor unions | [6], [13], [14], [22] |
| Lifetime employment | [2], [7], [9], [13], [14], [17], [22], [24], [27], [30], [31], [32], [34], [35], [36], [39], [41], [49], [52] |
| Training and Development | [8], [9], [13], [17], [39] |

tions/orders/memorandums than is common in the United States. Also, in-
terorganizational communication channels appear to be more flexible and
less rigidly contractual than is the norm in the United States.

   B. *Concern for employees.* Japanese managers are reported to have
a high level of genuine concern for their employees. Whether this stems
from a deeper concern for human relations management or from their lifetime employment system is not readily apparent.

C. *Creativity.* Creativity and innovative thinking are highly sought after in Japan and are seen as an avenue for work process improvements. Further, it is suggested that creativity is a consideration for promotion from middle management into the top management ranks.

D. *Decision-making process.* Japanese management commonly uses a collective, consensus method of making key decisions. This participatory method may have at least two advantages: (1) it allows for a greater number of reasonable alternatives to be considered; and (2) although it may be slow, once the decision is made, the implementation time required to sell/explain the decision is faster than in the United States.

E. *Financial controls.* It is reported that the Japanese enterprises are concerned with bottom-line accountability; but it is further mentioned that the opposite is also true.

F. *Inventory controls.* The Japanese seem to be very progressive with inventory control methods that provide a flexible response to market trends with just-in-time (JIT) minimal inventories and other applications.

G. *Planning.* The literature points out that the Japanese are good at both short-term and long-term planning. They do employ strategic planning, but remain extremely flexible and are able to adjust their plans. It is suggested that they make better use of emphasizing the long run and worrying less about a shorter (say, 3-month) accounting/financial period.

H. *Quality controls.* Much has been written about the Japanese methods of quality assurance with their so-called quality circle format. Japanese quality control is more in-line control than it is after-the-fact screening of defects. Management is keenly aware of product assurance and dictates that strong emphasis on quality be built into the product.

## Cultural and Environmental

A. *Adaptability.* The Japanese people seem to have an adaptable life pattern as influenced by their highly centralized educational system and by their avid curiosity about the rest of the world. From pre-school age, Japanese children are exposed to international situations. The Japanese television, newspapers, magazines, and educational emphasis is geared to overseas events. The result is that Japanese possess a greater awareness of the world outside their country than do Americans.

B. *Business-government relationships.* Government not only supports but works with business organizations toward a common goal. Government (via the MITI [Ministry of International Trade and Industry] and other agencies) provides advice and assistance to business.

C. *"Godfather" guidance.* The Japanese utilize a built-in senior mentor relationship to advise and steer the junior's development. The "godfather" is functionally available to directly counsel and aid the subordinate employee.

D. *Group loyalty.* Collectivism is inherent in Japanese historical development. In the Samurai days this tradition was manifested in the dominant life-style and became the accepted, built-in way of thinking.

E. *Harmonious, homogeneous, paternalistic people.* One national heritage, one race, one religious background, one language, all help explain this homogeneity. Although the Japanese people are individually competitive in some ways, their harmonious underpinnings are viewed by many authors as an advantage.

F. *Shared purpose.* The Japanese culture inbreeds a sense of common objective/goal development. Working relationships among superiors, peers, and subordinates seem able to hold to this unity of objective/goal idea. It is suggested that the Japanese are cultured in a manner that ensures their sense of belonging and their desire to contribute to the organization.

## CONCLUSIONS

In conclusion, the classification proposed permits the following:

    I. To face effectively the distinction between external/internal and lower/higher social, economic, and managerial structure.

    II. To give a rather realistic classification system of the reasons for Japanese management success.

    III. To provide a rather complete (although may be biased) list of the recent literature on the topic.

## BIBLIOGRAPHY

[1] Anderson, W. S. "Meeting the Japanese Economic Challenge." *Business Horizons,* Vol. 24, No. 2 (March/April 1981), pp. 56–62.

[2] Aonuma, Y. "A Japanese Explains Japan's Business Style." *Across the Board,* Vol. 18, No. 2 (February 1981), pp. 41–50.

[3] Bowen, W. "Why the Japanese Seem To Be Eight Feet Tall." *Fortune,* Vol. 100, No. 1 (July 16, 1979), pp. 179–82.

[4] Bryon, C. "How Japan Does It." *Time,* Vol. 117, No. 13 (March 30, 1981), pp. 54–60.

[5] Capon, N., Farley, J., and Hulbert, J. "International Discussion of Corporate Strategic Planning Practices." *Columbia Journal of World Business,* Vol. 15, No. 3 (Fall 1980), pp. 5–13.

[6] Cole, R. E. "Learning from the Japanese: Prospects and Pitfalls." *Management Review,* Vol. 69, No. 9 (September 1980), pp. 22–28.

[7] Cole, R. E. *Work, Mobility, and Participation: A Comparative Study of American and Japanese Industries.* Berkeley: University of California Press, 1979.

[8] Diebold, J. "Management Can Learn from the Japanese." *Business Week*, No. 2299 (September 29, 1973), pp. 14–19.

[9] Drucker, P. F. "What Can We Learn from Japanese Management." *Harvard Business Review*, Vol. 49, No. 2 (March–April 1971), pp. 110–22.

[10] Drucker, P. F. *Management: Tasks, Responsibilities, Practices*. New York: Harper & Row, 1974.

[11] Drucker, P. F. "The Price of Success, Japan Revisited." *Across the Board*, Vol. 15, No. 8 (August 1978), pp. 28–35.

[12] Drucker, P. F. "Behind Japan's Success." *Harvard Business Review*, Vol. 59, No. 1 (January/February 1981), pp. 83–90.

[13] Fox, W. M. "Japanese Management: Tradition under Strain." *Business Horizons*, Vol. 20, No. 4 (August 1977), pp. 76–85.

[14] Furstenberg, F. *Why the Japanese have been So Successful in Business*. London: Leviathan House, 1974.

[15] Givens, W. L., and Rapp, W. V. "What It Takes to Meet the Japanese Challenge." *Fortune*, Vol. 99, No. 12 (June 18, 1979), pp. 104 + .

[16] Hattori, I. "A Proposition of Efficient Decision-Making in the Japanese Corporation." *Columbia Journal of World Business*, Vol. 13, No. 2 (Summer 1978), pp. 7–15.

[17] Hatvany, N., and Pucik, V. "Japanese Management Practices and Productivity." *Organizational Dynamics*, Vol. 9, No. 4 (Spring 1981), pp. 4–21.

[18] Horvath, D., and McMillan, C. "Industrial Planning in Japan." *California Management Review*, Vol. 23, No. 1 (Fall 1980), pp. 11–21.

[19] Hunsicker, J. Q. "Can Top Management be Strategists." *Strategic Management Journal*, Vol. 1, No. 1 (January/March 1980), pp. 77–83.

[20] Ibuka, M. "By Merging American Techniques with Japanese Cultural Philosophies Better Management Can Develop." *Administrative Management*, Vol. 41, No. 5 (May 1980), p. 86.

[21] Johnson, R. T., and Ouchi, W. G. "Made in America (under Japanese Management)." *Harvard Business Review*, Vol. 52, No. 5 (September/October 1974), pp. 61–69.

[22] Krieger, J. L., and Lee, J. W. "Genesis of Japanese Management Success." Unpublished manuscript, Howard University (Washington, D.C.), 1981.

[23] Main, J. "The Battle for Quality Begins." *Fortune*, Vol. 102, No. 13 (December 29, 1980), pp. 28–33.

[24] Marsh, R., and Mannari, H. "Lifetime Commitment in Japan: Roles, Norms, and Values." *American Journal of Sociology*, Vol. 76, No. 5 (March 1971), pp. 795–812.

[25] Marengo, F. D. "Learning from the Japanese: What or How?" *Management International Review*, Vol. 19, No. 4 (1979), pp. 39–46.

[26] McClenehen, J. S. "Japan's Lessons." *Industry Week*, Vol. 208, No. 4 (February 23, 1981), pp. 69–73.

[27] McMillan, C. "Is Japanese Management Really So Different?" *Business Quarterly*, Vol. 45, No. 3 (Autumn 1980), pp. 26–31.

[28] Mochizuki, K. "Government-Business Relations in Japan and the United States: A Study in Contrasts," in D. Tasca, ed., *U.S.-Japanese Economic Relations: Coöperation, Competition, and Confrontation*. (New York: Pergamon Press, 1980), pp. 85–93.

[29] Murakami, T. "Recent Changes in Long Range Corporate Planning in Japan." *Long Range Planning*, Vol. 11, No. 2 (April 1978), pp. 2–5.

[30] Nakata, Y. "Three Keys to Success in the Japanese Market." *Business America*, Vol. 3, No. 13 (June 30, 1980), inside front cover.

[31] Nakayama, N. "The United States and Japan: Some Management Contrasts." *Computers and People*, Vol. 29, Nos. 11–12 (November/December 1980), pp. 8–10, 22.

[32] Noda, M. "Business Management in Japan." *Technology Review*, Vol. 81, No. 7 (June/July 1979), pp. 20–30.

[33] Nelson, J. "Quality Circles Become Contagious." *Industry Week*, Vol. 205, No. 1 (April 14, 1980), pp. 99 + .

[34] Ouchi, W. G. "Theory Z Corporations: Straddling U.S. and Japanese Molds," *Industry Week*, Vol. 209, No. 3 (May 4, 1981), pp. 48–54.

[35] Ouchi, W. G. "Going from A to Z . . . Thirteen Steps to a Theory Z Organization." *Management Review*, Vol. 70, No. 5 (May 1981), pp. 8–16.

[36] Ouchi, W. G., and Price, R. L. "Hierarchies, Clans, and Theory Z: A New Perspective on Organization Development." *Organizational Development*, Vol. 17, No. 2 (Autumn 1978), pp. 25–44.

[37] Pascale, R. T. "Zen and the Art of Management," *Harvard Business Review*, Vol. 56, No. 2 (March 1978), pp. 153–62.

[38] Patrick, H., and Rosovsky, H., eds., *Asia's New Giant, How the Japanese Economy Works*. Washington, D.C.: The Brooking Institute, 1976.

[39] Rehder, R. R. "Japanese Management: An American Challenge." *Human Resources Management*, Vol. 18, No. 4 (Winter 1979), pp. 21–27.

[40] Rehder, R. R. "What American and Japanese Managers are Learning from Each Other." *Business Horizons*, Vol. 24, No. 2 (March/April 1981), pp. 63–70.

[41] Reischaurer, E. O. "The Japanese Way." *Across the Board*, Vol. 14, No. 12 (December 1977), pp. 34–42.

[42] Ringle, W. M. "The American Who Remade 'Made in Japan'." *Industry Week*, Vol. 208, No. 4 (February 23, 1981), pp. 69–73.

[43] Rohlen, T. P. "The Company Work Group," in E. F. Vogel, ed., *Modern Japanese Organization and Decision Making*. Berkeley: University of California Press, 1975.

[44] Ross, S. "What is Japan, and What is Not Japan?" *Business and Society Review*, No. 37 (Spring 1980/1981), pp. 31–40.

[45] Schonberger, R. J. "The Transfer of Japanese Manufacturing Management Approaches to U.S. Industry." *Academy of Management*, annual national meeting, August 2–5, 1981, publication forthcoming.

[46] Seo, K. K. *Management in Japan and India*. New York: Praeger Publishers, 1977.

[47] Shelby, L., and Werner, R. A. "Quality Circles Forge a Link Between Labor and Management." *Defense Management Journal*, Vol. 17, No. 2 (Second Quarter 1981), pp. 40–45.

[48] Sklarewitz, N. "Japanese Executives in America: Two-Way Culture Shock." *Asia*, Vol. 3, No. 2 (July/August 1980), pp. 6–9 + .

[49] Stout, R. *Management of Control?* (Bloomington: Indiana University Press, 1980).

[50] Tanaka, H. "Learning Through Experience: A Trend in New Employee Education in Japan," in R. C. Huseman, ed., *Academy of Management Proceedings,* 1979, p. 419.

[51] Thompson, J. R. "How Japan Competes," *Dun's Review,* Vol. 114, No. 1 (July 1979), pp. 65–87.

[52] Tsurimi, Y. "The Best of Times and the Worst of Times: Japanese Management in America." *Columbia Journal of World Business,* Vol. 13, No. 2 (Summer 1978), pp. 56–61.

[53] Ueda, Y., and Craighead, G. P. "Patience in Human Relations: Keys to Doing Business in Japan." *Management Review,* Vol. 67, No. 10 (October 1978), pp. 57–59.

[54] Walsh, C. "Japan's Sure Road to Success." *Business America,* Vol. 4, No. 6 (March 23, 1981), pp. 3–4.

[55] Whitehill, A. M., and Takezawa, S. "Workplace Harmony: Another Japanese 'Miracle'?" *Columbia Journal of World Business,* Vol. 13, No. 3 (Fall 1978), pp. 25–40.

[56] Yang, C. Y. "Management Styles: American Vis-à-vis Japanese." *Columbia Journal of World Business.* Vol. 12, No. 3 (Fall 1977), pp. 23–31.

# 12

# Japanese Management Success: Implications for the Field of Organizational Development

ANSON SEERS

A search of the Organizational Development (OD) literature indicates a lack of research on Japanese organizations or the application of Japanese management concepts in U.S. OD programs. In fact, a search of the Journal of Applied Behavioral Science, perhaps the major OD journal, produced no such references. As a beginning toward filling this gap, the present paper reviews the development of OD, the increasing appearance of articles on Japanese management systems in the last decade, the commonly proposed explanations for the dramatic success of Japanese organizations, and the prognostications for business in the 1980s.

The development of OD has its roots in the small group research of Kurt Lewin and his associates [12]. The stimulus of this work led to the formation of the Research Center for Group Dynamics (RCGD) at the Massachusetts Institute of Technology in 1945, and the National Training Laboratory (NTL) in 1947. These organizations studied the effect of feedback to groups of information on the process characteristics of group interaction. Over the following decades, NTL became widely known for its work with sensitivity training and T-groups [2]. The popularity of sensitivity training peaked around 1970, but by then the literature was filled with a wide variety of approaches to organizational development that were based on interpersonal sensitivity training. The proliferation and differentiation of techniques led some observers to claim that the term "sensitivity training" had become so broad in definition that it was left with little real meaning [15]. Yet all these approaches to OD were somewhat alike to the outside observer. All stressed "experiential" learning as opposed to factual learning, focused on interaction processes between individuals in the context of a group, and carried the implicit assumption that individuals with improved interpersonal skills, greater insight and empathy, and more humanistic values would transform work organizations.

The major variable with respect to the differences among T-groups was the composition of the group undergoing training. To the extent that participants were unknown to one another (stranger labs), as opposed to members of an actual organizational unit (family labs), they were much more open and honest in their interaction. Yet, to the extent that stranger labs were ephemeral by nature, learning from such group experiences was least relevant to the realities of the "back home" organization.

While approaches based upon lab training are most widely known as OD methods, the field owes much to the development of survey research methodology. Early work in this area was conducted at the Survey Research Center of the University of Michigan [14]. This approach to OD became known as survey feedback, since the common approach was for a change agent to present the summarized results of attitude questionnaire data from employees to organizational groups with the supervisor present, with group discussion of possibilities for change ensuing. The key assumption of approaches based on survey feedback mechanisms is that employee participation and involvement will bring forth valid and necessary information for change, and will produce the necessary commitment to implement the desired changes. Effectiveness of survey feedback approach was limited, however, due to individual differences in receptivity to change and insight in the interpretation of findings, and also to the use of standardized questionnaire forms with no specific connection to the particular characteristics of a given company.

The development of OD over the years has progressed in the direction of the combination of techniques for broader impact on organizations. Increasingly, structural characteristics of organizations have become the targets of OD interventions. The rise in popularity of job redesign has led to a great deal of attention on the structuring of work activity. The welding of work design and OD owes as much, if not more, to the work of the Tavistock Institute researchers [7] as to the advocates of job enrichment [5, 9,

11]. It was the Tavistock researchers, advocating the socio-technical systems approach, who argued that social and technical characteristics of work systems needed to be integrated. Yet, integration, as such, is rarely attained. The popularity of work design is generally manifested as *redesign* of work: job enrichment. The presumption of job enrichment is that the industrial engineers have designed the work with concern only for technical factors, and the services of a change agent are needed to humanize the work so as to make it compatible with personal and interpersonal needs. In America, at least, we seem to have preserved a distinction between the role of the industrial engineer, who is to pursue technological efficiency, and the organizational psychologist, who is to pursue the opportunity for self-actualization by the work force. Thus, while the techniques of OD change agents have evolved, the overriding theme of the field remains advocacy of a humanistic philosophy of work.

## U.S. AWARENESS OF JAPANESE MANAGEMENT SUCCESS

A cursory review of management literature over the last decade produced 36 articles on Japanese business. Fully one half of these articles were less than one year old, and 75 percent were printed within the last three years. These are hardly startling figures, since it is only within the last few years that Americans have become aware of the impressive success story of Japanese business. Epitomizing these articles are three selections from the Harvard Business Review [6, 10, 20]. All seek the causes of the success of the Japanese. While different writers advocate different explanations for Japan's success, none offers more than impressionistic evidence. If the choice among explanatory factors is open to argument, at least most writers agree on similar lists of causal factors. These factors include cultural explanations, particularly emphasis on groups and interdependence as contrasted with the American ideal of the independent individual, traditions of permanent employment [3], and union organization by enterprise rather than by trade [19].

Other explanations focus on the institutional structures for business itself. The rise of big business in Japan began with the pre-World War II Zaibatsu, who, by some versions of history were largely responsible for Japan's entrance into the war. U.S. cold war policy in the late 1940s involved rebuilding Japanese economic institutions as a Westernized force in an area of the world that was viewed as highly susceptible to communist influence. Thus many of the major business figures prominent before the war as the Zaibatsu became the Zaikai — top business leaders after the war. Zaikai leaders were known for their jinmyaku, i.e., personal connections.

These leaders are now typically in their '70s and '80s, ages at which most American managers have long been put out to pasture. Thus, most Zaikai leaders have been working with their companies since the end of WWII. Their vision of a mighty Japan is a long-standing dream, and they have organized in its pursuit. With the blessing and, indeed, tangible support of America, Japanese business leaders sought strength through collective action, much as U.S. labor organizations pursued better pay and working conditions for the working man. Unlike American management groups, the Japanese groups have been used to orchestrate the development of economic sectors and to cultivate coöperative relations with government. It is just this kind of coöperation that some Americans refer to as "Japan, Inc." Rather than being an unfair advantage for the Japanese, the coöperation resulting in institutionalized planning above the level of individual companies is a product of debate and struggle [4].

While much attention has been given to quality circles in the popular press, few authors in business journals consider them to be responsible for Japan's success. Hayes [10], for example, claims that the Japanese have simply been more thorough and careful in their execution of the principles of production operations: material flows, machine maintenance, quality consciousness, and scheduling. Yet execution of production is but one element of business. Are we to presume that U.S. production managers have simply gotten lazy? I think not. Quality control circles have been an element in the success of the Japanese. Perhaps their key contribution is that they result in operational-level employees using concepts and methods of industrial engineering in what is essentially a participative management device. Thus the technical and personal aspects of work can be effectively integrated. While American managers balance the humanistic concerns of the organizational psychologists against the technological efficiency concerns of the engineers, Japanese workers in quality circles combine the principles advocated by such specialists in an implicit fashion as they deal with production problems.

Finally, let us be aware that much of the recent literature reflects simply the belated recognition of Japanese management success. Along with the burst of popular interest in Japanese management has come the question of what the "secret" of their success is. While this may be one of the easiest questions to ask, it is unlikely to lead us to useful knowledge. The Japanese and U.S. business systems differ in many ways. The principle of equifinality from systems theory tells us that complex systems can produce the same outcome with different inputs and different processes. The better analyses of the success of the Japanese, e.g., see [17], take into account the various institutional factors, cultural factors, and historical developments that have interacted in the Japanese experience.

# BUSINESS IN THE 1980s

As the decade began, a major concern in American business was the declining rate of growth of productivity. As this trend continued, we have seen actual decreases in productivity measures. These developments have certainly played a role in the sudden interest of many Americans in Japanese business. Yet our productivity statistics are only partially indicative of inefficiency. Consideration of our productivity measurement technique draws our attention to the changing business environment. Since economists define productivity as the ratio of goods and services produced to the amount of human labor used in the process, we should take particular note of changing patterns of work in the U.S.

The demographics of the workforce have changed considerably. The baby boom generation, having caused great changes in education as schools were first built and then closed, has become the largest group in the workforce. As the courts have found many groups to be the victims of social discrimination, the legal remedy has involved putting some individuals in business positions with less preparation and experience than needed. Also, both the cost of energy and the cost of money have risen dramatically. Where decision makers have had to choose between employing capital and employing labor, it has been rational for them to substitute labor for capital in many situations. The pressure for increase in the denominator of our productivity statistic helps to explain the lack of increase in the overall ratio.

Let us not forget that a few short years ago our economists were telling us we had reached the Affluent Society [8]. We have achieved levels of economic and social well-being never before seen. Then we began to herald the advance of the Post-Industrial Society [1]. The trends are clear enough. Business activity continues to shift from the production sector to the service sector. The blue collar workforce is shrinking, while the white collar force grows. Social roles are changing; the one wage earner family is an endangered species. People are living longer, population growth is slowing, and the standard of living may be ceasing to rise. Toffler [18] argues that the current changes parallel the Industrial Revolution in magnitude, but these changes will occur over a matter of decades, rather than centuries.

Romanticism aside, we won't return to a simpler past. Technology will continue to grow. We will outgrow the technology of mass as we develop the technology of energy. Rather than machines, railroads, and factories, electronics, computers, and nuclear power will shape our lives. The political changes observed in the Reagan presidency indicate that the government will play a smaller role in this future than we may have expected. Business will play a correspondingly larger role. The trend towards internationalism in business will continue. We may not be talking, in the future, of Japanese business versus U.S. business, but of truly multinational business.

## IMPLICATIONS FOR OD

The field of OD needs to mature if it will be of major use to organizational effectiveness in the 1980s. Its theme will continue to be the pursuit of greater organizational effectiveness through better human relations: greater employee participation, improved communication, opportunities for psychological growth and self-satisfaction; in short, the humanization of work. Increasing concern for the quality of work life will sustain a high level of interest in the area. The initials QWL will probably evoke wider recognition among managers than the initials OD.

Yet notable changes must occur in the substance of the field as well as the form. More cross cultural comparison studies are needed. The non-U.S. organizations typically examined in OD studies are predominantly European. What of the Japanese, the Arabs, and the Mexicans?

Further, OD needs to address organized labor. Unions traditionally have mistrusted OD as management-oriented. Their mistrust is not unfounded. If we look to the success of Japanese management, with their more harmonious labor relations and lack of involvement with the American and European OD movement, we can only ask if something more than mere coincidence is at work. While OD practitioners have advocated changes in organizations for improved effectiveness, the Japanese experience suggests that the organizations themselves be changed, rather than the people in them. Ouchi's [16] proposal for the Type Z organization argues that greater participation is the key to organizational success in the future. The claim is that greater participation will bring about more coöperation, greater trust, and attention to long-term considerations as opposed to short-term outcomes. Any student of Organizational Development must recognize this logic as a major theme in the evolution of the field. Such ideas are hardly novel in their application to U.S. business.

Resistance to change among union leaders signals underlying problems [13]. The underlying problems involve the suspicion that managers seek to use devices such as quality circles chiefly as a means to eliminate unions and their interference. Presumably, once the union is eliminated, management would then be unfettered in its exploitation of labor.

The adversarial system of labor and management is rooted in the political foundations of the American nation. The field of OD has not incorporated political dynamics either with respect to the environment in which they operate nor the internal mechanics of decision making. Should the

OD field continue to fail in such incorporation, we will be reading in our newspapers in the coming decade about the settlement of quality of work-life issues in the courtroom, much as today the hiring and firing issues are argued in points of law.

A conclusion of this chapter, then, is that the success of Japanese business does not indicate that organizations must simply become more humanistic. The relative success of Japanese and American businesses appears to be due as much to cultural, legal, and political factors as to worker motivation. Second, the history of application of humanistic management philosophy under the rubric of organizational development also argues that we can see some of the shortcomings of such approaches in U.S. business today. Believers in the human relations approach to organizations may take the occasion of the success of the Japanese for a revival of sorts, but the approach has seen its day. The challenge to American managers by the Japanese success is then no less than the challenge to the student of organizations. The future still belongs to those with fresh ideas.

# BIBLIOGRAPHY

[1] Bell, Daniel. *The Coming of Post-Industrial Society*. New York: Basic Books, 1973.

[2] Bradford, L. P. Biography of an Institution. *Journal of Applied Behavioral Science*, June, 1967, pp. 127–43.

[3] Cole, R. E. The Theory of Institutionalization: Permanent Employment and Tradition in Japan. *Economic Development and Cultural Change*, October, 1971, p. 60.

[4] Dahlby, T. Well-organized at the Top. *Far Eastern Economic Review*, April 24, 1981, pp. 76–80.

[5] Davis, L. E., and Cherns, A. B. *The Quality of Working Life*, Vols. 1 and 2. New York: Free Press, 1975.

[6] Drucker, P. F. Behind Japan's Success. *Harvard Business Review*, February, 1981, pp. 83–90.

[7] Emery, F. E. and Trist, E. L. Socio-technical Systems. In *Management Science Models and Techniques*, Vol. 2. London: Pergamon, 1960.

[8] Galbraith, J. K. *The Affluent Society*. Boston: Houghton Mifflin, 1958.

[9] Hackman, J. R., and Oldham, G. R. *Work Redesign*. Reading, Massachusetts: Addison-Wesley, 1980.

[10] Hayes, R. H. Why Japanese Factories Work. *Harvard Business Review*, August, 1981, pp. 56–66.

[11] Herzberg, F. One More Time: How Do You Motivate Employees? *Harvard Business Review*, 46, 1968, pp. 53–62.

[12] Lewin, K. Frontiers in Group Dynamics. *Human Relations*, 1, 1947, pp. 5–41.

[13] Lawrence, P. R. How to Deal with Resistance to Change. *Harvard Business Review*, 47, 1969, pp. 4–12.

[14] Mann, F. C. Studying and Creating Change: A Means to Understanding Social Organization. *Research in Industrial Human Relations*, Industrial Relations Research Association, *17*, 1957, pp. 146–67.

[15] Napier, R., and Gershenfeld, M. *Groups: Theory and Experience*. Boston: Houghton Mifflin, 1973.

[16] Ouchi, W. G., and Price, R. L. Hierarchies, Clans, and Theory Z: A New Perspective on Organizational Development. *Organizational Dynamics*, 7, 1978, (2), pp. 25–44.

[17] Patrick, H., and Rosovsky, H. *Asia's New Giant: How the Japanese Economy Works*. Washington, D.C.: The Brookings Institution, 1976.

[18] Toffler, A. *The Third Wave*. New York: William Morrow & Co., 1980.

[19] Tsurumi, Yoshi. *Japanese Business*. New York: Praeger, 1978.

[20] Wheelwright, S. C. Japan – Where Operations Really are Strategic. *Harvard Business Review*, August, 1981, pp. 67–74.

# 13

# Competition, Cooperation, and Technological Innovation in Japan

## LEONARD H. LYNN

The year 1970 marked the end of an era in world steelmaking. It ended more than half a century in which the open hearth had been the world's predominant steelmaking process. The new "mainstream" process was the basic oxygen furnace (BOF), a technology that was first commercialized by an Austrian steelmaker in 1952. BOF's are cheaper to build and operate than open hearths. Steelmakers, however, were not equally quick to recognize the advantages of the new technology. Some continued to build open hearths until about 1960. Nor were the steel industries in different countries equally quick to use the BOF. The U.S.S.R., for example, was notably slow.

How did U.S. and Japanese steelmakers compare in their response to the BOF? Although it has been argued that U.S. steelmakers were more aggressive than the Japanese in using this new technology, recent evidence suggests that the opposite was true.[1] During the period between 1954 and 1960, when steelmakers were not yet certain that the BOF was a more efficient steelmaking technology, U.S. steelmakers added steelmaking capacity at integrated plants fourteen times.[2] They built BOFs only four of those times, some 29 percent. During the same period, the Japanese built new steelmaking capacity at integrated plants nine times. In six of these nine instances they used the BOF, some 67 percent. By 1962 all of the major Japanese firms were operating BOFs, a milestone not attained in the U.S. until 1970. Indeed, by 1971 the Japanese had replaced all of the open hearths at their integrated plants — U.S. steelmakers have yet to do so [7].

Not only do the Japanese appear to have recognized the advantages of the BOF more quickly, they also appear to have contributed more to its subsequent development. The multi-hole lance that facilitated the scaling up of basic oxygen furnaces was developed in Japan. So was the OG system, which allows efficient pollution control and energy recovery. These are the two most important generally applicable advances in BOF technology. Reports in the literature also suggest that the Japanese are (and have been for some time) ahead in computerizing BOF operations. By three commonly used measures of performance, yield (the percentage of the pig iron in the BOF that is made into good steel), tap-to-tap time (the time required to make a heat of steel) and refractory consumption (which indicates how often furnaces have to be taken off-line to be relined with heat resistant refractory brick), the Japanese have long out-performed the Americans [8].

Elsewhere, I examine economic factors that affected the rate of diffusion of the BOF in the two countries [7], [8]. In this chapter I will argue that differences in the types of organizations involved in the introduction and development of new steelmaking technology in the two countries contributed to the superior performance of the Japanese.

## THE INNOVATION PROCESS

Organization theorists typically think of innovation as comprising decision and implementation stages [19]. Herbert Simon [17] divides the decision stage into three phases: search, the design and analysis of possible courses of action, and the choice of one of the alternatives. The implementation stage is less clearly conceptualized in the organizational literature. Although implementation is frequently taken to mean the mobilization of an organization to accept change, e.g., in Hage and Aiken [5], mobilization problems did not seem to be an important factor in the adoption of the BOF and may be relatively unimportant in technological innovation [8]. Economic historians, however, suggest the great importance of another aspect of implementation — solving problems to make a major new technology work [16]. This aspect of implementation was of considerable importance in the introduction of the BOF.[3] In this discussion, I will focus on the three phases of the decision phase defined by Simon and on the problem-solving required in adapting the BOF to the specific conditions facing early adopters.

## ACTION SETS AND INNOVATION

Much of the work of organization theorists on innovation has involved efforts to identify organizational characteristics leading to "innovativeness." Less attention is given outside organizations that affect both the decision to innovate and the implementation of that decision. This is a curious lapse. The inventors of better mousetraps do not wait for the world to beat a path to their door — they go out looking for potential customers. The developers of a new technology and their agents call on prospective users, write technical articles, present papers on it at engineering conferences, and exhibit it at trade fairs. Sometimes they contract agents. Sometimes go-betweens approach them. Similarly, the technical problem-solving capabilities of an organization are partly a function of the capabilities it can draw on from other organizations. Chandler [2], for example, discusses how the development of new marketing organizations facilitated the introduction of new production technologies in a range of industries. Rosenberg [16] points to numerous innovations that were made possible by the development of a machine tool industry. The adopter of a new technology is typically only part of an "action set," i.e., "a group of organizations formed into a temporary alliance for a limited purpose"[1].[4]

Markedly different "action sets" were responsible for the introduction of the BOF in the U.S. and Japan. Much of the difference can be attributed to differences in the histories of the two industries. The U.S. steel industry had been the world's largest since 1890. In the 1950s it produced approximately one hundred million tons of steel per year. Until the mid-1950s, Japan had never produced as much as ten million tons of steel in a year. A large industry had evolved in the U.S. to supply steelmakers with plant and equipment. Sales for this industry amounted to several billion dollars a year in the 1950s. Firms such as Koppers designed and built entire steel plants. Firms such as Open Hearth Combustion Co. (a Koppers subsidiary) specialized in the construction of open hearths. Lectromelt built electric furnaces. Pennsylvania Engineering was noted for its Bessemer converters. Mesta, Wean, and others built rolling mills. Large firms such as Harbison-Walker supplied the steel industry with the refractory brick it needed to line its iron and steelmaking furnaces. It was these supplier firms that were primarily responsible for introducing technological advances in the U.S. They were driven by competition to innovate. Foreign suppliers of steel plant and equipment were also interested in the U.S. market. It was the world's largest and it was relatively accessible. The U.S. had also evolved other mechanisms to promote the spread of technology, e.g., an independent technical and trade press, and professional associations with conferences for the purpose of information exchange.

In Japan, things were very different. The industry had not been large enough to encourage the evolution of a large industry to supply it. The steelmakers themselves built simpler equipment and imported more complex equipment from Germany or the United States. Since the Japanese market was relatively small, little effort was made on the part of foreign suppliers to sell in Japan — and, in any case, language and cultural difficulties presented far greater barriers than those surrounding the U.S. market. It was up to the Japanese to learn about new technology and to approach the suppliers. They would have to learn about new advances and evaluate them. In part this task was carried out by the steelmakers themselves: a task made somewhat easier by the ability of many Japanese engineers to read English or German. In part the information-scanning task was assumed by the trading companies. Mitsui had ties with Demag and Krupp, for example. Mitsubishi had established a European subsidiary back in the 1920s to watch for breakthroughs [14]. These and other firms also had engineers stationed overseas. Another part of the information-scanning task was assumed by the government. In the 1950s, the Ministry of International Trade and Industry (MITI) had to approve all technological imports.

## THE PROBLEM AND THE SEARCH FOR SOLUTIONS

The innovation process is typically seen as being triggered by a "performance gap." In the 1950s there was considerable dissatisfaction with the open hearth steelmaking process. Compared to other steelmaking processes such as the Bessemer and Thomas, the open hearth required expensive facilities and was slow to operate. It required the use of large tonnages of scrap for efficient operation, but the price of scrap in many areas was highly volatile, and supplies were uncertain. Despite these drawbacks, the open hearth continued its dominance because other contemporary steelmaking processes were severely limited with respect to the types of iron they could refine and the types of steel they could produce. Some steelmakers were attempting to improve the open hearth and other conventional processes. Others were developing new processes. Some of these solutions seemed promising and were used, but all had serious shortcomings, and none is now in widespread use. The real answer to the performance gap appeared in Austria in 1952 when a small steelmaker blew in the world's first commercial BOF.

The commercial BOF had been jointly developed by two Austrian steelmakers. Another firm, Brassert Oxygen Teknik, acted as their agent in selling license rights to the BOF. Brassert actively promoted the BOF world-wide, particularly in the U.S. — which was then by far the world's largest producer of steel. Brassert used personal contacts to make sure that those responsible for technological search at the U.S. steelmakers knew of the technology. It ensured that technical articles explaining the technology were published in leading journals. It made it easy for foreign engineers to visit the first BOF installations. Experiments were conducted and data published to demonstrate the compatibility of the technology with U.S. conditions. In May 1953, Brassert arranged for Kaiser Engineers to be its general licensee for the United States. Kaiser Engineers then began aggressively promoting the technology. By the end of 1953 many engineers from around the world knew about the BOF, and many of them had already visited the BOF installations in Austria [3]. Brassert's activities were less extensive in Japan, in part because Japan was not yet a major factor in the world steel industry, and in part because Brassert was less well-equipped to operate in Japan than in the United States.

By this time, however, the BOF had already been "discovered" by a Japanese steel firm.[5] Approximately a year and a half before the first commercial BOF went into service, an article describing a BOF pilot plant appeared in the German technical journal *Stahl und Eisen* — this was in December 1950. The article apparently did not attract widespread interest, but it did attract the interest of engineers at Nippon Kokan's Thomas steelmaking plant. These engineers then received information from a Mitsubishi Trading Company engineer who had recently returned from Europe. In June 1951, they embarked on a three-month tour of steel plants in Europe to learn more about the BOF (and other steelmaking technology). On returning to Japan, they fashioned a test converter and started to assess the feasibility of using a BOF in Japan. An internal company dispute blocked adoption of the technology, and there matters rested until 1956.

The second Japanese steelmaker to develop an active interest in the BOF was Yawata Steel, the largest firm in the industry. Yawata had been experimenting with another new steelmaking process, the turbo-hearth. By mid-1953, it was becoming clear that the experiments were not likely to be successful. Some of the engineers involved in the experiments read the articles that were beginning to appear about the BOF in British and German technical publications. Their test plant was changed to a pilot BOF plant. Information was sought through Okura Trading. Engineers were sent to Europe.

Three points are worthy of note here. 1) The BOF was discovered by NKK's engineers largely through their own initiative before the promoters of the technology had begun any efforts to sell it, indeed, before the first commercial plant was even in operation. 2) Both NKK and Yawata first learned of the existence of the BOF because of the ability of their engineers to read foreign languages. 3) Both firms were assisted in gathering preliminary information by the trading companies.

My focus in this paper is on the U.S. and Japanese steel industries. At this point, however, it becomes necessary to turn to a firm in another steel industry, the Canadian. It was Dofasco Steel of Ontario that brought the BOF to North America. And, it was due to Dofasco that the first U.S. adopter of the BOF learned about it. About a year after NKK's engineers returned to Japan with information on the BOF, a Dofasco Vice Chairman heard about the BOF while traveling in Europe. He instructed Dofasco's research department to find out more about the technology. In November 1952, Dofasco initiated tests and, in March 1953, Dofasco engineers went to Austria to find out more about the technology. In June 1953, Dofasco signed a license agreement giving it Canadian rights to the technology. Dofasco then completed other tests and started work on the first commercial BOF outside Austria.[6]

It was through Dofasco that the first American adopter of the BOF, McLouth Steel, learned about the BOF. A vice president of McLouth Steel was a close friend of the Dofasco Vice Chairman who had first developed an interest in the BOF. In April 1953, McLouth sent one of its engineers to Austria to investigate the BOF. Dofasco assisted McLouth in planning the trip, suggesting people that should be met and writing letters of introduction. McLouth quickly decided to use the technology. Indeed, while in October 1954 Dofasco became the first firm outside Austria to blow in a commercial BOF, McLouth had its BOFs in service in December 1954 [3].

The events at another steelmaker are of further interest in filling out our story. This steelmaker is Jones & Laughlin, the first major steelmaker in the United States to adopt the BOF. J&L, like McLouth, also first heard of the BOF in 1953. Information on the technology flowed through a personal connection: an agent of Brassert, the international sales agent for the technology, was a friend of a J&L vice president for technology. In the spring of 1953, two J&L engineers went to Austria to investigate the new technology. J&L put its BOF into service in September 1957, at virtually the same time as Yawata.

The Americans, then, found out about the BOF through personal connections and/or through the efforts of the promoters of the technology. The Japanese learned about it through a scanning of the technical literature, but with the help of trading companies.

## EVALUATION OF THE BOF

The efforts to analyze and evaluate the BOF before coming to a decision about whether or not to adopt it followed somewhat different courses at the different firms. Engineers at Dofasco, the Canadian firm, built pilot converters, to assess the viability of the technology in their specific situation.

Three concerns were of central importance. The first was whether or not pollution from BOFs could be controlled sufficiently to meet Canadian standards. The second was whether or not a refractory brick adequate for use with the BOF could be developed in Canada — the brick used in Austria was made of special materials that were not available in Canada and the cost of importing it would have been prohibitive. The third concern was the compatibility of BOF steel with Dofasco's rolling equipment and its customer's specifications. Because of these concerns Dofasco conducted extensive pilot plant experiments from late 1952 until its commercial BOFs were actually installed.

McLouth's engineers were less concerned about possible problems with the BOF. They did not intend to install BOFs as independent steel-making equipment, but rather to make a crude steel that could be further refined in McLouth's electric furnaces. They intended to use commercially available open hearth refractories (Dofasco had considered this course, but had become convinced in early pilot plant trials that it was impractical). McLouth's engineers also judged without pilot plant trials that pollution control would not present an insoluble problem.

Since Dofasco and McLouth were already operating BOFs at the time Jones & Laughlin was evaluating the technology, it was clear that some of the fundamental problems, e.g., those relating to pollution control and refractories, were soluble. J&L's engineers sought data from the other two firms. McLouth was becoming embroiled in a dispute over the BOF patents and was relatively uncoöperative, but Dofasco welcomed J&L engineers for plant visits and sold ingots to J&L so that tests could be made on J&L's rolling equipment with BOF steel. J&L also built a small test converter and conducted experiments at its central research laboratories.

At NKK, as was indicated above, a dispute slowed the process of evaluation of the BOF. Open hearth engineers in top management were unwilling to invest company resources in the technology until other firms had proven its viability. The engineers who had visited Austria in 1951 were determined that NKK would pioneer the BOF in Japan. Since they did not have the support of their superiors within the company, they carried out unauthorized tests with the help of people in the construction and research departments. They also published an unauthorized series of technical reports: giving the results of their experiments and publishing translations of articles from foreign journals about the BOF. Finally, they conducted other tests using operating Thomas converters, another unauthorized action and one that involved some risk to the equipment. In 1956, it was learned that Yawata's general manager of steelmaking was planning to visit Austria. Little was known about the experiments at Yawata, but there had been rumors that Yawata was experimenting with oxygen in converters and it was surmised that the Yawata manager might be seeking license rights to the BOF. NKK's president decided that NKK should act quickly. He dispatched two NKK engineers to North America and Europe to collect the final information needed in deciding whether or not to use the BOF. With the assistance of Mitsubishi Trading, the engineers visited Dofasco Steel in Canada, sought information from McLouth (though, because of the patent dispute, they were unable to visit the McLouth plant), and spoke to executives from other firms that were considering the use of the BOF. They were not only interested in technical information about the BOF, but also wanted to know the details about possible legal arrangements. Here Mitsubishi was particularly helpful. NKK's engineers learned that there was an intense three-way rivalry between BOT (Brassert Oxygen Teknik) and the two Austrian steelmakers that held the major patents for the BOF. NKK also learned that although Brassert was supposed to handle the international sale of BOF technology, in certain circumstances in which the purchase of other know-how was involved, foreign steelmakers could buy license rights directly from one of the Austrian steelmakers. With this information NKK was able to effectively exploit the rivalry between the three sellers of the BOF, and gain an unusually favorable license agreement.

Yawata Steel, like Dofasco, conducted extremely thorough pilot plant tests in evaluating the BOF — both of these firms made between 1,500 and 2,000 heats of BOF steel in their pilot plants, and both made BOF ingots large enough for rolling so that tests could be made of final products. Although Yawata engineers visited Austria and the BOF plant at Dofasco, they felt that conditions in Japan differed sufficiently from those in Europe and North America that the BOFs viability in Japan would have to be demonstrated before a commercial unit could be built. As was mentioned, in mid-1956 Yawata sent its general manager of steelmaking to Austria to gather the final information needed in coming to a decision on the BOF. The manager also collected information on refractories at Dofasco. With the assistance of Ohkura Trading Company, he also studied possible licensing arrangements. It seemed clear that the Austrian patents should be used, even though on the basis of Yawata's experience some Yawata engineers felt that the Austrian know-how was not really needed. Yawata's manager, however, was unable to negotiate a favorable license agreement and returned to Japan.

It is interesting to note that there was considerable exchange of information and advice among the North American firms. J&L gave a report on the 1953 visit to Austria by its engineers at the 1954 National Open Hearth Conference — a conference attended by engineers from all the companies [4]. Other reports on plant visits were given by engineers from Kaiser Steel and Dofasco. No such reports were published by Japanese firms until several years later. Yawata's engineers knew very little about NKK's activities, and NKK could only surmise what was happening at Yawata. Both firms knew that Fuji, Japan's second largest steelmaker, was conducting some experiments with steelmaking equipment, but did not know whether or not these were related to the BOF. On the other hand, Japanese were aggressive at seeking information from foreign firms. They were also aggressive in collecting information about the legal aspects of the BOF.

## IMPLEMENTATION

Once steelmakers had decided to adopt the BOF, they had to make legal arrangement for using the technology, secure a supply of refractory bricks so the furnaces could be kept in sustained operation, train crews, and purchase or build steelmaking equipment. Some of these activities had already been initiated before a final decision was actually made to use the BOF — decision-makers thought that at least the contours of solutions to problems were clear before they made a commitment. There were individual differences in how steel firms handled these problems — and, more generally, differences between how things were done in Japan and North America.

Dofasco Steel became the general licensee for Canada, agreeing to pay a running royalty of 25 cents per ton for every ton of BOF steel made. Dofasco then sought to get other Canadian steelmakers to use the technology — receiving a commission for every ton of BOF steel made by other Canadian steelmakers. McLouth and J&L received technical assistance from Kaiser Engineers, the U.S. general licensee for the BOF, but both companies later challenged the validity of the BOF patents. The patent dispute continued for seventeen years before it was finally settled — the patents were ruled invalid, though it seems likely that the costs of litigation far exceeded the royalties that had been sought.

As has been mentioned, NKK's engineers were tentatively offered a favorable license agreement that would make NKK the general licensee for Japan. The license cost $1.2 million in a lump sum, but included no running royalty. It was estimated at the time that this would be equivalent to about 7 cents per ton of BOF steel made, but Japanese production far exceeded expectations and the actual total was only a fraction of a cent per ton of steel made.

Yawata Steel, however, also wanted to become the Japanese general licensee for the technology. Indeed, some Yawata engineers in top management strongly felt that since Yawata had invested more in pilot plant research than NKK, Yawata should be the general licensee. At this point the Ministry of International Trade and Industry (MITI) became involved. Metallurgical engineers in MITI's iron and steel production division had long been interested in the BOF. It seemed that this new technology might help to reduce Japan's dependence on imported scrap. The director of the division had recently published articles on the BOF. MITI was concerned that competition between Yawata and NKK might drive up the price of the technology for Japan. Additionally, the ministry was anxious to prevent imports of foreign technology under conditions that would be unduly restrictive, e.g., those that might prevent Japanese firms that could profit from using a new technology from using it [8].[7]

At a meeting between the presidents of Yawata and NKK, an agreement was worked out whereby NKK would be the general licensee for the technology, but both NKK and Yawata would have the right to be in direct contact with the Austrians to seek technical guidance. All Japanese steelmakers would be allowed to purchase licenses to use the technology at the same cost per ton of steel paid by Yawata and NKK (royalties were assessed on each ton of steel produced and adjustments were regularly made until all users of the BOF had paid their share of the $1.2 million dollars by the end of the license period in 1970). Those purchasing licenses also agreed to share technology at biannual Japan BOF Group Meetings. Later users of the BOF were to send people for training to NKK and Yawata.

This arrangement effectively encouraged the early Japanese users of the BOF to overcome the relatively low inclination by Japanese steelmakers to share technology. It helped to promote the rapid diffusion of the technology in Japan. And, it helped to ensure that Japan got the technology at a very low cost. In contrast, the development of a patent dispute in the United States had the opposite effect. An existing inclination to share technology was somewhat inhibited.

Another problem for the early users of the BOF was that of securing an economical supply of the refractory brick used to line the furnaces. Refractory brick wears down a little each time a heat of steel is made. Furnaces periodically have to be taken out of operation so that they can be relined with brick. It is important that the brick be reasonably inexpensive (in a sense the brick can be seen as a "raw material" in steelmaking, since it is consumed in steel production) and that it be sufficiently durable to minimize disruptions in production.

Dofasco initially produced its own BOF refractories. The results were satisfactory, though Dofasco turned to outside suppliers when commercial brick became available. McLouth simply used open hearth brick. The results were highly unsatisfactory—though not enough to destroy the economic viability of the BOF. By the time J&L blew in its BOFs in 1957, refractories firms were supplying brick for the BOF in North America and this brick proved to be adequate. There was very little joint effort between the steelmakers and refractories firms in developing special brick for BOFs in North America. As a manager in charge refractories at one major U.S. steel firm put it: "We're not about to release many details of many of our processes to any of the refractories makers [10]." There was fear that important proprietary information would spread to competitors via the refractories firms since each of these firms typically supplied several of the steel firms.

In Japan, the situation was very different. Each of the three leading Japanese steelmakers had as an affiliate one of the three leading refractories firms. Yawata was largely supplied by Kurosaki, Fuji Steel by Harima and NKK by Shinagawa. The steelmakers owned a small percentage of the stock of these firms. In addition to purchasing some of its refractories from Shinagawa, NKK also produced some of its own brick — notably the brick it used in its Thomas converters. When NKK signed a license agreement for the BOF, Shinagawa attempted to capture the new market for brick by purchasing Austrian refractory technology. NKK, however, found that the brick it had been using in its Thomas converters was adequate for use in the BOFs. As it became apparent that special BOF brick offered advantages, however, NKK's refractories division was separated from the company and added to Shinagawa, which then supplied NKK's BOF brick.

The relationship between Yawata and its suppliers of refractories was crucial. Yawata had no recent experience with converter steelmaking and had more development work to complete in using the BOF. When early pilot plant experiments showed that refractories were likely to be a problem, Yawata initiated joint research programs with two of its suppliers, Kurosaki and Kyushu. Each of these programs pursued a separate line of development. In 1956 it became clear that Kurosaki's brick was likely to be the most suitable. Yawata increased its investment in Kurosaki, doubling the refractory firm's capital. Kurosaki used the additional funds to build a refractory plant near the Yawata Works to specialize in the production of BOF refractories. Interestingly, the ties between the steelmakers and the refractories were loose enough that Kurosaki was later able to sell brick to other of the major Japanese steel firms [6].

## CONCLUSIONS

While many implications can be drawn from this account, I would like to draw attention to two important respects in which the Japanese "organization action sets" involved in the introduction of the BOF differed from those of the U.S. First, the Japanese steelmakers strongly dominated their action sets, taking the initiative in the search, evaluation and problem-solving involved in major innovation. The U.S. steelmakers relied on suppliers of technology to bring them proposals for the latest technology. Second, the Japanese had far more efficient mechanisms for collecting and evaluating information on foreign technology.

The Japanese steelmakers took the lead in the search for new technology. It was the steelmakers who first learned of the existence of the BOF, and then actively collected information on it. In the United States (but not in the case of Dofasco, the Canadian steelmaker), there was a heavy reliance on suppliers. McLouth heard of the BOF through a personal connection, but then entrusted major engineering of its BOF to Kaiser Engineers. J&L became interested in the technology through a personal contact at Brassert. Similarly, NKK and Yawata sought their own answers to the problem of refractories. McLouth and J&L relied on suppliers.

In the United States there seemed to be an implicit assumption that vendors would bring complete information about their innovation, the steelmaker had only to compare the various proposals based on this information and then come to a decision. Competition both stimulated innovation on the part of suppliers, and ensured that the best new technology would be presented to the steelmaker. This was true whether the vendor was American or foreign. While there is some suspicion about the claims of vendors, it still seems to be felt that this adversarial system is preferable to other possibilities: e.g., more aggressive investigation by the steelmakers or actual control over vendors.

In Japan this way of doing things was not feasible. Japan did not have a strong domestic system of steel technology suppliers, and was not a large enough market to attract strong sales efforts by foreigners. On the other hand, overly heavy reliance on foreign suppliers without independent evaluation of their technology had led to serious difficulties in the past.[8] The Japanese steelmakers took the initiative in scanning technological developments.

Thus the Japanese found out about the BOF, and were actively investigating it more than a year before the first commercial BOF was blown in. The Americans essentially waited until information was brought to them. One of the firms they heavily relied on for technical advice on the construction of new steel plant equipment was Koppers, the largest American supplier of such equipment. It is interesting to note that Koppers was the first firm approached by Brassert about becoming a general licensee for the BOF. Two senior Koppers engineers were strongly interested in the BOF, but the company's top management turned down the opportunity to become licensee. Why did Koppers refuse to become licensee? Perhaps it would have been poor business for Koppers to destroy its open hearth construction business.[9] Open hearths cost twice as much per ton of capacity to build as BOFs. Furthermore, the ability to build open hearths was of little help in building BOFs, and this ability was made obsolete by the BOF. Did Koppers suffer serious losses by hesitating to promote the new technology? No, when the market for BOFs became a lucrative one a few years later Koppers quickly became the leading builder of BOFs in the United States.

Similarly, Yawata's aggressive approach in developing BOF refractories with its affiliates seems to have worked more efficiently than the waiting for a suitable brick to appear on the market by U.S. steelmakers. This relationship between steelmakers and refractories suppliers continues in Japan. It is an intriguing one. A central dilemma for the refractories firms is that the major point of competition for their product is durability at low cost. As durability increases, the total consumption of their product declines: indeed, they sell less than a third as much refractory material to steelmakers as they did twenty years ago. Worse yet, the steel industry is by far the largest customer for refractory brick, taking more than half of its product. Clearly there is a conflict of interest. In the U.S., the mechanism of competition is relied on to stimulate improvements in the brick. In Japan there is some competition, but there is also a much higher degree of control to force the refractories firms to work against their own interests. The Japanese now consume far less brick than the Americans to make a ton of steel.

Recently, considerable attention has been paid to the advantages of the Japanese "keiretsu" system and the systems of subcontractors for the implementation of quality control measures and inventory control. The case of the BOF suggests another area where a close association between vendors and their customers may have advantages — the introduction of major technological innovation. This runs somewhat counter to the conventional wisdom in the United States. Clearly there are also advantages to using the market to force competition and thus to foster progress. The Japanese seem to have found a way to efficiently combine competition and coöperation.

Another aspect of Japan's organization action sets involves its mechanisms for collecting detailed technical information. The trading companies played an important role in the case of the BOF. They continued to help Japanese steelmakers seek out new technology. One of these firms helped arrange U.S. Steel's sale of a bottom blown steelmaking process to Kawasaki a few years ago, for example. These firms also have been active in promoting the sale of Japanese technology outside Japan. The Japanese government also helped promote the BOF and helped force a domestic diffusion of information about it. It appears that MITI helped prevent at least one major Japanese steelmaker from adopting a steelmaking process that turned out to be unsuccessful [8]. MITI's power of control over technology imports has diminished since the time of the BOF, but the ministry still has a capable staff of metallurgical engineers contributing to foreign surveillance. In recent years, other organizations such as the Japan Iron and Steel Federation and the Iron and Steel Institute of Japan have also begun to play a role in the monitoring of international information on steelmaking. The federation publishes monthly abstracts of hundreds of articles appearing in the foreign press about steel. Translations are made available. The institute maintains libraries and computerized data systems. The U.S. analog to these organizations, the American Iron and Steel Institute, does nothing of the kind. Indeed, a few years ago it closed down the small library it had in Washington, D.C.

## FOOTNOTES

[1]For a summary of the literature arguing that the U.S. was a rapid adopter of the BOF, see [18]; the "recent evidence" is in [7].

[2]I specify "integrated plants," i.e., those with blast furnaces, because BOFs generally had to be used in combination with blast furnaces for economical operation.

[3]As Simon [17] and Mintzberg et al [13] note, the phases of the decision process are frequently interwoven. Technical problem solving also appears to occur throughout the process of innovation. Decision-makers may insist, for example, that the general direction of solutions to implementation problems be known before they will commit the organization to a decision.

[4]Aldrich distinguishes action sets from organization sets (organizations with which a local organization has direct links) and networks (all the organizations linked by a specified type of relationship).

[5]The description of events at the Japanese firms is primarily based on numerous interviews held in Japan in 1977–78 [8]. An account also appears in [15].

[6]The description of events at Dofasco is largely based on interviews with F. J. McMulkin, Vice President — Research of Dofasco, in December 1978.

[7]The ministry at times also used its power to control technology imports to limit access to new industries, and thus ensure that firms could attain a profitable scale.

[8]Both the Kamaishi and Yawata Works had been built with a heavy reliance on foreign advisers, both works had to be closed down for extended periods because of technical problems that were attributed to an insufficient familiarity with Japanese conditions on the part of foreigners [9].

[9]In 1957–58 Koppers built the last large new open hearth plant in the United States.

## BIBLIOGRAPHY

[1] Aldrich, H. E. *Organizations & Environments.* Englewood Cliffs, New Jersey: Prentice-Hall, Inc., 1979.

[2] Chandler, Alfred, Jr. *The Visible Hand.* Cambridge, Mass.: The Belknap Press, 1977.

[3] District Court, Eastern District, Michigan, S. Division. Henry J. Kaiser Co., et al v. McLouth Steel Corp. *257 Fed. Supp. 372,* 1966.

[4] Emerick, H. B. "Recent Developments in European Steelmaking Practices." *Proceedings,* National Open Hearth Conference, 1954.

[5] Hage, Jerald and Aiken, Michael. *Social Change in Complex Organizations.* New York: Random House, 1970.

[6] Kurosaki Yogyo Kabuski Kaisha. *Kurosaki Yodyo Gojunen-shi.* Kita Kyushu, Japan: Kurosaki, Yogyo, 1969.

[7] Lynn, L. H. "New Data on the Diffusion of the Basic Oxygen Process in the U.S. and Japan." *Journal of Industrial Economics* (forthcoming, 1982).

[8] Lynn, L. H. *How Japan Innovates.* Boulder, Colorado: Westview Press, 1982.

[9] Lynn, L. H. *Encyclopedia of Japan*, chapter on iron and steel industry (Kodansha, International, 1982).

[10] Malim, T. H. "Less Brick for More Hot Metal." *The Iron Age*, Volume 70 (October 1968).

[11] March, James and Simon, Herbert. *Organizations.* New York: John Wiley & Sons, 1958.

[12] McMulkin, F. J. "Oxygen Steelmaking in Canada." *Proceedings*, National Open Hearth Conference, 1955.

[13] Mintzberg, H., Raisinghani, D., and Theoret, D. "The Structure of 'Unstructured' Decision Processes." *Administrative Science Quarterly*, Volume 21, pp. 246–75, 1976.

[14] Miyamoto, M., Morikawa, H., Togai, Y., Mishima, Y., Katsura, Y., Sakudo, Y., and Uchida, K. *Sogo shosa no keieishi.* Tokyo, Japan: Toyo Keizai Shimposha, 1976.

[15] Nikkei Sangyo Shinbun. Gijutsu no Rirekisho — LD Tenro. *Nikkei Sangyo Shinbun* (October, 1976).

[16] Rosenberg, Nathan. *Perspectives on Technology.* Cambridge, England: Cambridge University Press, 1976.

[17] Simon, Herbert. *The New Science of Management Decision.* Englewood Cliffs, New Jersey: Prentice-Hall, 1977.

[18] U.S. Federal Trade Commission. *The United States Steel Industry and Its International Rivals.* Washington, D.C.: U.S. Government Printing Office, 1977.

[19] Zaltman, Gerald, Duncan, Robert and Holbek, Jonny. *Innovations & Organizations.* New York: John Wiley & Sons, 1973.

# 14

# Kazokushugi and Shudanshugi Management Approaches: Source of Concept Variance in Japanese Business Settings

MOTOFUSA MURAYAMA

## FAMILY-BASED MANAGEMENT SYSTEM — SOURCE OF CONCEPT VARIANCES

The *kazoku* system represents the peculiarities and historical continuity of the Japanese management system throughout the generations. Of course, there have been some changes in the patterns of the kazoku system according to the process of modernization and Westernization that took place in the industrialization period. But the core character of kazoku is preserved to a greater degree and is more apparent in business than in the modern Japanese family. This is indicative of a trend away from the "home kazoku system" to the "company kazoku system."

We must gain an understanding of the social patterns of "kazoku and management" before and during the Meiji Period, and then proceed to study the characteristics of management in Japan since the Meiji era. This is one of the essential areas to explore and study before the present managerial system can be satisfactorily discussed and understood; however, this has only been barely touched upon by Japanese management scholars.

Professor Tadashi Fukutake describes the concept of kazoku in his book as follows:[1] Kazoku must be considered within the total framework of Japanese society because the elements of the kazoku unit in the expanding family organization have been preconditioned by the political-economic and socio-cultural constraints of the concerned period. Not only is kazoku understood as an organization based upon kinship (shinzoku kankei) but is also recognized as the daily coöperative living center or social unit for production and consumption, guaranteeing the people's livelihood in the society.

According to Professor Chie Nakane, *Shinzoku* (kinship) is more dynamically defined as the following:[2] Shinzoku is the group of people chained together through blood-relation or marriage. Shinzoku differs from *Ketzuen shudan* (descent group), which is typified by a certain organization. Shinzoku is constituted rather by an individual-centered and driven blood or marriage relationship. While the functional behavior of shinzoku is usually centralized around a given individual (or a given family) at a given time with participation from a given individual or families, it is not expected that kazoku members stay within the fixed framework of the same shinzoku group. Furthermore, shinzoku is not the only kind of coöperative organization in Japan.

Both scholars recognized that shinzoku, or kazoku, is a functional group for the purpose of economic coöperation and survival, or the maintenance of the family, which suggests that the idea of coöperation descended from the blood-relation shinzoku.

In the feudal society prior to the Meiji Reformation, the Japanese business houses (*shoka*) and businessmen (*shonin*) had developed fairly refined management skills and an esprit de corps among themselves to motivate and carry on profitable businesses. The management patterns of shoka were taken from those of the family social unit and maintained in a similar way. The family business was supported by the prevailing social patterns of kazoku in those days; that is, the basic concept of any Japanese kazoku is an organization of genealogical continuity for maintenance and expansion. Thus, the kazoku organization takes precedence over its members. Consequently, this is the source of the pattern of Japanese management in which the values of groupism in terms of kazoku are superior to those of the individual member. This is illustrated by the shonin's typical attitude of "prosperity of trades and offsprings," whereby members are expected to aid one another for the prosperity of their kazoku, which in turn assures each member's life and place in society.

The feudal society had a variety of management patterns that continued well after the Meiji Period. In this era, the direct aim of management was the profit motive, which was characteristic of the strong capitalism of Mitsui, Mitsubishi, and Sumitomo in the Meiji years. Each commercial establishment was organized on the pattern of the family institution. The symbol of the family business was the *Noren*, which represented the tradition, confidence, and esteem of the house. This was passed on to succeeding generations, and such esteem for genealogical continuity survives, even when a women's garment store changes to a department store, a drug dealer to a pharmaceutical company, and an exchanger to a banking firm. Even present day enterprises highly esteem their long history and traditions. The maintenance of a business entity is the basic doctrine of the Japanese management system that has been symbolized in "noren."

This family style of management has the flexibility to absorb members according to the size of the business. According to kenchi-cho or soumon-ninbetsucho, there could be more than ten members in a big house. Some of these individuals were not kinfolk but live-in employees who were treated as though they were direct family members next in line to the owners' own children. For example, they were allowed to open a store as a subsidiary business. This has been the outstanding characteristic of the family management in Japan. Because of such a system the employees served faithfully.

The apprentice system was utilized in the management of a commercial house, and it usually consisted of three levels; head manager (*banto*), assistant (*tedai*) and apprentice (*detchi*).

According to Professor Hiroshi Hazama's research on a wholesale shop of textiles at Kiryu, Gumma-Ken, in the Tenpo Period (1830–1840),[3] there were status classifications in this management system. As Table 1 shows, there were six classifications in rank from boy workers to managers, and promotion was based on the years of service. This promotion was applied only to a *kogai* (employed from childhood). Those workers employed after their adult days were not promoted in the same manner, they were called middle-aged workers or men-servants. Not listed in Table 1 are the house boys and girls who were treated as an inferior class. This system apprenticed a 12-year-old boy and trained him to fill the manager position, the highest in the rankings, at 39 years of age, whence he would be regarded as a regular worker until 50 years old. After his retirement at 51 years, he would be allowed to work at his leisure and would be called leisure-time worker and would receive a stipend. Thus, the natural development of the lifetime employment pattern becomes clear.

With regard to a wage structure, Table 1 also shows that food, clothing, and shelter are guaranteed for nine years (six years as a boy worker and three years as a young fellow worker). No salary was paid but they were given outfit money and some gratuity. When a worker became an assistant (*tedai*), he was entitled to a yearly stipend; from this he would have to pay for his own needs. If he was a live-in servant, he received room and board. The salary was on an annual basis and was not paid at one time, but

TABLE 1   Classification of Ranks in a Wholesale Textile Shop in Kiryu, Gumma, Japan. Tenpo Period (1830–1840)

| | |
|---|---|
| Boy worker or *kodomo* (6 years period) | Outfit money provided. A gratuity as much as 200 biki at the fourth year after his starting service. Money income being entrusted by the store since 12 years of age. |
| Assistant worker or *koeki* (3 years period) | Outfit money given from 17 to 19 years of age. Gratuity of as much as 1 ryo. Rules are same as with boy-workers. Able to call these men by names. Reward will be given according to work performed. A *haori* (formal clothes) is not always necessary. |
| Young fellow or *wakamono* (9 years period) | From this position, personal belongings must be taken care of by themselves. Salary: 3 ryo from 20–26 years of age. Salary: 7 ryo from 27–31 years of age, money for supervising boy workers. |
| Appointed masters: | |
|   Assistant manager or *fukushihai* | 7 years from 32 to 37 or 38 years. Salary: 10 ryo. |
|   Manager or *shihai* | 10 years from 39 to 50 years of age. Salary: 20 ryo, a reward for supervising the young and fellow workers. |
|   Retired worker or *inkyo* | Leisure-time worker, after 51 years of age. Salary given according to working hours. |
|   Middle-aged servants or *chunenmono* | Equivalent to young fellow-workers. Reward given according to qualified service. |

*Source:* Hiroshi Hazama, "Nipponteki No Keifu" (Genealogy of Japanese Ways Management), Japan Management Association, Tokyo, 1963, pp. 41–45; and "History of the Silk Thread Industry," Gumma-Ken, 2nd Volume, 1954.

entrusted to the master who gave it out as he thought necessary. He paid the remainder of the money with interest when the employee became independent and was given his own shop. This summarizes Professor H. Hazama's research on the typical managerial system in the Edo Period. Here we note in this management pattern, which was passed down to succeeding generations, the existence of a class system, lifetime employment, a living expenses-salary award system, and a savings system. This management approach can be called *kazokushugi keiei*, or the family-based or family-type management.

This family-type management differs from a blood-affiliated family enterprise (*dozoku keiei*) in terms of its structure. In the case of a blood-affiliated family enterprise, the president was the head of a family and other members were chained by genealogy. The lineage was continued through the enterprise. Dozoku is hereby defined as the grouping concept applying to more than two families, which are chained through *honke* (original family) and *bunke* (extended family) relations within an economic setting.

In the case of a family-type management, the capitalist or the owner-oriented manager and majority of his employees were not blood-related. It was founded on a policy to form a coöperative or warm-hearted relation between capitalists and employees. Thus the shonin management policies of kazokushugi keiei played an important role in the formation of Japanese management ways in modern enterprises.

This kazokushugi management approach has been the basis for convincing and effective management policies uniting owners and workers in business operations. Workers were taught, "The company must be a quasi-family on the basis of parent and child relationships exactly similar to home kazoku of workers. Conflict of interest between owners and workers is not expected in the quasi-family structure. Sublime ideologies are available to the company as long as labor relations are directed towards the family organization and its behavior with the family background spirit."

For example, the following customs in the Japanese company management are closely identified with the Japanese family patterns:

## (1) The seniority system or nenko jyoretsu seido

In any Japanese home the elders come first and the younger follow the elder. (There are two exceptions: the female members are generally ignored with regard to economic support capacity, and direct descent is most respected.) This pattern in the family system is reflected in the company organization structure, and it sets the social order whereby the younger generation must wait patiently for promotion until his elder's promotion.

## (2) Lifetime employment system or shushinkoyo seido

The Japanese parent and child blood relationship exists as a lifetime association that cannot be denied unless some economic or emotional reasons justify a breakdown of this family bond. This idea extends to the company's philosophy and the general expectation that once a man gets a job he must stay for his lifetime. To quit would be considered "unthinkable;" this is unspoken but sensed as a silent social rule.

## (3) Family institutional pay scale for survival of kazokusei seizonkyu seido

The position of family members in the home is the basis for determination of employees' pay rates in the company. Both age and sex are the fundamental determinants for basic pay rate computation. The younger employees are usually dependent upon the parent due to the social recognition of lower status in social stratification. Therefore the company pays less to the younger generation. In a higher social stratification are the older group of workers ranging from 40 years through 60 years of age. They are given due respect and bear more responsibilities in the company and are paid on a higher scale accordingly.

### (4) Bonus allowance or Shoyo seido

The two periodical bonus distributions to the company staff employees each year are conceptualized as the parents' affection and warm-hearted consideration for the children rather than a materialistic distribution on the basis of a profit-sharing plan. They are also regarded as an adjustment for the lower basic pay rate or reward for the employees' sacrifice and endurance on account of the company. The employees believe in the employers' social and customary responsibility to carry out this bonus distribution as Japanese children anticipate *Otoshidama* or gift money at New Years.

### (5) Other fringe benefits or fukuri kosei seido

The company is a family and has to provide the house members (employees) with proper residences, medical care, gifts for marriage or birth of children, remuneration for employee's death, and pension plans. The retirement allowance and pension plan are intended to secure the later years of the retired employees after their lifelong sacrifice for the company.

Lower wage rates in the Japanese company are always preconditioned and precontrolled by the father's (company head) responsibility to protect the children (employees) in cases where there is a serious occurrence to the employee's life. Also, the average Japanese house structure is based upon the nuclear family concept. As long as the economic surrounding permits, departure from the large family unit is possible and all children excluding the first born son, who succeeds his father in the home and business, are looking for the opportunity to establish independent households in the metropolitan area. The Japanese companies function to fill this gap, helping those people who cannot remain in their parent's home to find independence. Therefore, the president's social responsibility is to create a home atmosphere in the company so that the employees can maintain a sense of belonging and develop the stability and loyalty necessary for the progress and expansion of the "home" company.

Regarding business rationalization in the Pre-Meiji Period, Saikaku Ihara in *Eitaigura* mentioned the prescription of the Millionaire Pill, a wonder drug that can make one richer—early to rise-5 ryo, doing family business well-20 ryo, night shift-8 ryo, economical behavior-10 ryo, and health-7 ryo. "You can be naturally of much use to the world if you obey this rule and do well your family business. Without trying to gain a profit, you cannot do well your family business." Doing family business well was thus highly esteemed from the quantitative viewpoint, as measured in monetary terms. An incidental but illustrative remark is made by one Edo writer, Baigan Ishida, in his *Questions and Answers in Cities and Countries, Both in China and Japan (Tohi Mondo)*, "It is a rule to gain profit through buying and selling and the profits got by the sweat of the brows should not be used up for selfish splendor but should be inherited as property from ancestors to descendants." Jyoken Nishikawa, in *Tradesman's Sack (Chonin No)* states, "Property is to be saved and inherited from generation to generation. So he is a great sinner who spends it for his splendor. To save well and leave property to one's children means to return what one was entrusted with to one's ancestors. This is the first step of filial piety." Thus, we could find that the merchants' greatest value in the family business was directed to the idea of prosperity of Business and Descendants, which can be traced back to the ancestor worship philosophy. The businessmen were motivated in this manner and set about to accumulate capital and multiply property that had been left from ancestors for future descendants.

In Europe, capitalism received spiritual support from Protestantism of the Calvin Sect. Protestantism was not influential in Japan, but the patterns of ancestor worship and the social unit of the house played an important part for a strong support of capitalism in Japan. It is often said that the Japanese commercial house lacked rationality. However, it is believed that the rationality of the enterprise lies in its ability to adjust itself to the present circumstances for survival and development.

A workable style of management was maintained and supported by the economical activities based on rationality as well as the inclination to avoid mistakes under an unstable management climate. For, in the feudal society, commerce was completely dependent on a goods-money economy and it was not as stable as the management of a self-sufficient agrarian society. Ideas (*saikaku*), computation (*sanyo*), and saving attitude (*shimatsu*) were developed by merchants in their efforts to adapt themselves in order to keep their businesses going in spite of feudal restraints. Traditionalism was certainly an overwhelming force, but so was rationalism as a means of existence and maintaining family (*kazoku*) continuity. For example, during the state of confusion in the last days of the shogunate, Mitsui-gumi drafted Rizaemon Minomura and Ono-gumi drafted Ichiemon Furu-kawa. Both men were middle-aged servants and not *kogai*; but because of their management skill, they were drafted — this was the rationalism of the merchants.

In the Meiji era, small businesses had a small number of live-in servants. They usually were able to get their own stores independently after
their training or after serving terms as apprentice or assistant or clerk
(there are not always formal and correct names).

This new-born store was called *bekke* (another house) or *makke* (tip
store) and was distinguished from *bunke* (the term used in kinship system
meaning house apart from the main branch). The bekke store was independent, and the funds and capital were given from the parent store according to the faithfulness of the employee. This can be considered a present from a warm-hearted employer. Even after independence, the bekke
exchanged greetings and participated in the ceremonial occasions of the
parent house, and it also received patronage from the parent family. They
tried to plan a mutual prosperity through coöperative life. The parent
family and bunke and bekke had their own stores and kept a common
noren and aided one another to maintain the whole. This was an affiliated
concern of a commercial house.

A large-scale commercial house has a different structure from that of
a small house. Generally speaking, it is an affiliated family group centralized for business purposes. Collateral relatives or live-in servants do not
become managers soon, but commute to the parent family and take part in
the family management, although they are independent as regards their
own households. In this way, the employer or parent family can prevent
the break-up of capital by the establishment of bekke.

As the scale of organization grows larger, it becomes necessary to
secure able managers inside their group. If there are branches in every
part of the nation, reliable and capable men are needed to take charge of
each management. The parent family usually appointed relatives to these
positions. These people ranked higher than clerks and were called managers, controllers, or directors. The people of bunke or bekke were not always used by the parent family but they were provided with capital by the
parent family in a collateral enterprise. Perhaps they became richer than
they would have been as independent managers of branches of the parent
family. They had a sense of superiority when, toward the end of the shogunate, even a samurai (a higher class) was helpless before the richness of a
big merchant (a lower class).

As the scale of organization grows still larger, house is separated
from store and the master begins to commute from home to office. Thus,
the separation of ownership from management was realized. The source of
capital was in the house of the master but the management or care of them
was left to the managers of bekke or bunke. As can be seen, managers in
Japan appeared from collateral management. They appeared as bekke
commuters or upstart clerks. As such they were always subordinate to the
owner of the capital and, though they were in charge of management, they

lacked gumption and enterprise. They were generally allegiant to the master. These managers differ from their Western counterparts, who are enterprising and persuade the rich to invest and control the businesses by themselves. However, in Japan, Eichi Shibusawa played an important part similar to the Western manager. He resigned from government service in the first years of Meiji to persuade Mitsui, Ono, and Shimada *gumis* (financial cliques) to establish the Dai-ichi Bank, Oji Paper Manufacturing Company, and Osaka Cotton Spinning Industry by investment of other entrepreneurs. As his book of *Gohon Shugui* shows, his actions were always directed by the sublime ideal of the national welfare.

There is a world of difference between him and the great clerks of Mitsui who managed the property of Mitsui and were busy accumulating private property and eager for world fame. In time, Western-type managers appeared from people under the control of Mitsui or rather from the collateral, for example, Ginjiro Fujiwara of Oji Paper Manufacturing or Sanji Muto of Kanebo.

In subsequent management developments, the idea of house becomes fainter in the enlarged kinsfolk management. The parent family, the center of this system, changed from owner-manager who is directly in charge of family business to mere owner by the separation of house from store. Constituents of the master's principal residence were all kith and kin, excluding servants and maids who did not participate in the family management and live-in servants who stayed at the store. As in the example of the Mitsui-group at the end of the Meiji Period, bekke was from store and not from house. Here bekke came to mean simply the independence of a household economy. Also, their finances did not come primarily from the master house. The relation between the master family and the bekke became quite individual, and it often ended in one generation. The fact that the employer had servants without blood-relation points out the gradual breakdown or deterioration of the affiliated family concern. When the scale of management grew larger, the number of members belonging to the apprentice system was no longer adequate for future managers either in quantity or quality.

Thus the master branch employed more middle-aged men and the other branches employed servants of their own. The employed were, as a rule, not for future management, but given the role to assist management. This could be called, as it were, the origin of office workers. As the number of those people increased, the structure of management changed from a complete affiliated family concern to one in which only the upper management were blood-related. As business practices became more sophisticated the *terakoya*'s type of education prior to the Meiji was not adequate, and other special knowledge and cultural studies became necessary. Colleges and professional schools were established to meet this need. Graduates of those higher institutions were employed as leading members for future business expansion. Here the old apprentice system, whereby able employees were trained through the ties of parent and child and treated as real members of the family until they could have independent shops, was denied. The competition among enterprises became stiff, and the managing ability of staff became more important.

Thus the limited range of blood-relation meant it could no longer be the sole supplier of staff. Hence the range was extended from kith and kin to friendship, alumni, or to persons from the same province. Even today this pattern of seeking employment through acquaintances exists to a limited extent.

The fundamental recruiting policies in the contemporary Japanese firm support the warm-hearted and traditional family patterns in attracting and hiring individual workers who consciously or unconsciously feel a void in the modern family unit due to the breakdown and deterioration of the traditional family system as a result of the quick pace of industrialization and post-war occupation policies. This implies that kazokushugi management is still a foundation for Japanese executive decision making, because the average Japanese man in a company organization can not be completely free from the family consciousness, as he lives in a modern nuclear family. The company kazoku system retrieves for him the lost traditional home kazoku relationship, which in turn supports the Japanese business value system and extends to the development of groupism or shudanshugi behavior in the Japanese management system.

## GROUP FORCE MANAGEMENT SYSTEM — SOURCE OF CONCEPT VARIANCE

### Introduction of Shudanshugi Management Theory

Shudanshugi can be literally translated as "group ideology" or "groupism." Shudanshugi is the basic value premise for the Japanese behavior, which is usually motivated by group consciousness, and defines the core of the Japanese personality characterized by paternalism or personalism toward a "we-group" or "we-feeling" and exclusivism or formalism toward the "they-group," or "they-feeling."

Shudanshugi in Japan has been unconsciously developed and taught as the concept of harmony or wa because it is the most effective means of pacifying the individual's dissatisfaction with unequal treatment in the group due to low social or economic status. Shudanshugi is a unique code of ethics developed by the Japanese group leaders to unify the members in the group who may be exposed to hardships in life. Group harmony is conceived in terms of the beauty in human life, an idea that can be traced back to the political value system of the feudal period in Japan. The maintenance of a strong group consciousness also allows the individuals in a group to share in the psychological stability afforded to those belonging to it. In most cases, the Japanese people are fearful of being independent from the group to which they primarily belong.

The psychological tendency here, then, is toward weakness in the individual, but this is advantageous for organizations based on collective behavior. Therefore, the weakness found in the Japanese way of shudanshugi is liable to invite group fallacy in the regular decision-making process. Group fallacy is usually perpetrated by the well-informed minority group in order to consolidate the uninformed majority group.

Before proceeding further, a general definition of group, or *shudan*, is necessary. A group is defined in the psychological and social-psychological sense as the phenomenon wherein constituent members have a definite recognition of a functional interrelationship. Moreover, this becomes obvious when the following conditions are present: (a) interdependence, (b) face to face interaction, (c) communication, (d) we-feeling, (e) identification, (f) unity, (g) privilege, and (h) specific norm.

Now let us consider the group concept in Japanese terms. Of course, shudanshugi is not peculiar only to Japan, but the framework of the Japanese cultural heritage is not comparable to other standards because the nature of a group is the product of environmental setting, conditioned by the frequency of social contact among the individuals involved, and dependent on the following variables: (a) common interest (*kanshin*), (b) common demand (*rigai* and *yokyu*), (c) locational proximity, and (d) common mediaries for communication.

The above four variables not only determine the formation of a group in general, but also our frame of reference in evaluating the characteristic qualities of shudan, which are as follows:

(1) Informal but forced participation
(2) Strong group consciousness and cohesiveness
(3) Minority ego-involvement leadership
(4) Remodeling by breach of personal faith
(5) Confucian norm in appearance and emotional norm in reality
(6) Group rationalism in place of individual rationalism
(7) Group personality development
(8) Homogeneity-absorption and heterogeneity-rejection trend

These are the eight criteria for measuring the quality of shudan. Shudanshugi management theory is derived from the aforesaid shudan formation and development principle to respond to the unique business environment of Japan.

## Structure of Shudan

Shudan is generally classified into primary and secondary groups, ingroup and out-group, formal and informal groups, or face-to-face and coacting groups. In the course of analyzing the implementations of shudan, the author had to develop another theoretical framework to visualize the hidden characteristics in the shudan within the Japanese company.

The shudan of inner company organization is conditioned by political, economic, cultural, social, legal, educational, religious, and technological factors. Shudan is always double-faced in that indirect (unspoken) goals, and direct (spoken) goals are both inherent to it.

Shudan is both an emotional system, which can be translated as the we-group (we-feeling or *nakama ishiki*), and a goal-oriented system. The atheistic state of mind among Japanese individuals is conducive to group feeling or group mind. Thus, we-feeling and goal-attainment are essential for the realization of individual security in spiritual and material life. Shudan is in a position to function as "god" because the Japanese people have lost communication with the churches and temples, and finally, a common belief in God (or gods).

The danger in shudan ideology occurs when all the shudan members lose their personality and individuality due to complete absorption into the shudan thereby ignoring the environmental constraints that guide their daily lives as individuals. This is due to the superior influence of the shudan fallacy or shudan egoism which prevents the we-group from being automatically controlled by the fair-justice or universal norms of any external shudan (they-group).

Empirically speaking, direct and rational expression and behavior have been successfully rejected in shudan communication. The we-feeling shudan is a most emotional entity, motivated by sensing and feeling (*sassuru* and *omoiyari*). This implies that functional rationalism may be inferior to personal emotionalism at the first stage of communication. Gradually, personal emotionalism is transmitted to group consciousness (emotionalism), which becomes the basis of group rationalism in achieving the group goal. This process could be called the "neutralization" function by the shudan leaders.

As illustrated in Figure 1, the core characteristic of shudan is goal attainment through situational rationalism. Shudan rationalism found in the Japanese organization is usually expressed indirectly through the emotional elements shown by the inner octagonal belt in Figure 1. While the inner belt contains the policies for group behavior, the outer belt consists

FIGURE 1 Structure of *Shudan*

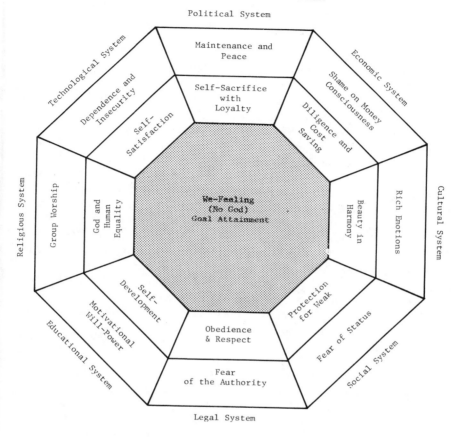

Notes: (1) Inner belt represents emotional forces, and policy-execution aspects of indirectly spoken instruction.

(2) Outer belt represents motivational forces to inaugurate group behavior and constraints of socially unspoken instructions.

of unspoken motivational guides for decision-making by the leading minority group. Thus the structure of shudan in Japan has developed a rationalism within an irrationalism (*rigai no ri*).

## Shudanshugi-Based Management Theories (I)

There have been many evaluations and criticisms of the Japanese economy by people in Europe, America and Asia, but the general consensus of all is that the Japanese have rehabilitated themselves through "imitation" and "cheap labor."

It is true that the Japanese people have been especially receptive to new productive techniques, and have not only mastered new ideas, but frequently managed to improve on them, thereby providing the same products at a cheaper cost. This can be exasperating to the Western observers who, having spent many years on costly research, are suddenly faced with competition at rates they cannot match. Imitation is an effective method of study whereby less developed countries may catch up to the industrially advanced countries. The Japanese people have handled this well but have been more effective than just that, because the Japanese strategy is beyond that of simple imitation. Imitation has its limitations and at present there is a trend in large Japanese enterprises to allocate more funds toward research and new product development areas.

Although Western productive techniques have been rapidly assimilated, management for high efficiency and high wages has not become part of the Japanese business system. It is clear at least that wages in Japan are lower than in America, England, and West Germany.

It has been said that "the Japanese people have a talent for using men at low wages," and it is established that most workers in Japan are very industrious. Although Westernization and Americanization in Japanese society is increasing, the Japanese have their own unique and characteristic personnel management system, as discussed before.

There is a fundamental difference between European and American management and that of the Japanese. The former is based upon the principle of individualism and impersonalism and the latter implements the principles of group- and personal-relation-based behavior.

When work is done by the group, it is difficult to evaluate an employee. This is done by measuring length of service, the most objective standard at hand. What is measured in this way is the individual's social attitude, his character, loyalty, sincerity, and effort, and not his contribution in terms of achievement and ability. Often this type of personnel evaluation is not uncommon: "That man works well and does his best, but his attitude is bad." This idea prevails among the salaried men and conditions their work attitudes. Thus they support the following three rules: not to be late, not to be absent, and not to complain at work.

In Europe and America, they try to evaluate one part of personal duty as manpower, or an accomplishment of duty, but in Japan the value of personality is considered most. The former is called the system of function and accomplishment, and the latter is called the system of mentality and efforts.

In Japan, the ability and achievement of an employee is not evaluated at a definite point, but they recognize his achievement in terms of his efforts. Or, when he is employed, if he has sincerity he is expected to do his best, even though he may have little ability. The meaning of lifetime employment in relation to that becomes clear.

A few who have ability complain strongly about this way of personnel evaluation, but for most people it is preferable because it makes them feel secure in the group. This is not to say that ability is ignored; however the method of personnel evaluation in shudanshugi management is different from that in America and Europe.

Recently, criticism has been raised against the evaluation of employees by length of service. The reasons are many, but generally four are pointed out. First is distrust against a senior staff member (*jyoshi*). Personnel evaluation is usually controlled by an evaluator, a man who judges other persons in his organizational unit. So, if the employee has no confidence in the evaluator, his anxiety is great. There is only a vague reliance on authority in Japan, in contrast to the complete trust and awe accorded to one's seniors in pre-war times. The young (post-war youth) are searching for a more objective means of evaluation.

Second, there is a negative feeling about evaluating a man over a long time, since "a man cannot predict the uncertain future." The young think that it would be more rational to evaluate a person at each point and reward him accordingly.

Third, in terms of the principle of equality, many of the young are against evaluating an individual by length of service because they have been educated in democratic and egalitarian ideologies Japanized during the post-war period.

Fourth is the position of the intellectual elite, called the criticism against the principle of equality. The position of the titled and social elite was abolished after World War II, and the starting point of people who graduated from any kind of university was equal. Since the military no longer exists, and the official world and the academic circles do not attract these people, they gather in the business world. However, they can no longer rely on their family backgrounds for immediate advancement.

Personnel management in any Japanese organization consists of "groupism and personalism superiority." In big European and American organizations the bureaucracy takes care of the personnel problem because it sets the norms to motivate and standardize organizational behavior. The bureaucracy popularizes and develops in management its "technological superiority" (accuracy and speed in organizational management, cost cutting, and solution of personnel problems). On grounds of the "technological superiority," objective standards establish the human relations of members within the organization through the principle of division of labor. Thus, division of labor can be more scientifically improved with a technology-oriented mind. In other words, "technological superiority" becomes a very impersonal matter, and the duty that is given to the individual in the organization surely has impersonal characteristics. So, duty is a very impersonal thing and this is typically seen at automated work places where unskilled laborers repeat simple, mechanical jobs.

Furthermore, having designated the duty in the Western organization, each unit of organization is individual to the very end or, more accurately, each task accomplished through individual power. The way of thinking, which strictly classifies the individual's share in the mass-living, may be fundamentally connected with European and American culture. Within this context, others are essentially thought of as competitors, and their shares are made clear and established as impersonal and objective. This division of labor leads to the avoidance of conflicts in human relations. In other words, a goal is clearly visible and rational to participants in this division of labor and it serves as a common communication tool to consolidate work and separate individuals.

In large European bureaucracies, which are based on the premises of individualism and impersonalism, there is a feeling of powerlessness on the part of the individual as a single unit within the big organization, and an antipathy grows up against the impersonal treatment shown to them.

In Japan, individual responsibility exists, but the substantial unit of the work force consists of the group responsibility with the group privilege. Work is accomplished through the mutual aid of members of the work place. Thus, the individualistic human relations seen in Europe and America are rarely observed. In the West, rarely does a worker help his partner because his own work is delayed and he may increase the other's wages by doing so. He may even request a change when he is troubled with the slowness of his partner's work. At the work place in Japan, however, even when somebody has trouble with his partner, he will complain about it only behind his back, and will try to cover his partner in relation to other work places. Or, as in the post-war trend, if he talks about his partner's weakness to a senior official, this is received with criticism, "You are actively breaking a joint of the laborer's class." The atmosphere of "harmony" is an ideal condition in the Japanese work place.

Both personalism in human relations seen in we-feeling group of employees or management staff and groupism of human relations between employers and employees are a form of paternalism, containing the *kazokushugi* management system (family-based management philosophy) and the welfarism management system (humanity-based management philosophy). Although an individual confronts a big organization through the mid-group by groupism, he does not confront it directly, and he is given a kind of emotional satisfaction from the managerial organization by the personalism that pervades groupism and can not be independent from a group-feeling. This condition is somewhat mitigated, of course, by the large scale of organization and the classical struggle of employers and employees, both of which have an influence on many laborers in Japan.

The Japanese tend to be progressive in the course of idea development, but conservative in the course of regular activities. For example, the dissatisfaction with low wages is surely there; however, it does not take on explosive proportions. The paternalistic policy of serving one firm all one's life gives a certain kind of stability, especially in respect to the absence of the anxiety of unemployment, and the bright prospect of a future life with gradual wage increases over the long term. In other words, the workers in big enterprises can establish their living plan for their future lives, though wages are low, and this is the basis of the system's stability. Thus, although they may support socialism in theory, in reality they don't want to revolutionize the social system. This makes it quite confusing for a foreigner to communicate with a Japanese organizational man. A Japanese scholar called such an attitude "opportunism," which is the basis for progress.

Since the Meiji era, many capitalists and managers in Japan have been introducing the various technologies of the more developed countries of the West. Management technology has also been introduced, but its adoption has not been as smooth, for its objects are people and not commodities. A progressive selection, modification, and absorption of the new knowledge has been going on. The author has defined this as a primitive process (*dochakuka gensho*) that has been built in the Japanese society.

Management is, so to speak, a living thing, and it is meaningful only by its successful function in the real world. Japanese management, which has supported the urgent development of Japanese capitalism, has publicly introduced the new knowledge from Europe and America as well as developing its own methods by promoting the fusion of both groups through trial and error with less adherence to Japanese traditions. New knowledge changes with the age; tradition is never fixed. Therefore, Japanese shudanshugi management has been flexible in its adjustment to the modern social and technological structure and has developed into an effective device for corporate survival.

## Shudanshugi-based Management Theories (II)

It is often said that rights and responsibilities are not clearly defined in Japanese enterprises, and that a spelled-out duty shows the limit of a job objectively. In contrast to the shudanshugi management philosophy, clear definition of individual responsibilities and privilege in a Japanese organization creates unfavorable and impersonal effects. A job is one's life in each Japanese business entity, but its contents are not very clear. Each man has a different duty. The man who has ability and good personal contact with the bosses always has work, even if a job has to be made for him. (For example, in the life-long employment system, employers have to make new jobs for those who become surplus personnel, using the rationale of self-improvement.)

In Japan, the work position of each unit is organized by the human-centered group, rather than by individuals. Thus, the typical pattern of organization is different in Japan and America (Figure 2).

The system of education for life-long employment in the company prepares an individual for this group-centered activity. In Japan, firms do not select a man with the ability to do his job, when locating him at a certain position, but they will employ a man who has a faithful character and moderate way of thinking and will cultivate him in the enterprise for life-

FIGURE 2   Typical Structure of Organization in Japan and the West: (a) Japanese organization—structure of partial and group responsibility; (b) Western organization—structure of authorized and individual responsibilities.

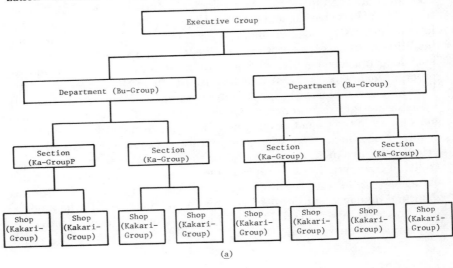

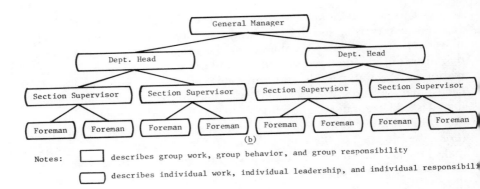

Notes:   ☐ describes group work, group behavior, and group responsibility

☐ describes individual work, individual leadership, and individual responsibili

long service. Once he loses his ability to work, he will be kept until retirement age. So, one's position in the company organization is only roughly based on ability. For example, when viewing people at the same position in the formal procedure, there will be people who do not have enough knowledge and experience. The older workers with knowledge and experience will assist people who are completely incapable or who are weak physically and mentally. In general, the people who get the work done are those who have enough experience and knowledge; however, as everybody has some merit, people at the same position help each other to act out the duties that are given them by their organization. There, the terms *otagaisama* (to help one another) and *okagesama* (help by another person's generosity) represent common courtesy.

As each job is carried out within the work place, *accommodation*, or *kandai*, is generated by we-group feeling and leads to unconscious violation of the code of conduct, because accepting another's feelings is regarded as a virtue as well as symbol of partnership in the same shudan. Thus people at the same position often illegally accommodate each other, leading, for example, to many accidents while driving without a license in Japan. Accommodation can not be denied in shudan, on account of the effects it would have on traditional human relationship, but the mistaken application of the accommodation principle has become one of the most common sources of corrupt shudan.

In any work center, man's harmony is thoroughly emphasized everywhere as the most important value. Suppose there are capable and incapable men sharing the same position in a department. Under these conditions, various complaints about the work center occur. Then, "harmony" becomes important in order to ease the strained relations among workers and encourage them to act together as a unit to get the work done.

As regards "workers' harmony," the role of the senior staff member is very important as long as he is in the supervising position. What is expected of him is not simply knowledge and teaching ability, but his experience in human relations and his character in shudan. Often the leader who seemingly has no ability in shudan is unexpectedly popular with the junior staff and consequently shows good results as the leader of the group. On the other hand there may be a section chief who is not popular with his own staff, though he has great ability and is active on the job. His demonstration of abilities may be quite disgusting to the related group members. If he has less ability to a certain degree, he will give the job to his subordinates and then they will be given the satisfaction of work because of the heavy responsibility, or be aware of their rapidly increasing ability. Furthermore, if he accepts the responsibility for his subordinates or through a senior worker's mistake, he can win their trust, another important part of shudanshugi management. Therefore, the prime responsibility of work

FIGURE 3   Japan-America Chemical Co., Ltd. Organization Chart

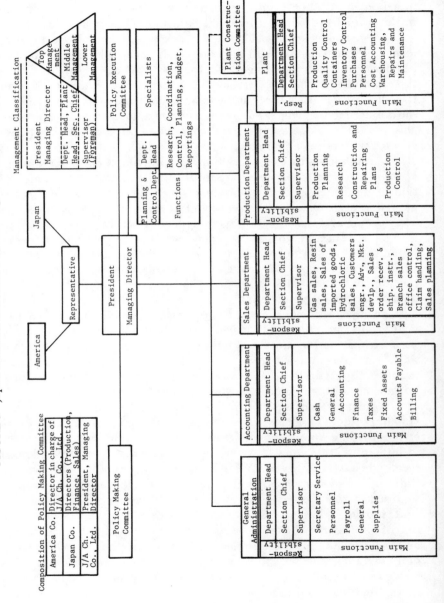

leaders is to create harmony so that their staff and employees will be motivated to assist the leaders with group-feelings.

Considering that experience is more important than knowledge to the manager, it does not seem irrational that managerial position is decided according to length of service years. Anyway, the leader in a Japanese shudan's biggest responsibility is as the coördinator of the group, rather than as expert or professional on the job. Thus, coördinating abilities in shudanshugi management is a necessary qualification for leadership in Japan.

Many books explain that the leader rules with the right of "tough father," or "tyrannically." Except in various small enterprises, conditions of the Japanese business environment have changed this. Very few laborers work today with strong feelings of "graciousness" toward their senior men. A number of them, rather, have the feeling of "don't give yourself airs" and "be wary of the power of our labor union." In some ways, there may be a tendency to take for granted the authority of senior men because many managerial systems in Japan are centralistic and also, the leader in shudan is not given the right to employ and discharge subordinates as in the U.S. There is a substantial equality of group members in the work place in Japan. Then, how does the leader supervise his workers? Efficient leadership is based upon a warm-hearted concern for each worker that is very personal, even taking into consideration family affairs. And such feelings as "let's follow what our boss man says" or "it is pitiful to make trouble for our boss, though I am against it as the order of the company" have found a right place in the order of coördinating irrational factors in the work place.

Figure 3 shows the organization of a joint venture between a U.S. and a Japanese firm. This chart illustrates the group responsibility system of an international business organization, as based upon a job analysis of individuals in the company "shudan." Here, man, job, and position are not clearly distinguished due to the expectation of the shudanshugi approach that the system will protect weak and vulnerable individuals against the Western professionalism in terms of internationalization or management innovation.

# FOOTNOTES

[1]Tadashi Fukutake, "Nihon No Shakai" (Japanese Society) Tokyo: Yuhikaku, 1951.

[2]Chie Nakane, "Kazoku No Kozo" (Family Structure) Tokyo: Tokyo University Press, 1971.

[3]Hiroshi Hazama, "Nipponteki Keiei No Keifu" (Genealogy of Japanese Ways of Management) Tokyo: Japan Management Association, 1963.

# BIBLIOGRAPHY

## Sources compiled by Non-Japanese Experts*

[1] R. N. Beller. *Nippon no Kindaika to Shukyo Rinri (The Japanese Religions in the Tokugawa Era)*. Tokyo: Mirai Sha, 1962.

[2] E. Blunden. *Nippon Henro (Pilgrimage of Japan)*. Tokyo: Asahi, 1950.

[3] Bluno and Taught. *Kaitei Nipponbi no Saihakken (A Revised Edition — Rediscovery of Japanese Beauty)*. Tokyo: Iwanami Shoten, 1962.

[4] Bluno and Taught. *Nippon (Japan)*. Tokyo: Iwanami Shoten, 1959.

[5] E. F. Boyel. *Nippon no Shin Chukan Kaikyu (The New Middle Class in Japan)*. Tokyo: Seishin Shobo, 1968.

[6] J. Caculp. *Nippon no Insho (Impression of Japan)*. Tokyo: Nanun Do, 1964.

[7] K. Carlelgy. *Tairiku Nippon (The Continental Japan)*. Tokyo: Ushio Shuppan, 1970.

[8] Isiah Ben Dassun. *Nipponjin to Yudayajin (Japanese and Jew)*. Tokyo: Yamamoto Shoten, 1965.

[9] Yan Demnan. *Tokyo Joho (Tokyo Information)*. Tokyo: Oizumi, 1962.

[10] M. E. Demock. *Nippon no Tekunokurato (A Japanese Technocrat)*. Tokyo: Time Life, 1969.

[11] P. P. Dore. *Toshi no Nipponjin (Japanese in the City)*. Tokyo: Iwanami, 1962.

[12] Dunlop, Harbison, and Myers. *Indasutorizumu (Industrialism)*. Tokyo: Toyokeigaishinpo Sha, 1963.

[13] Mark Gain. *Nippon Nikki (The Diary in Japan)*. Tokyo: Chikuma Shobo, 1951.

[14] R. Gilan. *Daisan no Taikoku, Nippon (The Third Powerful Nation; Japan)*. Tokyo: Asahi, 1969.

[15] W. A. Grotus. *Watashi wa Nipponjin ni Naritai (I want to Be a Japanese)*. Tokyo: Chikuma Shobo, 1964.

[16] R. Halloran. *Nippon-Mikake to Shinso (Japan-Out-look and Truth)*. Tokyo: Jiji Tsushin Sha, 1965.

[17] F. H. Harbison and C. A. Myers. *Keizai Seicho to Ningen Noryoku no Kaihatsu (Economic Growth and Development of Human Resources)*. Tokyo: Diamond, 1964.

[18] F. H. Harbison and C. A. Myers. *Kogyoka to Keieisha (Industrialization and Executives)*. Tokyo: Diamond, 1961.

[19] H. Hedberg. *Nippon no Tyosen (The Challenge of Japan)*. Tokyo: Maninichi Shinbun Sha, 1965.

[20] J. Hirschmeier. *Nippon ni Okeru Kigyosha Seishin no Seisei (The Origins of Entrepreneurship in Meiji Japan)*. Tokyo: Toyokeizaishinop Sha, 1966.

[21] M. B. Hohnsen (ed.). *Nippon ni Okeru Kindaika no Mondai (Problems of Modernization in Japan)*. Tokyo: Iwanami, 1968.

[22] H. Hoiveles. *Nippon deno Yonju Kenkan (Forty Years in Japan)*. Tokyo: Shunju Sha, 1964.

[23] M. B. Johnsen. *Sakamoto Ryoma to Meiji Ishin (Ryoma Sakamoto and Meiji Reformation)*. Tokyo: Jiji Tsuchin Sha, 1965.

---

*English title of book is a literal translation of the Japanese book title.

[24] H. Kahn. *Cho Taikoku Nippon no Chosen (The Japanese Challenge)*. Tokyo: Diamond, 1970.

[25] H. Kahn. *Nippon Mirai Ron (The Theory of Japanese Future)*. Tokyo: Yomiuri Shinbun Sha, 1965.

[26] D. Keene. *Nipponjin no Seiyo Hakken (Discovery of the West by Japanese)*. Tokyo: Chuokoron, 1968.

[27] N. Kiping and J. Whitehorn. *Nippon Ikken (A Glance Over Japan)*. Tokyo: Keidanren, 1961.

[28] W. W. Lochwood (ed.) *Nippon Keizai Kindaika no Hyakunen (Hundred Years Modernization of Japanese Economy)*. Tokyo: Nihonkeizai Shibun Sha, 1966.

[29] W. W. Lockwood. *Nippon no Atarashi Shihonshugi (New Capitalism in Japan)*. Tokyo: Diamond, 1964.

[30] W. W. Lockwood. *Nippon no Keizai Hatten (Economic Development in Japan)*. Tokyo: Toyokeizai, 1958.

[31] The London Economist. *Nippon wa Nobotta (Japan Has Risen)*. Tokyo: Takeuchi Shoten, 1967.

[32] The London Economist. *Soredemo Nippon wa Susumu (But Japan Goes on)*. Tokyo: Takeuchi Shoten, 1965.

[33] The London Economist. *Odorokubeki Nippon (Surprising Japan)*. Tokyo: Takeuchi Shoten, 1963.

[34] O. Kerry. *Nippon no Wakai Mono (Young People in Japan)*. Tokyo: Hibiya Shuppansha, 1950.

[35] B. K. Marshall. *Nippon Shihonshugi to Nationarizumu (Japanese Capitalism and Nationalism)*. Tokyo: Diamond, 1968.

[36] R. Miner. *Nippon o Utsusu Shisana Kagami (Small Mirror Reflecting Japan)*. Tokyo: Chikuma, 1961.

[37] E. Myner. *Seiyo Bungaku no Nippon Hakken (Discovery of Japan in Western Literature)*. Tokyo: Chikuma Shobo, 1959.

[38] The Noposte. *Yuko no Homon (A Visit of Friendship)*. Tokyo: Toe Shoin, 1964.

[39] E. H. Norman. *Nippon ni Okeru Kindai Kokka no Seiritsu (Establishment of a Modern Nation in Japan)*. Tokyo: Iwanami Shoten, 1947.

[40] H. Passing. *Nippon Kindaika to Kyoiku (Modernization and Education in Japan)*. Tokyo: Saimaru Shuppankai, 1969.

[41] J. Pitau. *Inoue Takeshi to Kindai Nippon no Keisei (Takeshi Inoue and the Formation of Modern Japan)*. Tokyo: Jiji Tsushin Sha, 1965.

[42] J. Pitau. *Nippon-Daiyakushin (Japan – The Great Progress)*. Tokyo: Jiji Tsushin Sha, 1965.

[43] J. Rambert. *Komo Nippon Dangi (Foreigners' Talk about Japan)*. Tokyo: Mainichi Shinbun Sha, 1965.

[44] E. O. Reischave. *Nippon Kindaika no Atarashii Mikata (The New View of Modernization in Japan)*. Tokyo: Kodan Sha, 1967.

[45] E. O. Reischave. *Raishawa no Mita Nippon (Japan Observed by Mr. Reischave)*. Tokyo: Tokuma, 1967.

[46] E. O. Reischave. *Nippon – Kako to Genzai (Japan – Past and Today)*. Tokyo: Jiji Tsushin Sha, 1967.

[47] E. O. Reischave. *Patonashippu (Partnership)*. Tokyo: Jiji Tsushin Sha, 1963.

[48] E. O. Reischave. *Nippon tono Taiwa (Conversation with Japan)*. Tokyo: Jiji Tsushin Sha, 1961.

[49] D. & E. Reisman. *Nippon Nikki (The Diary in Japan)*. Tokyo: Misuzo Shobo, 1968.

[50] W. W. Rostow. *Keizai Seicho no Shokankai (The Stages of Economic Growth)*. Tokyo: Diamond, 1961.

[51] E. Sandestecher. *Nippon (Japan)*. Tokyo: Jiji Tsushin Sha, 1962.

[52] C. B. Sansom. *Seiou Sekai to Nippon (The Western World and Japan)*. Tokyo: Chikuma, 1966.

[53] E. O. Sansom. *Taiheiyo no Higan-Nichibei Kankei no Shiteki Kento (A Historical Examination of the U.S. and Japan Relations)*. Tokyo: Nippon Zaiseikai, 1958.

[54] C. B. Sansom. *Sekaishi ni Okeru Nippon (Japan in the World History)*. Tokyo: Iwanami Shoten, 1950.

[55] O. Stattler. *Nippon Rekishi no Yado*. Tokyo: Jinbutsuorai Sha, 1961.

[56] J. Stechell. *Kiku to Katana Naki Nippon (Japan without Chrysanthemum and Sword)*. Tokyo: Hirano Shoten, 1957.

[57] H. Tiltmon. *Nippon Hodo Sanju Nen (Thirty Years of News Casting of Japan)*. Tokyo: Shincho Sha, 1965.

[58] H. W. Valfelt. *Ichioku Nin no Autosaida (A Hundred Million Outsiders)*. Tokyo: Toyokeizai, 1969.

[59] I. Y. Vant. *Nippon no Bunka (Culture of Japan)*. Tokyo: Misuzu Shobo, 1963.

## Sources compiled by Japanese Nationals

[60] Aida, Yuji. *Nipponjin no Ishiki Kozo (The Structure of Japanese Consciousness)*. Tokyo: Kodan Sha, 1970.

[61] Aida, Yuji. *Gorishugi (Rationalism)*. Tokyo: Kodan Sha, 1966.

[62] Aida, Yuji. *Aron Shuyoio (Alone Camp)*. Tokyo: Chuo Koron Sha, 1962.

[63] Cho, Yukio (ed.). *Jitsugyo no Shiso (Thoughts of Business)*. Tokyo: Chikuma Shobo, 1964.

[64] Fujita, Ichihara, Funabashi, *Nippongata Rodokumiai to Nenkoseido (Japanese Trade-Union and Shiniority System)*. Tokyo: Toyo Keizaisinpo Sha, 1960.

[65] Hasegawa, Nyozekan. *Nipponteki Seikaku (The Japanese Character)*. Tokyo: Iwanami, 1938–1942.

[66] Hazama, Hiroshi (ed.). *Zaikaijin no Rodokan (Business Community Representatives View Toward Laborers)*. Tokyo: Diamond, 1970.

[67] Hazama, Hiroshi. *Nippon Romu Kanrishi Kenkyu (Historical Studies of Japanese Personnel Management)*. Tokyo: Diamond, 1964.

[68] Hazama, Hiroshi. *Nipponteki Keiei no Keifu (Economy of Japanese Management)*. Tokyo: Nippon Noritsu Kyokai, 1963.

[69] Hidaka, Rokuro (ed.). *Nippon no Kindaika (Modernization in Japan)*. Tokyo: Shisei, 1963.

[70] Hoga, Yaichi. *Nipponjin (Japanese)*. Tokyo: Fuzan Shobo, 1939.

[71] Hori, Hidehiko. *Nipponjin no Ikikata (The Way of Living of Japanese)*. Tokyo: Shincho Sha, 1962.

[72] Horie, Yasuzo. *Meiji Ishin to Keizai Kindaika (The Meiji Reformation and*

*Economic Modernization).* Tokyo: Shibun, 1963.

[73] Inoue, Kiyoshi. *Nippon no "Kindaika" to Gunkoku Shugi (Modernization and Fascism in Japan).* Tokyo: Shin-Nihon Shuppansha, 1966.

[74] Inukai, Michiko. *Kurashi no Naka no Nippon Tanken (The Expedition of Japan in Life).* Tokyo: Chuo Koron Sha, 1963.

[75] Ito, Nagamasa. *Shudan Shugi no Saihakken (Rediscovery of Groupism).* Tokyo: Diamond, 1969.

[76] Kaizuda, Shigeki. *Nippon to Nipponjin (Japan to Japanese).* Tokyo: Bungei-shunju Sha, 1965.

[77] Kamei, Katsuichiro. *Nipponjin no Seishinshi Kenkyu (The Studies on History of Japanese Minds).* Tokyo: Bungeishunju Sha, 1963.

[78] Kamiyoshi, Sadakazu. *Akindo Keiei (Merchant Management).* Tokyo: Diamond, 1969.

[79] Kamiyoshi, Sadakazu. *Keiei no Naka no Nippon Hakken (Discovery of Japan in Management).* Tokyo: Diamond, 1967.

[80] Kamiyoshi, Sadakazu. *Nipponteki Keiei (Japanese Ways of Management).* Tokyo: Diamond, 1965.

[81] Kamiyoshi, Sadakazu. *Hesomagari no Keiei (Irregular Management).* Tokyo: Chuokeizai Sha, 1960.

[82] Kaneko, Mitsuharu. *Nipponjin ni Tsuite (The Japanese).* Tokyo: Shunju Sha, 1959.

[83] Karaki, Junzo. *Nipponjin no Kokoro no Rekishi (The History of Japanese Spirits).* Tokyo: Chikuma Shobo, 1970.

[84] Kitagawa, J. M. *Toyo no Shukyo — Kindaika o Meguru Kurushimi (Oriental Religions — Difficulties about Modernization).* Tokyo: Miraisha, 1963.

[85] Kasa, Shintaro. *Kasa Shintaro Zenshu (The Complete Works of Shintaro Kasa).* Tokyo: Asahi Shinbun.

[86] Kasa, Shintaro. *Mono no Mikata ni Tsuite (The Ways of Viewing Things).* Tokyo: Kawade Shobo, 1950.

[87] Kato, Shuichi (ed.). *Gaikokujin no Mita Nippon (Japan Seen by Foreigners).* Tokyo: Chikuma Shobo, 1961.

[88] Kawara, Hiroshi (ed.). *Tenkanki no Shiso — Nippon Kindaika o Megutte (Thoughts in Turning Points — Modernization in Japan).* Tokyo: Waseda Dai-gaku Shuppankai, 1963.

[89] Keizai Gakkai of Keio University (ed.). *Nippon Keizai no Kindaika (Modernization in the Japanese Economy).* Tokyo: Toyokeizai, 1968.

[90] Kishida, Kokushi. *Nipponjin Towa? (What is Japanese?).* Tokyo: Kodokawa, 1952.

[91] Kishida, Kokushi. *Nipponjin Kikei Setsu (The Theory of Malformation of the Japanese).* Tokyo: Hyoron Sha, 1968.

[92] Kojima, Ryoichi. *Nipponjin de Aru Koto (To Be a Japanese).* Tokyo: Fuzan Shobo, 1962.

[93] Kuki, Shuzo. *"Iki" no Kozo (The Structure of Iki).* Tokyo: Iwanami, 1930.

[94] Matsuo, Hiroshi. *Kogyoka no Siteki Tenkai (Historical Development in Industrialization).* Tokyo: Yajima Shoten, 1960.

[95] Matsushima, Shizuo. *Romukanri no Nipponteki Tokushitsu to Hensen (Japa-

*nese Characteristic and Changes in Personnel Management).* Tokyo: Diamond, 1962.

[96] Minami, Hiroshi. *Nipponjin no Shinri (Japanese Psychology).* Tokyo: Iwanami, 1953.

[97] Mitsushima, Shizuo. *Rodo Shakaigaku Josetsu (Introduction of Labor Sociology).* Tokyo: Fukumura Shoten, 1951.

[98] Miyamoto, Mataji. *Kansai Bunmei to Fudo (Civilization and Climate of Kansai).* Tokyo: Shiseido, 1971.

[99] Miyamoto, Mataji, and Okamoto, Yukio. *Nipponteki Keiei Towa Nanika? (What is Japanese Management?)* Osaka: Yukon Sha, 1968.

[100] Miyamoto, Mataji. *Amerika no Nihon Kenkyu (The Research on Japan in the United States).* Tokyo: Toyokeizai, 1970.

[101] Mori, Goro. *Sengo Nippon no Romukanri (Personnel Management in Japan after the War).* Tokyo: Diamond, 1961.

[102] Nada, Kazuo. *Keiei Kanri Kan (The View of Management).* Tokyo: Diamond, 1970.

[103] Nakagawa, Keiichiro, and Yui, Tsunehiko (ed.). *Keiei Tetsugaku, Keiei Rinen (Management Philosophy, Management Doctrine).*

[104] Nakayama Ichiro. *Nippon no Kogyoka to Roshi Kankei (Industrialization and Industrial Relations in Japan).* Toyko: Nippon Rodo Kyokai, 1960.

[105] Nakayama, Ichiro. *Nippon no Roshi Kankei to Rodokumiai (Industrial Relations and Labor Unions in Japan).* Tokyo: Nippon Rodokyokai, 1959.

[106] Nakayama, Ichiro. *Nippon no Kindaika (Modernization in Japan).* Tokyo: Kodan Sha, 1965.

[107] Nippon Kindaika Kenkyukai (ed.). *Nippon Kindaida to Sono Kokusai Kankyo (Modernization in Japan and Its International Settings).* Tokyo: Kyoyobu of Tokyo University, 1965.

[108] The Nippon Bunka Form (ed.). *Rosto Riron to Nippon Keizai no Kindaika (Theory of Rostow and Modernization of Japanese Economy).* Tokyo: Shincho, 1962.

[109] Nishida, Ikutaro. *Nishida Ikutaro Zenshu (The Complete Works of Ikutaro Nishida).* Tokyo: Iwanami, 1930.

[110] Nishida, Ikutaro. *Nihon Bunka no Mondai (The Problems of Japanese Culture).* Tokyo: Iwanami, 1940.

[111] Oda, Minoru. *Nippon no Kangaeru (The Ways of Japan).* Tokyo: Kawade Shobo, 1963.

[112] Okada, Akio. *Nippon Yon Hyaku Nen — Gaikokujin no Kenbun (400 years in Japan — Foreigners' Observation).* Tokyo: Nippon Hosokyokai, 1964.

[113] Okamoto, Hideaki. *Kogyoka to Genbakantokusha (Industrialization and Field Foreman).* Tokyo: Nippon Rodo Kyokai, 1966.

[114] Okochi, Kazuo. *Nippon no Keiei to Rodo (Management and Labor in Japan).* Tokyo: Yuhikaku, 1961.

[115] Ono, Toyoaki. *Nipponteki Keiei to Ringi Seido (Japanese Management and Ringi System).* Tokyo: Diamond, 1960.

[116] Ono, Toyoaki. *Nipponteki Keiei no Tankyu (Search for Japanese Ways of Management).* Tokyo: Diamond, 1964.

[117] Sabata, Toyoyuki. *Nikushoku no Shiso (The Thoughts of Meat-Eating)*. Tokyo: Chuo Koron Sha, 1966.

[118] Sabata, Toyoyuki. *Nippon o Minaosu (Rediscovery of Japan)*. Tokyo: Kodan Sha, 1964.

[119] Saegusa, H. *Kindaika to Dento (Modernization and Tradition)*. Tokyo: Chikuma, 1969.

[120] Saegusa, H. *Seioka Nippon no Kenkyu (Studies in Westernized Japan)*. Tokyo: Chuokoron Sha, 1958.

[121] Sakata, Yoshio. *Shikon Shosai (Samurai Spirit and Merchant Talent)*. Tokyo: Mirai Sha, 1964.

[122] Samon Kinpara (ed.). *"Nippon Kindaika" Ron no Rekishizo (The Historical Image of Japanese "Modernization Theories")*. Tokyo: Chuo University Press, 1968.

[123] Sera, Masatoshi. *Nipponjin no Warai (Smiles of the Japanese)*. Tokyo: Hosei University Press, 1959.

[124] Sera, Masatoshi. *Hadaka no Nihonjin (The Naded Japanese)*. Tokyo: Kodan Sha, 1960.

[125] Shimizu, Ikutaro. *Nippon Teki Naru Mono (The Ways of the Japanese)*. Tokyo: Ushio Sha, 1968.

[126] Sofue, Takao. *Nipponjin — Sono Kozo Bunseki (Japanese — The Analysis of Their Structures)*. Tokyo: Shiseido, 1970.

[127] Sumiya, Mikio. *Nipponjin no Keizai Kodo (Economic Behavior of Japanese)*. Tokyo: Toyokeizai Shinpo Sha, 1969.

[128] Sumiya, Mikio. *Nippon no Rodo Mondai (Labor Problems in Japan)*. Tokyo: Tokyo University Press, 1967.

[129] Sumiya, Mikio (ed.). *Nippon Kindaika no Shosokumen (The Aspects of Modernization in Japan)*. Tokyo: Japan YMCA, 1965.

[130] Suzuki, Taisetsu. *Suzuki Taisetsu Zenshu (The Complete Works of Taisetsu Suzuki)*. Tokyo: Shunju Sha.

[131] Suzuki, Munenori. *Nippon no Kindaika no "On" no Shiso (Thoughts of "On" in Japanese Modernization)*. Tokyo: Horitsubunkasha, 1964.

[132] Suzuki, Taisetsu. *Zen to Nihonbunka (Zen and Japanese Culture)*. Tokyo: Iwanami, 1940.

[133] Sofue, Takao. *Nipponjin no Kokoro (The Heart of Japanese)*. Tokyo: Shiseido, 1966.

[134] Takada, Kiyoko (ed.). *Hikaku Kindaika Ron (Comparative Modernization Theories)*. Tokyo: Mirai Sha, 1970.

[135] Takagi, Masataka. *Nipponjin no Shinri (Japanese Psychology)*. Tokyo: Iwanami, 1953.

[136] Takagi, Masataka. *Nipponjin (The Japanese)*. Tokyo: Kawade Shobo, 1955.

[137] Takeyama, Yasuo. *Nippon no Keiei (Management of Japan)*. Tokyo: Kazimashuppankai, 1965.

[138] Toke Suri Kenkyujo (ed.). *Nipponjin no Kokuminsei (Japanese Nationality)*. Tokyo: Shiseifo, 1961.

[139] Tohata, Seiichi. *Nihon Shihonshugi no Keiseisha (The Creator of Japanese Capitalism)*. Tokyo: Iwanami, 1964.

[140] Tohata, Seiichi (ed.). *Modernization of Japan*. Tokyo: Asia Keizai, 1966.

[141] Tominaga, Saburo. *Rekishika no Mita Nippon Bunda (Japanese Culture Seen by a Historian)*. Tokyo: Bungeishunju Sha, 1967.

[142] Tsuchiya, Takao. *Nihon ni Okeru Keieisha Seishin no Hattatsu (Development of Executive Spirits in Japan)*. Tokyo: Keiei Shobo, 1958.

[143] Tsuchiya, Takao. *Nihon no Keieirinen Shi (The History of Management Doctrines in Japan)*. Tokyo: Nihonkeizai Shinbunsha, 1964.

[144] Tsuchiya, Takao. *Nihon Shihonshugi no Keieishiteki Kenkyu (Management-Historical Studies of Japanese Capitalism)*. Tokyo: Mimizu Shobo, 1954.

[145] Tsuchiya, Takao. *Nihon no Keieisha Seishin (Japanese Executives' Spirit)*. Tokyo: Keizaiorai Sha, 1959.

[146] Tsuda, Sokichi. *Tsuda Sokichi Zenshu (The Complete Works of Sokichi Tsuda)*. Tokyo: Iwanami.

[147] Tsuda, S. *Nippon no Romu Kanri (Japanese Personnel Management)*. Tokyo: Tokyo University Press, 1970.

[148] Tsuda, S. *Nenkoteki Roshi Kankei (Industrial Relation Through Seniority System)*. Kyoto: Mineruba, 1968.

[149] Tsude, Sokichi. *Nihonjin no Shisoteki Taido (The Ideological Attitude of the Japanese)*. Tokyo: Chuo Koron Sha, 1948.

[150] Tsukuba, Tsuneharu. *Nipponjin no Shiso (Thoughts of the Japanese)*. Tokyo: Sanishi Shobo, 1961.

[151] Tsukuda, Tsuneharu. *Beshoku, Nikushoku no Bunmei (The Civilization of Rice-Eating, Meat-Eating)*. Tokyo: Nippon Hosokyokai, 1969.

[152] Tsurumi, P. *Nipponjin eno Adobaisu (Advice to the Japanese)*. Tokyo: Hyoron Sha, 1964.

[153] Uchida, Yoshihiko. *Nion Shihonshugi no Shisozo (Ideological Images of Japanese Capitalism)*. Tokyo: Iwanami, 1968.

[154] Ujihara, Shizuro. *Nippon no Roshikankei (Industrial Relations in Japan)*. Tokyo: Tokyo University Press, 1961.

[155] Usui, Yoshimi (ed.). *Nipponjin (Japanese)*. Tokyo: Chikuma Shobo, 1960.

[156] Watsuji, Tetsuro. *Watsuji Testsuro Zenshu (The Complete Works of Testsuro Watsuji)*. Tokyo: Iwanami.

[157] Yoshida, Mitsukuni. *Zaikaijin no Gijitsukan (The Business Community Representatives' View toward Technologies)*. Tokyo: Diamond, 1970.

[158] Yoshikawa, Yukijiro. *Nipponjin no Shinjo (Feeling of the Japanese)*. Tokyo: Chincho Sha, 1960.

# 15

# Education, the Foundation of the Japanese Productive System?

ALLAN S. BAILLIE

If there were some kind of comparative I.Q. testing of various national intelligentsias, I suspect that the Japanese would win. Like the general population's literacy level, their level of perception, sensibility, and general academic competence is close to the world's highest. [1]

There is a general recognition in Japan that the country's most important natural resource is its people and, as might be expected, the basic school system is designed to offer the entire population an unparalleled level of education (Figure 1). This chapter attempts to show the essential connection between Japan's basic educational system and the country's phenomenal success in manufacturing. In a school system that produces perhaps the most literate population in the world few fail yet all meet certain minimum standards. Little wonder, then, that the Japanese business system produces the highest quality products while minimizing inventories, space requirements, and waste. The Japanese educational system is an integral part of the employment and promotion system, as shown in Figure 2, and seems to have a direct bearing on the nation's productivity.

FIGURE 1   Japanese Educational System

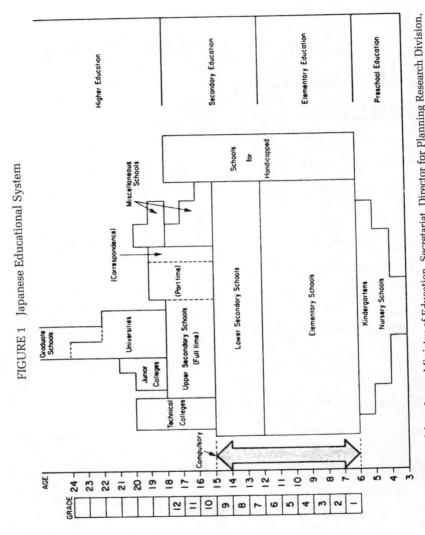

Source: Adapted from Japan, Ministry of Education, Secretariat, Director for Planning Research Division, Education in Japan, 1968–70, Tokyo, August 1971, p. 93.

FIGURE 2    Interrelated Factors that Influence Japanese Job Performance

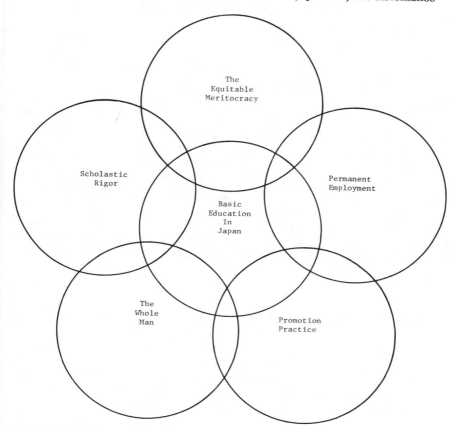

## THE GOAL ORIENTATION OF JAPANESE EDUCATION

It is good to emphasize the development of individual ability and independent study. On the other hand, is there not any danger of lowering the level of achievement as a whole on account of the lack of standards for common learning. [2, p. 7]

The formulation of goals and objectives for education is apparent at all levels of society, from the Ministry of Education down to individual classrooms. Japanese teachers visiting the United States are struck immediately by the lack of overall goals evidenced here. In Japan there are differences of opinion about the best way to educate children—debates in which the teachers union and Ministry of Education are at loggerheads. However, there is a consensus in Japanese society recognizing the need for the school system to produce highly qualified manpower and the need to maintain high standards. Even this latter goal is not always apparent in the U.S. school system. In spite of the fact that about 30 percent of the population is involved in the educational process, there is really little effort to install legitimate standards of education. Student curriculums vary from school-to-school and, really, from student-to-student. National goals for the system relate more to social objectives than to specific coursework needed to attain a basic education. Recently, a few states such as California have decided students should attain certain basic skills before graduating from high school, but the test employed is laughable since an average ninth grader passes it without difficulty. Perhaps more to the point is that, even with extensive tutoring in the tenth, eleventh, and twelfth grades, some California high school students do not graduate because they cannot pass this basic test of literacy and mathematical skill. In Japan, even the worst students must prove literacy in a complicated language like Japanese. There, national tests are given covering basic subjects to ascertain if students can graduate from middle school (compulsory education ends with the ninth grade) and high school.

## THE EQUITABLE MERITOCRACY

> Tests, tests, tests . . . They have dominated our student days. [3, p. 231]
> Japanese people believe that their individual life chances hinge on success in these exams. Thus, families devote a surprising proportion of their resources toward assisting their children in exam preparation and children devote long hours day after day to study. [3, p. 206]

Although a major goal of basic education in Japan is the promotion of egalitarian social change and thus it is available to all who are qualified. But the system is also oriented toward identifying prospective elites. Partly as a result of government policy and partly because of the Japanese families concern for the child's success in the schools, the national examinations and various school examinations have become screening devices, often referred to as the "exam hell." For good reason the University of Tokyo is generally perceived as the top educational institution in Japan. Japanese families simply see that the elite has graduated from this institution. This perception is so perverse that in one survey the Japanese public ranked the University's president directly below the prime minister in status. Ambitious Japanese students wishing to attend this institution will carefully select their high school on the basis of its success in placing graduates in this and several other elite universities.

    However, to gain entry into a high school like Nada in Kobe it is necessary to attend one of the high-ranking middle schools, and, in turn, success in gaining entry into the best middle schools usually means the student should attend a top primary school and kindergarten. Since success in school is a reflection on the success of family, mothers push youngsters into these elite schools at considerable expense to the family.

Testing is apparent at all levels in this system from the I.Q. Test administered to students entering primary schools through the examinations for the University of Tokyo. As the student progresses in the system more study is required. Supplemental schools are attended to help students score well on exams and it is often said that the best students only have time to sleep four hours a night. The relative ranking of educational institutions is well known in Japanese society so that much of an individual's status in the Japanese society can be attributed to the schools attended. As might be expected, the various companies are also ranked, as are the various agencies of the government. Top students from the elite schools opt first for government agencies such as MITI and then for large banks or highly regarded companies. Of course the school attended and even the year attended play a role in the student's career, since he is most likely to socialize with former classmates.

## SCHOLASTIC RIGOR

The level of subject matter taught in [U.S.] private high schools is, in some cases, higher than that of Japanese schools. In contrast with this, the level of mathematics in the [U.S.] public high schools is extremely low. [2, p. 125]

The Japanese school year is approximately one-third longer than that found in the United States. The curriculum is primarily set by the Ministry of Education, which also approves textbooks (Table 1). Supplementary schools are often attended by high school students to gain an edge in national examinations, which cover the Japanese language, science, the English language, mathematics, and social science. In addition to these subjects, Japanese schools cover music, art and handicraft, physical education, and moral education at all grades in the system. School is attended six days a week. Students in the lower secondary schools are required to participate in extracurricular sports, although inter-scholastic sports are not emphasized.

In Japan, there is little evidence of grade inflation found in the U.S. Although few 'F' grades are given, most students (60 percent) in the system receive what would be a 'C' grade in the United States. Studies have indicated that the grades given are reasonably good predictors of student scholastic success in Japan, but are not as important as examinations in determining a student's eligibility to attend an elite university.

The fact that Japanese students rank at the top of international tests in

TABLE 1   Academic Schedules in Japanese Basic Education System

Elementary School (effective from 1971/72 school year)

| COURSE | FIRST GRADE | SECOND GRADE | THIRD GRADE | FOURTH GRADE | FIFTH GRADE | SIXTH GRADE | SEVENTH GRADE | EIGHTH GRADE | NINTH GRADE |
|---|---|---|---|---|---|---|---|---|---|
| Japanese language | 7 | 9 | 8 | 8 | 7 | 7 | | | |
| Social studies | 2 | 2 | 3 | 4 | 4 | 4 | | | |
| Arithmetic | 3 | 4 | 5 | 6 | 6 | 6 | | | |
| Science | 2 | 2 | 3 | 3 | 4 | 4 | | | |
| Music | 3 | 2 | 2 | 2 | 2 | 2 | | | |
| Art and handicrafts | 3 | 2 | 2 | 2 | 2 | 2 | | | |
| Homemaking | – | – | – | – | 2 | 2 | | | |
| Physical education | 3 | 3 | 3 | 3 | 3 | 3 | | | |
| Moral education | 1 | 1 | 1 | 1 | 1 | 1 | | | |
| Total[1] | 24 | 25 | 27 | 29 | 31 | 31 | | | |

*Lower Secondary School (effective from 1972/73 school year)*

| | | | |
|---|---|---|---|
| Japanese language | 5 | 5 | 5 |
| Social studies | 4 | 4 | 5 |
| Mathematics | 4 | 4 | 4 |
| Science | 4 | 4 | 4 |
| Music | 2 | 2 | 1 |
| Fine arts | 2 | 2 | 1 |
| Health and physical education | 3.5 | 3.5 | 3.5 |
| Industrial arts or homemaking | 3 | 3 | 3 |
| Moral education | 1 | 1 | 1 |
| Extracurricular activities | 1.5 | 1.5 | 1.5 |
| Elective subjects[2] | 4 | 4 | 4 |
| Total | 34 | 34 | 33 |

[1]One school hour represents forty-five minutes for elementary schools, and fifty minutes for lower secondary schools. The tables show the standard number of school hours per week, with assumption that instruction is given for thirty-five weeks a year.

[2]Pupils may choose more than one subject from among: foreign language (English and French), vocational subjects, and other subjects determined by local education authorities in light of local needs and abilities of pupils.

*Source:* Adapted from "Japan's Education System Under Scrutiny: Reform a Major Political Issue of 70s," *Japan Report* (New York, Consulate General of Japan), XIX, No. 5, March 1, 1973, p. 2.

science and mathematics suggest this rigorous system is accomplishing what it purports to do. More important, the large number of students trying to find places in top universities not only accumulate substantial knowledge that can be useful in their careers; they also acquire work habits and a devotion to goals very important to their employers. Students are accustomed to long hours, few absences, and short vacations (three weeks) because this is the way they have conducted themselves in school. This very demanding system with its high scholastic expectations tends to influence the students' subsequent behavior in the business world. Such Japanese manufacturing techniques as Quality Circles,[1] Just-in-Time,[2] and Autonomation[3] presume that individual Japanese workers and their foreman will solve problems as they occur and that they have the ability to use rather complicated techniques.

## THE "WHOLE MAN" CONCEPT

> We raised questions to many persons on many occasions but we received almost no intelligible answers. With feelings of embarrassment and irritation we tried to approach this problem from various angles. [2, p. 35]

In Japan the "Whole Man" concept means a type of person harmoniously developed, a well-rounded person in terms of the physical, intellectual, emotional, spiritual, and technical dimensions of personality and knowledge. Japanese teachers are very much aware of this concept and find it totally lacking in U.S. schools. In reference to American schools, one teacher was quoted, "We felt that the school exists not simply as an agency for transmitting knowledge but also as a place where the personality of the student is formed." Another was quoted as saying U.S. schools appeared to be "more or less negative" on the question of moral education. It should be noted that, although moral training is a part of the curriculum, the Japanese school routines are themselves vehicles for moral education. Teachers explain to students that classroom behavior is a way of showing respect for fellow students. By relying on peer pressure, the teacher gets the students to appreciate the worth of their fellows. Much of the school activity is oriented toward the same goal. Monday mornings, students line up and, after announcements, the principal presents a small talk with some moral message in it. Students are rotated in unpaid jobs, serving lunch to fellow students and helping clean up the classroom. The emphasis on working for their classmates helps reinforce the idea that all work is dignified. Trips to shrines and overnight trips are actually designed to promote fellowship among students and memorable common experiences. The virtue of such activity is not difficult to see. Teaching people how to get along and to feel a community of interests will be very useful in the work setting. In the prestige companies, each morning employees sing the company song and exercise together while standing beside their machines. A U.S. consultant told me that after working on a shop floor for a week or so he started doing the exercises too.

Problem-solving and personal improvement follows patterns instilled in school. There is a great effort to achieve a consensus on the best possible solution. This helps avoid embarrassing anyone for failures. The pattern is set in school as the teacher relies on peer pressure and general comments about proper behavior and what is expected to accomplish many learning objectives.

## PERMANENT EMPLOYMENT

A worker entering a company from school or college is checked over like an applicant for membership in the Union Club. School, background, family, health are all rigorously examined — even in Japan's competitive work market. [4, p. 183]

Firstly, recruits do not choose a firm for the job or the monetary reward but as a place to live in. [5, p. 31]

Permanent employment or lifetime employment is peculiar to the larger companies. Since these companies perceive themselves as large families, they are very careful in hiring permanent employees. As part of the procedure, teachers are interviewed, the candidates' whole family is investigated and interviewed, and the health record of the prospective employee examined. Typically, the large companies are interested primarily in candidates only from the best schools. In the past, workers for the shop floor were hired from middle schools, and high schools provided the clerical help. With the vast majority of Japanese now attending either vocational school or high school and many more going on to the university, the education level on factory floors has changed. Today, the new hiree for a shop position is likely to be a high school graduate occasionally with some junior college training. Actually, there is a real shortage of middle school graduates. This has probably led to a narrowing of wage differentials between graduates of middle schools and high schools. As a result, an attempt has been made to pay college graduates at a level above the middle school graduate, who has naturally been with the company while the college graduate received his additional schooling. Of course, it is still generally assumed that pay will increase with tenure.

Companies have become more aggressive in hiring better college students, trying to get them to commit themselves to the firm before the fall interviews. This practice has fallen into disrupt, and now students may contact potential employers during the summer, but they will not take their entrance examinations or interviews until October. This usually means they can only talk in earnest with one big company. By November 1st, most students know if they have been selected. Clearly, the emphasis on merit by the system is recognized by the large companies and used to their advantage.

## PROMOTION PRACTICE

> I took the Kakaricho examination two years ago but failed it because it needs someone who is a high school graduate, or even with some college. [6] While I was Kumicho, my written reports were poor. The factory manager wrote critical comments on them so I couldn't sleep nights. I resigned as Kumicho. [6, p. 162]

Seniority is a primary factor in the promotion schemes of most Japanese firms, but clerical jobs and management positions are reserved for high school and college graduates, respectively. Studies of Japanese firms disclose there is a close correlation between rank and seniority and education. The reason is understandable, since attainment of higher ranks require a certain amount of seniority and the ability to pass rather difficult examinations. Figure 3 depicts the criteria used for promotion in one electronics firm. (In the firm covered by the Table, 400 took the Kararicho Exam but only 20 passed.) The examinations are really a screening device with the evaluations by the superiors the major consideration. Actually, the times shown are misleading; many subsection chiefs indicate they have been with this firm as much as fifteen years before promotion to section chief.

As the manager moves up in the organization, his technical skills become less important and his communication skills more essential. Many candidates who are middle school or high school graduates fail to do well on the examinations because they simply cannot compete with the general knowledge and ability of the college graduates. Clearly then, education and the ability to pass examinations are critical for promotion in the Japanese firm. Promotion examinations are rarely used in U.S. companies.

## CONCLUSION

It should be quite clear that education in Japan is a serious business. A student's ability to gain enrollment at a top university is essential for a successful career in either business or government. The use of examinations in both the schools and business indicates a strong desire to reward the most knowl-

FIGURE 3   Promotion Criteria in an Electronics Firm

| RANK | EXPERIENCE (IN LOWER POSITIONS) | MINIMUM REQUIREMENTS | |
| --- | --- | --- | --- |
| | | EVALUATIONS BY | EXAMINATION |
| *Members of the Union* | | | |
| 1st level foreman | 2 years | Kumiche, Bucho, Kacho | General knowledge, electricity, mechanics |
| 2nd level foreman | 1 year | Supervisor, Bucho, Kacho | General knowledge |
| Subsection chief | 1 year | Supervisor, Evaluation Committee, Jigyobucho | General knowledge, math, Japanese language |
| *Management Level* | | | |
| Section chief | 4 years | same | same |

edgeable individuals with the highest positions. In Japanese society, knowledge is assumed to be the key to problem-solving and decision making. These examinations force candidates to learn as much as they can about a subject. As a direct result there is a tremendous interest among Japanese about new discoveries in their fields. After all, knowledge and the ability to pass examinations are basic to virtually all occupations. Consequently, the Japanese tend to assume that new techniques, new theories, new knowledge are the key to solving problems. Certainly taking the time to gather adequate information and consider various viewpoints are fundamental to Japanese decision making. As one businessman remarked, it is the only society where a ditch digger can be found reading the New York Times (Japanese Edition). As some authorities have pointed out, Japan may be the first post-industrial society. It appears that Japanese industry is functioning on a level difficult to replicate because of the workforce's ability to quickly introduce new concepts and the way foremen and workmen on the factory floor apply themselves to make their productive system work. Firms in other industrialized countries don't even try to operate without inventories or minimum set-up time, or to eliminate waste. Japanese firms use an elaborate supplier system which sometimes involves ten levels of suppliers. To complicate matters, this supplier system often operates on the basis of small lots of various components assemblies delivered on an hourly basis. Much of the explanation for the remarkable achievements of the Japanese in working with this complex and demanding system can be found in the nature of the Japanese educational system, possibly the most competitive in the world. The high standards apparent in this system would suggest that any country wishing to adopt Japanese methods of manufacture would ultimately need an equally well-educated workforce.

## FOOTNOTES

[1]QC Circle activity involves the use of Pareto analysis, cause and effect diagrams, and statistical quality control.

[2]Just-in-Time means that all quantities for the production process must arrive at the correct time exactly as ordered (this includes the supplier network that involves the bulk of the end product value).

[3]Autonomation or autonomous defects control involves Bakayoke (an automatic stop device to halt the production line in case of a problem. When the line is halted, nearby workers and foreman react quickly to help solve the problem.

## BIBLIOGRAPHY

[1] Gibney, Frank. *Japan, The Fragile Super Power*. New York, W. W. Norton & Company, Inc., 1979, p. 221.

[2] George, Z. F. Bereday and Masui, Shigeo, *American Education Through Japanese Eyes.* Honolulu, The University Press of Hawaii, 1973.

[3] Cummings, William K. *Education and Equality in Japan.* Princeton, N.J., Princeton University Press, 1980.

[4] Gibney, Frank. *Japan, The Fragile Super Power.* New York, William Morrow and Company, Inc. 1979, p. 183.

[5] Saski, Naoto. *Management and Industrial Structure in Japan.* London, Pergamon Press, Ltd., 1981, p. 31.

[6] Marsh, Robert M. & Mannari, Hiroshi. *Modernization and the Japanese Factory.* Princeton, N.J., Princeton University Press, 1976.

# 16

# Differences in Japanese and American Corporate Tax Incentives and Their Investment Implications

STEVEN B. JOHNSON

In recent years many Japanese firms have invested more than their U.S. counterparts in product research and development and in the development of foreign markets for their goods and services. While there may be many reasons for the discrepancy, this study examines the extent to which differences in Japanese and American tax incentives may have contributed to it. Specifically, it is hypothesized that two tax incentives available only to Japanese firms during the period between 1967 and 1980 may have contributed to this discrepancy: (1) the availability of a tax credit for firms that increase their level of investment in product research and development; and (2) the availability of a percentage of sales deduction for the development and collection of revenue from overseas markets.[1]

The plausibility of this hypothesis is studied by means of a modified version of the Hall-Jorgensen model (HJM) [3]. A description of the model and the basic research methodology utilized is provided in section one. Next, the plausibility of the hypothesized relationship between the tax incentives of interest and differences in Japanese and American firms' investment strategies is assessed in section two. Finally, the findings and implications of the study are discussed in section three.

# MODEL AND METHODOLOGY

The potential relationship between the tax incentives of interest and this investment discrepancy between many Japanese and American firms is studied within the context of a modified version of the HJM. The HJM is built on the assumption that corporate decision makers seek to maximize the after-tax rate of return earned by the set of investments made by the firm. Since after-tax rate of return is a function of the revenues generated by each investment less the implicit rental price of the capital invested, differences in the implicit rental price of the capital for alternative investment opportunities can influence the set of investments selected. It follows that since tax incentives can lower the implicit rental price of capital for eligible investment opportunities vis-à-vis ineligible opportunities, corporate decision makers tend, over time, to adopt investment strategies that take advantage of available tax incentives.

Stated in equation form, the implicit rental price of capital (c) for a particular investment alternative (e.g., purchasing advertising, investing in product research and development, etc.) is:

$$c = \frac{q(r + \delta)\ (1 - k - uz)}{(1 - u)} \tag{1}$$

where $q \equiv$ the amount required to be initially invested in the alternative
$r \equiv$ the market discount rate
$\delta \equiv$ the length of time over which returns can be earned on the initial investment
$k \equiv$ the effective research and development credit rate for an eligible investment
$u \equiv$ the effective corporate income tax rate for a particular investment's contribution to the firm's taxable income
$z \equiv$ the present value of the deduction for amortizing (for tax purposes) the amount initially invested in the alternative

An examination of Equation 1 reveals that the tax credit available to eligible Japanese firms for increasing their level of product research and development (k) serves to reduce the amount invested initially in this alternative (a), and hence reduces the implicit rental price of capital (c) for this alternative. It also reveals that the percentage of sales deduction available to eligible Japanese firms that invest in the development of overseas markets serves to increase the present value of the deductions for amortizing such investments (z), thus reducing the implicit rental price of capital (c) for this alternative.

The allowance of such tax credits and deductions tends, over time, not only to shift the investment strategies of eligible firms, but also to increase the overall level of discretionary investment capital available. This increase in the level of discretionary investment capital is attributable to the lower overall tax burden imposed on firms that adopt investment strategies that take advantage of the tax incentives available. Stated in equation form, this increase in the level of discretionary investment capital (K) is:

$$K = \alpha \frac{pQ}{c} \tag{2}$$

where $\alpha \equiv$ the degree to which firms conform their investment strategies to take advantage of the tax incentives available

$pQ \equiv$ the increase in sales due to the new or improved product or the expansion into foreign markets + the increase in the firms' inventories (valued at selling price, not cost)

$c \equiv$ the implicit rental price of capital from Equation 1

An examination of Equation 2 reveals that the greater the degree to which eligible Japanese firms conform their investment strategies to qualify for the tax credit for product research and development and the deduction for the development of overseas markets ($\alpha$), the greater the increase in the level of discretionary investment capital available (K).

While firms are induced to adopt investment strategies that are tax incentive compatible when such credits and/or deductions are available, this adjustment does not occur instantaneously. Because of the lag effect associated with such an adjustment, the variables described are best viewed as intertemporally related. Changes in the investment strategies of eligible firms as of period t are a function of the degree to which firms can recycle discretionary investment capital available to take advantage of tax incentives, and the rate at which this recycling takes place. Stated in equation form, the tax incentive compatible changes in the investment strategies of eligible firms as of period t ($I_t$) are:

$$I_t = \sum_{s=0}^{\infty} \Delta I_{t-s} \tag{3}$$

where $\Delta I_{t-s} \equiv$ the degree to which firms conform their investment strategies to be tax incentive compatible in each of the periods preceding period t

An examination of Equation 3 reveals that the faster eligible Japanese firms can recycle discretionary investment capital, and the greater the degree to which this recycled investment capital is utilized to take advantage of the tax credit for product research and development and the deductions for the development of overseas markets, the greater will be the change in firms' investment strategies as of any point in time subsequent to the enactment of these tax incentives.

This modified version of the HJM is utilized in the next section to examine the plausibility of the hypothesis that these Japanese tax incentives have contributed to the discrepancy of interest. Circumstantial and other evidence is utilized in order to obtain a preliminary assessment of the plausibility of hypothesized relationship. Consequently, for purposes of the study, the empirical validity of the model is assumed, and its explanatory power is taken to be adequate to support the analysis and findings.

## ASSESSING THE PLAUSIBILITY OF THE HYPOTHESIZED RELATIONSHIP

Even given the empirical validity (and explanatory power) of the model, in order for the hypothesized relationship between the Japanese tax incentives and the investment discrepancy to exist three conditions must have been present during the period under consideration:

1. The credit for increasing product research and development and the deductions for the development of overseas markets must have been significant enough to have induced firms to adapt their investment strategies to be compatible with the tax incentives;
2. eligible Japanese must have been in a position to recycle or raise discretionary investment capital in order to be able to adapt their investment strategies to be compatible with the tax incentives; and
3. the tax incentives must have been available long enough to compensate for any lag association with the efforts of eligible Japanese firms to adjust their investment strategies accordingly.

Since the presence of these conditions is prerequisite to the existence of the hypothesized relationship, this section evaluates its plausibility by examining circumstantial and other evidence as to whether they were present or not.

Evidence of the first condition is provided by noting potential tax savings available to eligible Japanese firms that adopted tax incentive compatible investment strategies. The credit for increasing product research and development, for example, is 20 percent of the increase over the highest previous expenditure for such purposes since the taxable year preceding the taxable year in which January 1, 1967 fell, limited to a maximum of 10 percent of a firm's tax before the credit. The annual percentage of sales deduction for the development and collection of revenues from overseas markets is summarized in Table 1. Given the magnitude of these tax incentives, there is little doubt that the first condition was present during the period under consideration.

Circumstantial evidence of the second condition is provided by two

TABLE 1    Percentage of Sales Deduction Available to Japanese Firms (1967–1980)

|  | PERCENT OF SALES IN OVERSEAS MARKETS FOR WHICH A DEDUCTION IS ALLOWED | |
|---|---|---|
|  | TRADING FIRMS | MANUFACTURING FIRMS |
| Non-corporate firms | 1.7 | 2.3 |
| Corporations with stated capitol of: | | |
| 100 million yen or less | 1.7 | 2.3 |
| 100 million to 1 billion yen | .85 | 1.15 |

observations: (1) many Japanese firms did invest substantial amounts in product research and development, and in the development of overseas markets, during the period of interest (i.e., approximately 1967 through 1980); and (2) many Japanese firms appear to have made their greatest improvements in product quality and innovation, and to have captured their greatest share of overseas markets, during this period. While other possible inferences can be drawn from these observations, it seems reasonable to infer that many eligible Japanese firms were in a position to recycle or raise discretionary investment capital during this period in order to adopt investment strategies that were more tax incentive compatible.

Finally, evidence of the third condition is provided by noting that both the credit for increasing product research and development and the percentage of sales deduction for the development of overseas markets were enacted (and initially made available) around 1967. Studies of the lag function associated with the enactment of the investment tax credit in the United States indicate that the adjustment process generally takes between 1 and 5 years (depending on economic conditions, industry factors, etc.) [2]. Assuming that a comparable lag function applies to the tax incentives of interest in this study, eligible Japanese firms should have had sufficient lead time to adjust their investment strategies accordingly.

## FINDINGS AND IMPLICATIONS

Although the evidence is circumstantial at best, it does support the plausibility of the hypothesized relationship. Consequently, the study provides no basis for rejecting the hypothesis that differences in the investment strategies of many Japanese firms vis-à-vis their American counterparts may be attributable, in part at least, to tax incentives available only to the former during the period of interest.

In evaluating the results of the study, however, at least three additional limitations should also be considered. First, the tax incentives examined represent only one small difference in the overall socio-economic environments in which Japanese and American firms formulate investment strategy. Second, the modified HJM is in need of empirical testing to determine its validity and explanatory power. Finally, it should be reemphasized that tax incentives of this sort impact on the selection of investment strategies in only a marginal fashion. Hence, a study of tax incentives can provide only a partial examination of the total set of variables that are determinative of a given investment fashion. In spite of its limitations, however, this study can have implications for U.S. tax policy. For example, if the Japanese tax credit has contributed to the discrepancy between many Japanese firms and their American counterparts, there is reason to expect that the tax credit for increased product research and development recently enacted in the U.S. (as part of the Economic Recovery Act of 1981[2]) should help alleviate this difference. Similarly, if the percentage of sales deduction available to Japanese firms for developing their overseas markets has contributed to the discrepancy between Japanese and American firms, perhaps U.S. policy makers ought to consider the enactment of a similar deduction for American firms.

In order to provide guidance to U.S. policy makers, however, further research is needed. In addition to rigorous empirical testing of the suggested model itself, further corroborating evidence is needed to determine whether each of the prerequisite conditions considered in section two was actually present during the period of interest. Then, and only then, can it be concluded that the availability of such tax incentives influenced, to some degree at least, the investment strategies of eligible Japanese firms during this period.

As a basis for providing guidance to U.S. policy makers it is not, however, sufficient to merely establish that such tax incentives influenced the investment strategies of Japanese firms during the period between 1967 and 1980. In order to determine whether such tax incentives would work equally well in the U.S., it is necessary to examine the total environments within which Japanese and American firms formulate their investment strategies to ascertain whether any potentially overriding sociological, legal, or economic differences exist [4]. The possibility of any intertemporal differences should also be considered.

## CONCLUSION

The findings reported in this paper represent the beginning stages of a more extensive effort to study the investment implications of differences in the Japanese and U.S. tax systems. The anticipated study will attempt to corroborate the validity and explanatory power of the suggested model in a more rigorous fashion. In addition, it will attempt to gather more convincing evidence of the presence of the three prerequisite conditions during the period of interest.

In searching the literature it is surprising to note that only limited research along this line has been conducted to date, yet there may be potentially significant insights to be gained by policy makers in both nations. For example, by being able to study the actual consequences of a tax incentive scheme implemented in one nation, but not the other, policy makers in the latter are afforded the opportunity to learn from the experiences of the former. Conversely, if both nations implement substantially identical tax incentive schemes, yet experience different investment consequences, it may be possible to learn more about the importance of the various sociological, legal, or economic differences that exist.

The comparative experiences of past, present, and future Japanese and American tax incentive schemes represent a vast reservoir of potential insights into the determinants of investment strategy by firms in both nations. It is only by means of further research along the lines suggested, however, that the lessons available can be learned and appreciated.

## FOOTNOTES

[1]The tax credit is available to: "Corporations that file blue returns [and have] increases in research and experimental expenditures related to the manufacture of products or technical improvements. The credit is 20 percent of the increase over the highest previous expenditure for such purposes in any period, beginning with the period before the period in which January 1, 1967, fell. This tax credit is limited to a maximum of 10 percent of the corporation tax before such credit" [1, p. 9]. The percentage of sales deduction for the development and collection of revenues from overseas marketing . . ." [1, pp. 34–35]. For greater detail as to the actual percentage of sales deduction available to firms, see Table 1 on page 216. It might also be noted that "exporting firms are allowed certain deductions from revenues received in foreign exchange or its equivalent from foreign transactions as follows: 35 percent of revenues from patents, know-how, etc., resulting from research; 20 percent of revenues from copyrights; 20 percent of revenues for technical services relating to the construction of production of buildings, plant, machinery, and equipment, provided the revenue from such services is at least two million yen for each contract. The minimum allowable deduction is 50 percent of the corporation's taxable income for the accounting period, excluding income from real property and capital gains on fixed assets and securities" [1, pp. 8–9].

[2]Section 221 of the Economic Recovery Tax Act of 1981 provides that "There shall be allowed a credit . . . equal to 25 percent of the excess (if any) of: (1) the qualified research expenses for the taxable year, over (2) the [average] base period research expenses" [5, p. 392]. This recently enacted tax credit is substantially the same as the preexisting Japanese credit except for two distinguishing features: (1) the new U.S. credit is 25 percent of the increase in product research and development, while the Japanese credit is 20 percent; and (2) the increase for purposes of the U.S. tax credit is determined by comparing the current year's expenditures with the average expenditure for each of the three previous years, while the increase for purposes of the Japanese credit is determined by comparing the current year's expenditures with the largest annual expenditure since the passage of the credit (around 1967).

# BIBLIOGRAPHY

[1] Deloitte, Haskins, & Sells. *Taxation in Japan*. New York: Deloitte, Haskins, and Sells, 1979.

[2] Fralich, J. S. "A Microeconometric Analysis of the Impact of Tax Policy on Investment Expenditures." Ph.D. Dissertation, Syracuse University, 1970.

[3] Hall, R. E. and D. W. Jorgensen. "Tax Policy and Investment Behavior," *American Economic Review*, (June 1967), pp. 391–414.

[4] Smelser, N. J. "Notes on the Methodology of Comparative Analysis of Economic Activity." *The Social Sciences: Problems and Orientations*. The Hague: Mouton & Co., 1968, pp. 145–59.

[5] West Publishing Co. *Selected Federal Taxation Statutes and Regulations, 1981 Edition*, M. D. Rose, ed. West Publishing Co., 1981.

# 17

# Toward Consumption in Mercantilist Japan

HOWARD W. BARNES and CLAYNE L. POPE

## INTRODUCTION

Europe and the United States are overreacting to the threat of the "Japanese Challenge." The enormous economic growth that has occurred in Japan in the three and a half decades following World War II has led many to believe that Japan can never be matched in its productive efficiency. In part this is attributed to the dedication and discipline of the workers and managers and the extraordinary coöperation that exists among business, government, and labor in this, the last of the great mercantilist societies.

Notwithstanding the impressive growth that has taken place in a short period, the industrialization of Japan is not the first time that a nation has undergone rapid fundamental change, nor is there any reason to believe that the dramatic increases of the past will inevitably continue in the future. Japan is changing, not only in wealth, but in its disposition to consume. Departing from traditional simplicity, the Japanese household is demanding more in comforts and conveniences, and access to additional public goods. The consequence of this drive to increased consumption portends a decrease in the portion of national income available for savings and investment.

# THE ISSUES

Americans and Europeans are generally concerned about the advantages that Japanese industry seems to enjoy in producing quality products at competitive prices. Included in this issue is the apparent superiority of Japan's labor force, with its underlying cohesiveness and shared values, which make the needs of the individual coherent with those of the company and the nation. The success enjoyed by Japan in the past leads many to think that the future will be merely an extrapolation of the last three decades. A study of economic history leads to a different conclusion. Historically, mercantilism has been a transition phase between feudalism and a market economy during which the needs of the consumer are almost always subordinated to that of the producer. Because Japanese economic development has been at an accelerated pace, it would appear that the nation's mercantilist period will be of shorter duration than that experienced in Europe and the United States. Economic indicators clearly demonstrate that Japan is shifting from a producer to a consumer orientation.

# EMPLOYMENT AND CAPITAL FORMATION

Dramatic change is occurring in the Japanese labor force. Not only has the work force swelled by 23 percent since 1960, but there has likewise been a significant shift in sector employment. Table 1 indicates that 31.2 percent of the labor force was engaged in agriculture in 1960; ten years later it was reduced almost in half to 16.5 percent, with a further reduction to 10.4 per-

TABLE 1  Percent Employment by Industry, 1960, 1970, and 1979

|  | 1960 | 1970 | 1979 |
|---|---|---|---|
| Agriculture and forestry | 31.2 | 16.5 | 10.4 |
| Fisheries and aquaculture | 1.3 | .9 | .8 |
| Mining | 1.1 | .4 | .2 |
| Construction | 5.3 | 8.0 | 9.8 |
| Manufacturing | 21.3 | 27.0 | 24.3 |
| Wholesale and retail trade | 19.0 | 19.8 | 22.5 |
| Finance, insurance, and real estate | | 2.6 | 3.4 |
| Public utilities | 5.5 | 6.9 | 7.0 |
| Services | 12.4 | 14.7 | 17.9 |
| Government | 2.9 | 3.2 | 3.7 |

Source: *Japan Statistical Yearbook*, 1980. Bureau of Statistics, Office of the Prime Minister, p. 51.

cent in 1979. In all, more than six million farm workers sought employment in other industries [2, p. 56–67]. Table 1 further reveals that manufacturing was a primary beneficiary of the agricultural worker exodus with an increase from 21.3 to 27.0 percent of the labor force, while significant gains were also reported in construction, trade, and services.

Clearly the largest employment growth in the nineteen-year period ending in 1979 was in the service industry, which increased from 12.4 percent in 1960 to 17.9 percent in the most recent year. Unlike other sectors of the economy, services are not only labor-intensive, but at the same time offer less potential for improvements in worker efficiency. Finally, only a small portion of services created in Japan are "exportable"; hence growth in the service industry is in large measure at the expense of potential export sales.

Upon closer examination of Table 1 it would appear that an anomaly is found in manufacturing employment. Between 1960 and 1970 more than four million workers were added to the industrial labor force, which peaked in the latter year at 27 percent. However, between 1970 and 1979 the manufacturing workforce actually decreased by almost one-half million people, this in spite of a three-fold increase in the nation's gross national product and continually rising export sales. Of course, most of this can be explained by improvements in production efficiency resulting from the increased use of mechanized and automated manufacturing processes. But this explanation is not complete. With increasing prosperity, workers received higher wages and were inclined to spend more on current consumption of goods and services, which is evident in the growth of employment in wholesale and retail trade; finance insurance and real estate, public utilities, and services [4]. Again, domestic consumption was obtained at the cost of export sales.

Also noteworthy in this shift from production to consumption is a reduction in the work week. In 1968, the average Japanese worker spent 45 hours per week on the job [1]. Eleven years later the work week had decreased to 41 hours, approximately the same as in Europe and the United States. Like most industrialized nations, Japan has found that as its wealth and standard of living increased, money lost some of its motivating power. The marginal utility of leisure thus exceeds the marginal value of additional income.

The rate of capital formation presented in Table 2 provides additional evidence that the rapid economic growth, which prevailed in the sixties and mid-seventies, is beginning to slow. By comparison with measures of capital formation in Europe, and particularly the United States, the share of national income invested in new plants and equipment is exceedingly large. For example, one cannot find a period in U.S. economic history when investment equalled or exceeded 30 percent, although instances can

TABLE 2    Fixed Capital Formation (billions of yen)

| YEAR | FIXED CAPITAL FORMATION | GROSS NATIONAL PRODUCT | CAPTIAL FORMATION |
|------|------------------------|------------------------|-------------------|
| 1955 | 1,778  | 8,865   | 20.1 |
| 1960 | 5,048  | 16,207  | 31.1 |
| 1965 | 9,916  | 32,814  | 30.2 |
| 1970 | 26,043 | 73,503  | 35.4 |
| 1972 | 31,524 | 92,754  | 34.0 |
| 1973 | 41,339 | 113,090 | 36.6 |
| 1974 | 46,960 | 135,065 | 34.8 |
| 1975 | 47,972 | 148,798 | 32.2 |
| 1976 | 51,792 | 167,795 | 31.0 |
| 1977 | 56,026 | 186,209 | 30.1 |
| 1978 | 61,935 | 205,046 | 30.2 |

Source: *Japan Statistical Yearbook*, 1976 and 1980. Bureau of Statistics, Office of the Prime Minister, pp. 496–97.

be found in Europe following the Second World War when some nations approached this level. The capital-formation ratios for Japan appear to have peaked in the early seventies. This impressive record of investment could not be sustained indefinitely in the face of employee demands for increased wages and salaries and a more equitable participation in the bounties of rising national wealth.

## RISING SOCIAL COSTS

The high rate of capital formation shown in Table 2 obscures an issue of mounting concern to public policy in Japan. In comparison with the social democracies in the West, Japanese wealth transfers constitute a relatively small part of its gross national product. In large measure rising social costs may be attributed to industrialization and the breakdown of the traditional three-generation family. The previously mentioned exodus of six million agricultural workers has generated a massive movement from rural and small urban areas to metropolitan centers. Retired people who could formerly look to children in the extended family to provide assistance in their advanced years are now obliged to turn to public welfare for much of their sustenance.

Evidence of the diffusion of the Japanese family is suggested by a comparison of the number of family members per household in 1960 with those in 1975, the most recent year data is available. In 1960, the average household had 4.54 members; ten years later it had fallen to 3.69, and subsequently to 3.45 in 1975 [2, p. 30]. The decrease in family size is not explained by a declining birth rate because the number of live births per 1,000 population changed from 17.2 in 1960 to 17.1 in 1975. In fact the number of live births have increased from 1.6 million in 1960 to 1.9 million in 1975, suggesting again that a reduction in the average family size can be attributed to a break-up in the traditional structure. At the same time the percentage of the population over 65 has been rising steadily, from 4.7 percent in 1940 to 8.9 percent in 1979. It is estimated that it will rise to 12 percent by 1993, the same as Sweden, currently the most aged nation [5]. The social costs in connection with caring for a growing elderly population will impose a heavy burden on a nation which only recently has begun to prepare for its aged.

In addition to the demands posed by an aging population and a breakdown of traditional extended families, Japan must also meet other costs attendant to its population migration, including public sanitation, recreation, and transportation. Costs relating to the infrastructure have been long deferred. For example, only 46 percent of Japanese homes in 1978 were reported to have flush toilets, which Westerners consider the barest minimum for convenience and health [2, p. 441].

## CHANGING CONSUMPTION PATTERNS

A study of consumer expenditures gives further evidence of the rapidly changing patterns. Although household expenditures for food have increased with inflation in the past decade, the ratio of food purchases to total expenditures has fallen from 36.2 percent in 1965 to 28.9 percent in 1978. Table 3 reveals changes predicted by the nineteenth-century Prussian statistician, Ernst Engel. In his study of 153 Belgian families it was observed that as real incomes rise, families devote a smaller portion of their income to food, although total food expenditures increase. There is also evidence that housing expenditures remain more or less constant in relation to total income, while discretionary expenditures rise correspondingly. In the case of Japan, the ratio of housing expenditures in 1978 was almost the same as that in 1965, although there was a rise to 11.2 percent in 1970. Discretionary purchases, including transportation, recreation, and social expenses increased faster than incomes, which is consistent with the theory of income elasticity.

The effects of mercantilism are readily evident when Japanese household expenditures for food are compared with other countries, especially the United States. In traditional form, food producers have allied themselves with government to prevent unbridled competition from abroad. Os-

TABLE 3    Household Expenditures (As a Percent of Total Household Expenditures)

|  | 1965 | 1970 | 1978 |
|---|---|---|---|
| Food | 33.5 | 29.0 | 25.1 |
| Food away from home | 2.7 | 3.1 | 3.8 |
| Housing | 9.8 | 11.2 | 9.3 |
| Fuel and light | 4.4 | 3.7 | 3.9 |
| Clothing | 11.5 | 10.6 | 9.5 |
| Medical care | 2.5 | 2.6 | 2.5 |
| Personal care | 3.0 | 2.7 | 2.5 |
| Transportation and communications | 2.6 | 3.0 | 3.8 |
| Private transportation | 1.0 | 2.5 | 4.3 |
| Education | 3.5 | 2.3 | 2.7 |
| Recreation and reading | 6.5 | 7.7 | 8.3 |
| Tobacco | .9 | .8 | .6 |
| Remittances | 1.2 | 1.8 | 1.8 |
| Social expenses | 6.0 | 6.9 | 8.1 |
| Personal business | 1.1 | 1.1 | 1.4 |
| Other | 9.8 | 11.0 | 12.4 |

Source: *Japan Statistical Yearbook*, 1980, pp. 418–19.

tensibly this was done to protect jobs, preserve family farms, and maintain a degree of food self-sufficiency. While the objectives appear noble, the consequence of protectionism is higher food prices and less consumer capacity to purchase other goods and services.

Not only has the ratio of incomes spent on food decreased in recent years, but there has also been a significant shift in the types consumed. For example, Table 4 reveals that the daily per capita consumption of rice has fallen from 302.5 grams in 1965 to 223.5 grams in 1978.

TABLE 4    Selected Food Items for Daily Per Capita Consumption (in Grams)

|  | 1965 | 1970 | 1978 |
|---|---|---|---|
| Rice | 302.6 | 260.5 | 223.5 |
| Meat | 24.3 | 36.6 | 58.5 |
| Eggs | 31.7 | 40.7 | 40.7 |
| Dairy products | 102.8 | 137.2 | 162.5 |
| Green vegetables | 300.5 | 316.1 | 314.7 |
| Fruits | 77.9 | 104.7 | 110.8 |

Source: *Japan Statistical Yearbook*, 1980, pp. 240–41.

# STRUCTURAL TRANSFORMATION

Japan's pattern of economic growth is neither unique, nor will the particular pattern of growth continue unabated in the future. In part it is the rapidity of change that is astonishing, if not threatening, to other nations. From a broader historical perspective, however, it is obvious that all industrialized nations have gone through similar transformations, but in the more distant past and at perhaps slower rates of change. Roughly speaking, economic growth characterized by increases in per capita income generates structural change in an economy so that production gradually shifts from concentration in agriculture to emphasis on manufacturers and, ultimately, services. Writing in 1890, Alfred Marshall noted that, in the Middle Ages, "three-fourths of the people were reckoned as agriculturists" [3]. At the turn of the century in England only about 10 percent of the population was listed as farmers or farm workers on the census rolls. High rates of agricultural employment tend to obscure the fact that, in primitive societies wanting in the specialization of labor, much of the manufacturing, cloth making, and other crafts were performed on the farm in the home. As Marshall observed, "The real diminution then of England's agriculture is not so great as at first sight appears; but there has been a change in its distribution" [3].

Changes in agriculture are the first and most obvious transformation which takes place when a nation industrializes and later moves towards mass-consumption. The shift out of agriculture is really based on the fact that man can only eat so much. Consequently, rises in income lead to less than proportional increases in the demand for agricultural products. (In the jargon of economists, one would say that the income elasticity for food is very low.) Two forces may ameliorate the structural shift of the labor force out of agriculture. Productivity change may be slow in agriculture relative to other sectors of the economy so that the labor requirements in agriculture continue. Also, an economy that exports agricultural products will not undergo as much decline in the relative position of agriculture. Nevertheless, all industrialized nations have gone through the same essential transformation from agricultural dominance to focus on manufacturing and services. Figure 1 reveals the dramatic reduction in Japan's agricultural force which occurred between 1960 and 1979. Even at 10.4 percent of the labor force, Japan's current agricultural employment remains high in comparison with that of Germany, the United States, and the United Kingdom. As dictated by public policy, the reduction of the farm labor force may not continue its rapid descent, owning to a consensus that the nation should retain a degree of food self-sufficiency. At the same time, Japan's mountainous terrain requires a much higher component of labor than in the United States and the more efficient food producing nations in Europe.

FIGURE 1    Agriculture: Percent Employment of Labor Force

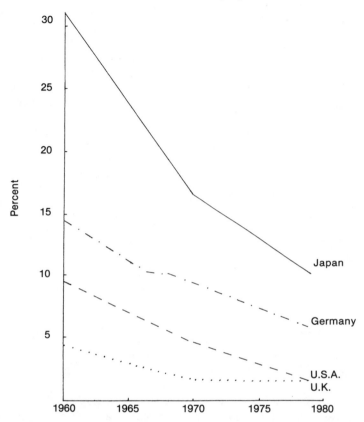

Sources: *Japan Statistical Yearbook, Statistisches Jahrbuch für die Bundesrepublik, Statistical Abstract of the United States,* and *Annual Abstract of Statistics.*

Clearly, the first benefactor of the structural change is the manufacturing sector. In 1960, Japan trailed Germany, the United Kingdom, and the United States in the percentage of the labor force engaged in manufacturing. As shown in Figure 2, the ratio of manufacturing employment to total employment increased steadily in Japan until about 1970, when it coincided with the figure reported for the United States. Interestingly, the proportion of workers in manufacturing in neither Japan nor the United States ever reached the post-war levels of Germany and the United Kingdom. Much of this can be attributed to the lower efficiency of production processes in the European countries. After 1970, the rate of manufacturing employment continued to fall in Japan, as it did in the United States, not

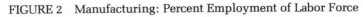

FIGURE 2    Manufacturing: Percent Employment of Labor Force

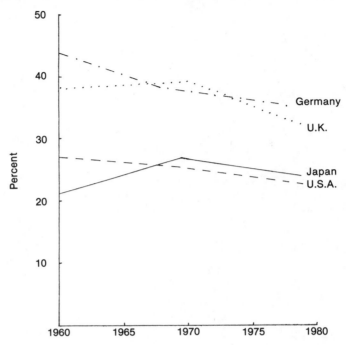

*Sources: Annual Abstract of Statistics, Statistisches Jahrbuch für die Bundesrepublik, Japan Statistical Yearbook,* and *Statistical Abstract of the United States.*

because of falling production levels, but as a consequence of the introduction of greater mechanization and automation, as well as increasing demand for workers in other sectors of the economy. Interestingly, manufacturing employment as a percentage of total employment peaked in the United States at about 26 percent in 1920, a percentage similar to the apparent peak for Japan.

As income per capita rises, much of the increased demand is in the form of services rather than manufacturing or agricultural products. From Figure 3 it is evident that each of the four industrialized nations have increasingly become services-oriented. Japan and the United States are more or less comparable in both the ratio of service workers and the rate of change. In large measure, services employment has grown at the expense of other sectors, principally agriculture and manufacturing. Growth in services signals important fundamental changes in the economy of a nation since it suggests that the basic needs of the society, including food, clothing, and shelter, have been largely satisfied and that a surplus of resources exists which may be consumed in the form of pleasure and personal enrichment. Because services are consumption-directed, they contribute little to the economic infrastructure of a nation; hence a diversion of these resources necessarily involves an opportunity cost. Such consumption is often purchased at the cost of increased manufacturing capacity.

In addition to foregoing additional investment, services are generally produced and consumed by the indigenous population. It is true that international tourism involves the exporting of services, but this is not as important in Japan as it is in Western Europe, owing to the fewer numbers of foreigners coming to their shores. Other services, including insurance, research, and education, generally do not draw other nationals to Japan, at least in comparison with Europe and the United States. Accordingly, it would appear that the growth of the services sector in the Japanese economy implies a far-reaching redirection of resources, consistent with the the-

FIGURE 3    Services: Percent Employment of Labor Force

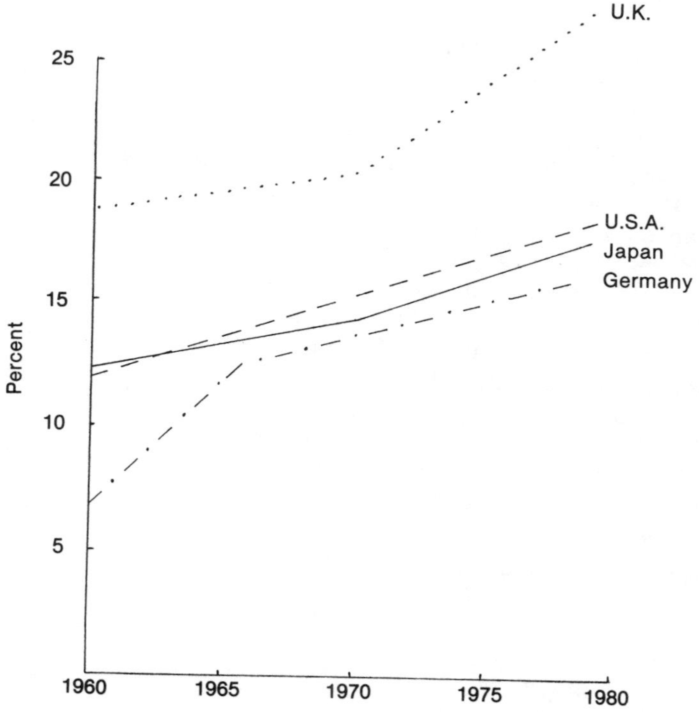

Sources: Annual Abstract of Statistics, Statistical Abstract of the United States, Japan Statistical Yearbook, and Statistisches Jahrbuch für die Bundesrepublik.

sis of this chapter that the nation is moving steadily from an almost sole occupation with manufacturing to a similar focus on services.

The shift toward services presents an economy interested in rapid economic growth with a difficult challenge. Productivity advances in services
are apparently more difficult than improvement in manufacturing. The
gains from new technologies, scientific developments, or new processes are
rare in services. Instead, services appear to be labor intensive so that unit
cost rises with the process of economic growth. Thus, all industrialized nations including Japan appear to be caught in the same conundrum — higher
incomes imply higher demand for services that can only be supplied at
higher labor costs. The computer provides the most optimistic possibilities
for escape from the slow growth path implied by the structural shift toward
services. Japan, like all other advanced economies, faces the task of sustain-
ing growth.

## CONCLUSIONS

Change has occurred in Japan, at a pace which is unparalleled in history.
From the chaos of the forties the nation has risen, like the mythical phoenix, to become the third major economic power in the world. The rebirth of
Japan can be attributed to the dedicated work of its labor force, the quality
of its managers, and the favorable political environment provided by its
government. By deferring consumption, Japan has been able to save and
invest an astonishingly large portion of its national income. For almost
three decades workers and households were willing to sacrifice, but in the
1970s a new mood began to sweep across the land. No longer willing to defer consumption indefinitely, consumers began to purchase goods and services in ever-increasing quantities. In turn, workers demanded and obtained
increased incomes from employers, with the consequence that the rate of
capital formation began to decline in the mid-1970s.

The rise in incomes has generated structural changes inside the Japanese economy that will alter the pace and pattern of growth. Services are
likely to become an increasingly dominant use of resources with slower productivity gains.

Departing from traditional practices, Japan has become increasingly
oriented towards consumption. This desire to acquire is insatiable. As one
need is satisfied another will take its place to the limit the productivity of
the nation will allow.

Concurrent with the disposition of households to consume is the recognition that the nation is bereft of many public goods, including sanitation, adequate facilities for culture and recreation, and roads and freeways
to accommodate its increasing stock of automobiles and other motor vehi-

cles. Public goods are also consumption goods, in that the purchase necessarily involves an allocation of the nation's capital resources, which could have been used to acquire additional plant and equipment.

Additional demands will also be placed on the Japanese economy to assume some of the social costs which have been imposed by the break-up of the traditional three-generation family. Not only are the aged not receiving public assistance at a level common in the United States and Western Europe, but the numbers of elderly citizens are growing rapidly. Within the next two decades Japan may overtake Sweden as the world's most aged nation.

Japan has grown rapidly, but it has been at the cost of deferred consumption and postponed expenditures for public goods and services. The Japanese are not a people apart from others in the advanced nations, and it is evident that they behave in a manner remarkably similar to that observed by classical economists.

> Consumption is the sole end and purpose of all production; and the interests of the producer ought to be attended to, only so far as it may be necessary for promoting that of the consumer. The maxim is so perfectly self-evident, that it would be absurd to attempt to prove it. But in the mercantile system, the interest of the consumer is almost constantly sacrificed to that of the producer; and it seems to consider production, and not consumption, as the ultimate end and object of all industry and commerce.
>
> — Adam Smith, *Wealth of Nations*, 1776

# BIBLIOGRAPHY

[1] Bureau of Statistics, *Japan Statistical Yearbook*. Tokyo: Prime-minister's Office, 1972, p. 74, 1980, p. 72.
[2] Bureau of Statistics, *Japan Statistical Yearbook*. Tokyo: Prime-minister's Office, 1980, pp. 30, 56–57, 432, 433, 441, and 496–97.
[3] Marshall, Alfred. *Principles of Economics*, 8th ed. revised. London: McMillan and Company, 1920, p. 136.
[4] The Oriental Economist. *Japan Economic Yearbook 1980–1981*. Tokyo p. 68–69.
[5] Shioya Ko. "The Graying of Japan: A Hidden Crisis." *Asia*, August 1981, p. 39.

# 18

# Education, Transport Capital, and Productivity Change: The Case for Japan's Experience Since the Meiji Era

TOSHIYUKI TAMURA and SOHTARO KUNIHISA

## INTRODUCTION

This chapter examines the long-term effect of the accumulation of human and non-human social capital on economic output in Japan since the *Meiji Restoration*. Special emphasis will be put upon transport capital and education, since these are considered to have contributed in a major way to the country's sustained rise in productivity. The argument is presented within a macroeconomic framework, and econometric techniques are employed in order to assess its more intricate and long-ranged aspects.

The authors are grateful to Professors S. M. Lee and K. E. Kendall of the University of Nebraska–Lincoln, and to Professors M. Kaji of the University of Tokyo and L. S. Hiraoka of the Kean College of New Jersey for their helpful comments and suggestions. Thanks are also due to Professors M. Kaiyama of Saitama University and M. Kurasawa of Yokohama National University for their inspiring discussions with the authors, and to Mr. H. Ueda and Ms. F. Takamatsu of the Institute of Behavioral Sciences for their continuous collaboration. Needless to say, all the remaining errors and misunderstandings are those of the present authors.

In the following section, we briefly review a century of industrialization in Japan. In the third section we build a simple econometric model to help us understand interrelationships among the factors that have determined the observed path of economic development. In the fourth section, we appraise the estimated results of the previous section, and also engage in an 'ex-post' simulation study. The last section is the conclusion.

# A BRIEF HISTORICAL RETROSPECTIVE

In this section we will give a brief historical sketch of the industrialization process in Japan.[1] For this purpose, it is convenient to divide the period involved into four subperiods or stages, making use of the "end-of-the War years" as dividing lines. We define Period I, Period II, and Period III as 1868–1895, 1896–1919, and 1920–1945, respectively. Period IV covers the remaining postwar years.

*Period I.* The so-called modernization policies of the Japanese economy and society was pushed forward with the well-known four-character slogan *Fukoku Kyohei* (Rich Country, Strong Military). In 1878, the new Meiji Government commenced the reformation of the educational system, the railway enterprise between Tokyo and Yokohama, and the government-owned silk mill at Tomioka in Gunma Prefecture. The Education Act was laid down in 1879, and the four-year system of compulsory education started in 1886. In 1893, vocational schools were established. With regard to transportation, the Railway Construction Act of 1892 was a turning point in that it paved the way for substitution of overland transport for marine transport, which formerly played a leading role.

*Period II.* It is often said that Japanese industrialization began to "regularize" owing to reparations from China. The Shipbuilding Promotion Act was set in 1896 in order to cope with the marine transportation boom of those days. The Railway Nationalization Act of 1906 and the Road Act of 1919 seem to reflect the increased demand for overland transport on one hand and the intensified military considerations on the other. As for education, compulsory education was extended to the six-year system in 1906. The University Act[2] and the Highschool Act were made public in 1918, and municipal and private universities were given authorization.

*Period III.* A considerable share of Japan's social and economic policies began to be "distorted" for military purposes. The Automotive Traffic Enterprise Act and the Overland Traffic Enterprises Adjustment Act were promulgated in 1931 and 1938, respectively, to reinforce the government's control. On the other hand, the Adolescent School Act took effect in 1935 in order to integrate the former vocational education system with the system for military training. Elementary schools changed the name from *Shogakko* (Primary School) to *Kokumin Gakko* (National School).

*Period IV*. Japan's postwar rehabilitation took advantage of the *Toku-ju* (emergency procurement demand) a result of the outbreak of the Korean War (1950). The National Railway Act was put in force in the preceding year, and the Road Act of 1952 raised the curtain on the "highway age." Five-Year Plans for the improvement of roads, railways, and harbors started in succession in the late '50s. The Income Doubling Plan of 1960 brought about times of rapid economic growth. With respect to education, it should be noted that the postwar reformation of the school system converted the multiplicity of the prewar system into a homogeneous structure. In accordance with the enforcement of the Fundamentals of Education Act and the School Education Act in 1947, the new system introduced coeducation and nine-year compulsory attendance.

Tables 1 and 2 will suggest that the demand for, and investment in, transport facilities and education began to increase at relatively early stages of industrialization. Statistical figures in these tables almost parallel the steady increase in industrial output. In the following two sections, we evaluate this point by means of a very long-range econometric model.

# A MACROECONOMETRIC MODEL

In this section, we build a very simple macroeconometric model to help us understand the interrelationships among key factors in the development of the Japanese economy. The structural estimation is performed by OLS method, making use of the statistical data for 91 years ranging from 1885 to 1975. For several years immediately before and after World War II, however, some of the statistical figures are not available, and we are forced to

TABLE 1   Rate of Attendance for Compulsory Education and Number of Graduates Following Higher Courses

| YEAR | RATE OF ATTENDANCE FOR COMPULSORY EDUCATION (%) | NUMBER OF GRADUATES FOLLOWING HIGHER COURSES (%) |
|------|------|------|
| 1873 | 28.13 | |
| 1880 | 41.06 | |
| 1890 | 48.93 | 4.3* |
| 1900 | 81.48 | 8.6 |
| 1910 | 98.14 | 13.9 |
| 1920 | 99.03 | 19.7 |
| 1930 | 99.51 | 21.1 |
| 1940 | 99.64 | 28.0 |

*1895

Source: Ministry of Education [4].

TABLE 2    Major Traffic Statistics

| YEARS | TOTAL LENGTH OF LINES OF NATIONAL RAILWAYS (km) | NUMBER OF VEHICLES (1000 units) | TONNAGE OF VESSELS OWNED (1000 G.T.) |
|---|---|---|---|
| 1870 | 29[a] | | 15.5 |
| 1880 | 158 | | 41.2 |
| 1890 | 984 | | 93.8 |
| 1900 | 1,626 | | 543.4 |
| 1910 | 7,838 | 1.2 | 1,234 |
| 1920 | 10,436 | 7.9 | 5,810 |
| 1930 | 14,575 | 88.7 | 8,511 |
| 1940 | 18,400 | 217 | 5,683[b] |

[a]1872

[b]Merchant Fleet.

Source: The Bank of Japan, Hundred-Year Statistics of the Japanese Economy, 1966.

exclude these years from the sample period. Moreover, for simplicity of the model structure and because of the scarcity of consistent time-series data, we have allowed ourselves to employ duplicate interpretations for the identical variables.

Let us first assume the following saving function:

$$S_t = -536171 + (0.309556 + 0.065253 \, Z)V_t \tag{1}$$
$$(17.12) \qquad (22.86)$$
$$R = 0.917, \text{D.W.} = 1.86$$

where $S_t$ and $V_t$ are, respectively, real gross saving and real GNP at year t, and Z is a dummy variable that assumes 0 for the prewar period and 1 for postwar years. Since the saving-investment gap in any given year is equal to the current foreign surplus of the year $(B_t)$, $S_t$ in the L.H.S. of Eq. (1) must satisfy the identity

$$S_t = IP_t + IH_t + IG_t + B_t$$
$$= IP_t + IH_t + IGA_t + IGB_t + B_t \tag{2}$$

In Eq. (2), the sum of the gross private investment[3] $(IP_t)$, the gross private housing investment $(IH_t)$ and the gross investment $(IG_t)$ defines the total investment at year t. The government investment is divided into the investment in transportation facilities $(IGA_t)$ and the remaining public investment $(IGB_t)$. Needless to say, the latter includes the public investment in educational facilities.

The accumulated stock of private investment $(KP_t)$ and that of government investment $(KGA_t$ and $KGB_t)$ depreciate at the rates equal to one minus coefficients of the following capital stock function:

$$KP_t = 0.948973\,KP_{t-1} + IP_t \qquad R = 0.997, D.W. = 1.75 \qquad (3\text{-}1)$$
$$(174.21)$$

$$KGA_t = 0.997616\,KGA_{t-1} + IGA_t \qquad R = 0.999, D.W. = 1.85 \qquad (3\text{-}2)$$
$$(360.83)$$

$$KGB_t = 0.958946\,KGB_{t-1} + IGB_t \qquad R = 0.999, D.W. = 1.51 \qquad (3\text{-}3)$$
$$(257.44)$$

Since the housing investment ($IH_t$) seems to have little or no effect on production, we isolate it from other investment categories and assume that the housing investment function is of the form

$$IH_t/POP_t = -2.18687 + 0.076348\,V_t/POP_t \qquad R = 0.924, \qquad (3\text{-}4)$$
$$(20.22)$$
$$D.W. = 1.86$$

We now proceed to the estimation of the effects on production of human and nonhuman social capital. We first define the stock of nonhuman social capital ($KG_t$) as a linear combination of transport capital ($KGA_t$) and other social capital ($KGB_t$), i.e.,

$$KG_t = \lambda KGA_t + (1 - \lambda)KGB_t \qquad (4)$$

This is because we have no *a priori* information concerning the productivity effects of the two different social capital. The parameter $\lambda$ used in Eq. (4) will be determined in terms of the fitness to actual data.

The stock of social human capital can safely be approximated by the number of educated laborers. We denote by $LE_t$ the annual number of graduates from higher educational institutions.[4] Hence the corresponding "stock" concept of the educated labor might be represented by the total number of graduates in the labor force. In view of the resulting decrease in the sample period and the degree of freedom, we restrict the range of summation to the past ten years and define the accumulated educated labor by

$$ALE_t = \sum_{\tau=1}^{10} LE_{t-\tau} \qquad (5)$$

The production function is assumed to be of linear, homogeneous Cobb-Douglas type:

$$V_t/L_t = Exp[\alpha_0 + \alpha_1 T](KP_{t-1}/L_t)^\delta \qquad (6)$$

where T is a time variable. The technical progress might be thought of as embodied in labor ($L_t$) and private capital ($KP_t$). Hence we assume that the technical progress term $\alpha_1 T$ is related to the human and nonhuman social capital in the following way:[5]

$$\text{Exp}[\alpha_1 T] = (ALE_t/POP_t)^\beta (KG_{t-1}/POP_{t-1})^\gamma \tag{7}$$

$POP_t$ being the population at year t.

The estimation procedure is three-staged. We first estimate the production function (6), and then proceed to the estimation of the technical progress function (7) after substituting the estimated rate of technical progress $(\alpha_1)$ into the L.H.S. of Eq. (7). We let the parameter $\lambda$ vary from 0.0 to 1.0 by steps of 0.1, and adopt the one that gives the maximum coefficient of correlation (R). The relationship between $\lambda$ and R is as illustrated in Figure 1. Setting $\lambda = 0.6$, we finally reëstimate the production function to obtain[6]

$$\ell n(V_t/L_t) = 3.85164 + 0.100893 \; \ell n(ALE_t/POP_t) \tag{8}$$
$$\phantom{\ell n(V_t/L_t) = } (6.16) \quad\quad (2.55)$$

$$+ 0.00372353 \; \ell n(KG_{t-1}/POP_{t-1})$$
$$(6.43)$$

$$+ 0.372253 \; \ell n(KP_{t-1}/L_t) \quad\quad R = 0.978, \text{ D.W.} = 1.88$$
$$(3.87)$$

The labor supply function is as follows:

$$\ell n(L_t/POP_t) = -1.70983 + 0.100289 \; \ell n(V_{t-1}/POP_{t-1}) \tag{9}$$
$$\phantom{\ell n(L_t/POP_t) = } (22.35) \quad\quad (8.40)$$
$$- (0.0806661 + 0.00244384 \; Z) \; \ell n(LE_{t-1}/POP_{t-1})$$
$$\phantom{-} (16.00) \quad\quad\quad (8.62)$$
$$R = 0.902, \text{ D.W.} = 1.88$$

In Eq. (9), the rate of employment $(L_t/POP_t)$ is regressed against per capita income $(V_{t-1}/POP_{t-1})$ and the rate of attendance for higher schools $(LE_{t-1}/POP_{t-1})$ of the previous year. Note here that $LE_t$ is reinterpreted as a proxy variable for attendance to school, and the rate of attendance is measured in terms of the whole population.

The demand for education will increase as people get richer and richer, and accordingly one might well explain it by some income-related concept. Since education should be seen as investment in human capital rather than annual consumption, and since school education owes to a considerable extent to government and private investment activities in educational facilities, we relate the rate of attendance to higher schools to per capita saving. We have in fact

$$\ell n(LE_t/POP_t) = -7.95738 + 1.46995 \; Z + 0.480511 \; \ell n(S_{t-1}/ \tag{10}$$
$$\phantom{\ell n(LE_t/POP_t) = } (21.38) \quad (4.21) \quad\quad (3.69)$$
$$POP_{t-1}) \quad\quad R = 0.998, \text{ D.W.} = 1.71$$

Implicit in this equation is, therefore, the demand and supply relationship

FIGURE 1    The Relationship between λ and R

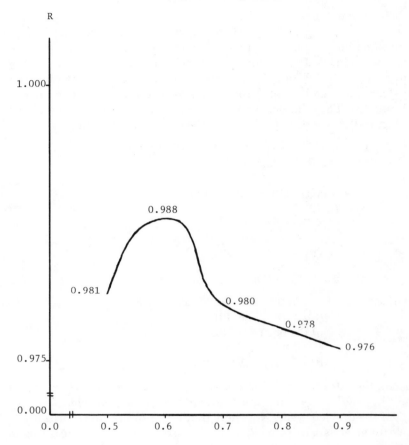

in the market for school education. As suggested above, we are treating the post-school education and OJT as embodied in the human social capital ($ALE_t$).

Finally, we must specify the manner in which investment is performed. Let

$$IP_t/IG_t = IP_t/(IGA_t + IGB_t) = \beta_t \tag{11}$$

and

$$IGA_t/IG_t = \alpha_t \qquad (IGB_t/IG_t = 1 - \alpha_t) \tag{12}$$

Eq. (11) assumes that the government investment is performed so as to keep pace with, or to induce, private investment, and that the ratio $\beta_t$ between them is determined by exogenous factors.[7] Similarly, we treat as exogenous the ratio $\alpha_t$ in Eq. (12), which shows how the government investment is allocated between $IGA_t$ and $IGB_t$. We substitute into these ratios the actually observed values, unless we are concerned with a simulation study. In addition, we regard the population ($POP_t$) and the current foreign surplus ($B_t$) as exogenous variables.

The whole structure of the model is illustrated in Figure 2, where solid lines imply the simultaneous relations and broken lines the lagged ones. There are 18 variables in all, of which 14 are endogenous and the remaining 4 are exogenous.

## APPRAISAL AND EXPERIMENT

The saving function (1) in the previous section tells us that the marginal propensity to save showed a slight upward turn after the end of World War II. We also know from Eqs. (3-1)–(3-3) that the private capital stock depreciates faster than the stock of social capital, and that the transport capital is the most durable among the three. Furthermore, Eqs. (9) and (10) demonstrate the cause and effect relationships among income, saving, the rate of attendance, and the rate of employment. Namely, a growth of per capita income accompanies an increase in per capita saving and a rise in the rate of employment, but the former exerts a negative effect on the latter. This is because per capita saving is positively related to the rate of attendance, which has negative correlation with the employment rate. What is interesting here is that, due to the increased demand for higher education caused by the rapid economic growth in Period IV, the rate of school attendance effected the rate of employment even more adversely.

The production function (8) deserves special attention. When we speak of the effect on production of social physical capital as a "cluster," the relative importance of the transport capital can be thought to be about 60 percent, if we are permitted to argue in terms of the maximum coefficient of correlation. Moreover, capital and labor elasticities of production suggest that, under the assumption of competitive markets, the relative income share of capital is 37 percent, and that of labor 63 percent.

Let us now try to examine how the Japanese economy would have worked if the government's behavior had been different. We propose to compare three different cases within the framework of our model.[8] *Case 1* simply traces out the actual working of the economy, while the remaining two cases are concerned with the hypothetical cases. More precisely, *Case 1* assumes that $\alpha_t$ in Eq. (12) takes the values identical with what actually occurred. In *Case 2*, however, $\alpha_t$ is assumed to be 1.5 times greater than what it has been throughout the whole sample period. Finally, *Case 3* assumes that $\alpha_t$ is 1.5 times greater than reality only for Periods I and II, and returns

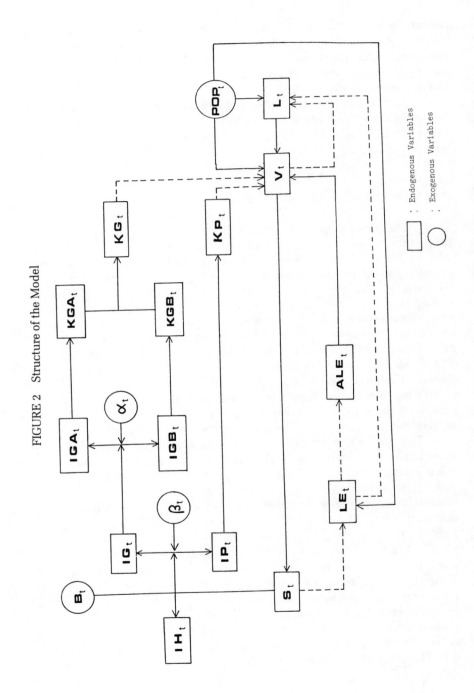

FIGURE 2  Structure of the Model

□ : Endogenous Variables

○ : Exogenous Variables

to the actual level in Periods III and IV. Since nothing has been said to $\beta_t$, the budget restraint of the government requires that an increase in $IGA_t$ should be "passed" to the corresponding decrease in $IGB_t$.

The structural stability and the explanatory power of the model can be confirmed by the final test with respect to *Case 1*. The final test result proves to be almost satisfactory in that the coefficients of correlation between the observed and the estimated values of endogenous variables lie between 0.985 of $KGA_t$ and 0.915 of $IP_t$. Table 3 summarizes the simulation results in the form of cumulative sums of the differences between Cases with respect to major variables and for specific periods. By assumption, the cumulative sums of *Case 3 − Case 1* take the same values as of *Case 2 − Case 1* for the period between 1896 and 1910.

There are several points to be noted in Table 3. In the first place, the effects of 50 percent increase in $\alpha_t$ in Periods I and II (*Case 3*) are very persistent and remain effective even in Periods III and IV, although the magnitudes are attenuated. This suggests that the transport-oriented policy taken by the Meiji government, which preceded the actual burst of the large-scale traffic demand, contributed to the output increase in later periods. Second, the increase in output is brought about not only by the direct effect on productivity of the higher rate of transport capital accumulation, but also by the accelerated accumulation of private capital, which seems to be induced by an increased demand for goods and services. In fact, Figure 3 enables us to compare the paths of $V_t$, again in the form of the differences between cases. Stagnant movement in Period III and drastic upward turns in 1950 and 1960 of the broken curve in the figure endorse the points made above. Finally, $LE_t$ shows a slight increase both in *Case 2 − Case 1* and in *Case 3 − Case 1*, far from being decreased by the curtailment of $IGB_t$. This might also be interpreted as a result of an increased income.

Needless to say, one cannot rely too heavily upon the results we have obtained. A preliminary conclusion we can safely draw from the above ex-

TABLE 3   Simulation Results (1)−Cumulative Sums of Differences between Cases (Units: 100 persons, million yen)

|  | CASE 2−CASE 1 | | | CASE 3−CASE 1 | |
|---|---|---|---|---|---|
|  | 1896–1910 | 1920–1945 | 1946–1975 | 1920–1945 | 1946–1975 |
| $V_t$ ( $\times 10^3$) | 56 | 205 | 1,183 | 148 | 358 |
| $KP_t$ ( $\times 10^3$) | 34 | 197 | 1,116 | 163 | 448 |
| $KG_t$ ( $\times 10^3$) | 6,214 | 36,164 | 159,112 | 20,988 | 29,037 |
| $LE_t$ | 0.6 | 1.9 | 23.6 | 1.4 | 8.1 |
| $L_t$ | 11.0 | 42.6 | 79.8 | 30.8 | 28.4 |

FIGURE 3   Simulation Results (2) — Increment of GNP in Differences between Cases

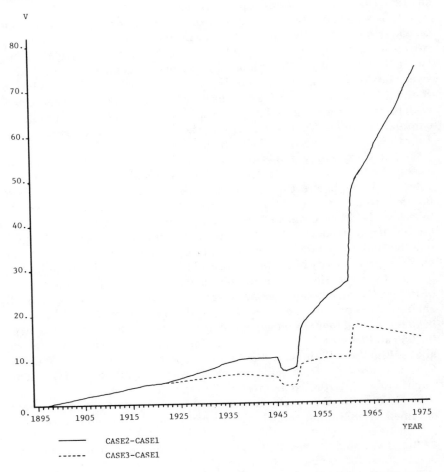

periment seems to be that the transport-oriented (and perhaps education-oriented) accumulation of social capital has contributed to the industrialization of Japan and not the other way round.

## CONCLUSION

In the second section we took a bird's eye view of Japan's industrialization over a century. What we found was that education and the accumulation of transport capital have kept pace with the economic development. In Section 3 we constructed a simple econometric model in order to examine the interrelationships among these variables. Working with this model, we learned in Section 4 that it is the effort to educate people and accumulate transport capital that has contributed to the industrialization of Japan, and not the opposite.

From various points of view, the model in this paper could be revised or extended in several directions. First, the investment behavior of entrepreneurs and of the government could be made explicit. Second, the model could be broken down so as to make it possible to deal with industrial structure and other microeconomic factors. Third, fiscal and financial aspects could be incorporated. Finally, the model could be enlarged geographically in order to examine relationships with foreign countries, especially Korea and Taiwan. Although these modifications are attractive, they remain beyond the scope of the present chapter.

## APPENDIX: DATA SOURCES

a) $V_t$, $S_t$, and $B_t$.

We have taken GNP figures for the period between 1885 and 1940 from K. Ohkawa et al. (eds.), *Estimates of Long-Term Economic Statistics of Japan since 1868*, Vol. I, Toyo Keizai Shimpo-Sha, 1974, and the GNP deflator from Vol. VIII of the same edition. Corresponding figures for the years 1941 to 1975 are taken from the Economic Planning Agency (EPA) *Yearbook for National Income Statistics*. We linked the prewar and postwar GNP deflators by means of a magnification factor, and set 1970 as a base year. Variables in yen units in this paper are all evaluated at 1970 prices. Data for foreign surplus are taken from Vol. XIV of Ohkawa et al., *Estimates*, and those for gross saving are calculated according to definition (2) in the text.

b) $IGA_t$, $IGB_t$, $IG_t$, $KGA_t$, $KGB_t$, and $KG_t$.

Data related to public investment are taken from EPA, *Estimation of Government Fixed Capital Formation and Government Capital Stock*, 1966, and *Estimation of Social Capital Stock*, 1977. $IGA_t$ includes investment in roads, railways and harbors, while military expenditures are subtracted from the government investment figures.

c) $IP_t$, $KP_t$, $IH_t$, $KH_t$.

Figures in EPA, *Private Firms' Stock of Capital*, 1978, and Vol. IV of Ohkawa et al., op. cit., are employed after redeflating for the 1970 basis. In view of the effect on production, we subtract from $IP_t$ and $KP_t$ housing investment $IH_t$ and stock of houses $KH_t$. Data for $IH_t$ and $KH_t$ are taken from Vols. III and IV of Ohkawa et al., op. cit.

d) $L_t$ and $POP_t$.

Data on working population are available in *Census Reports* since 1920 by five year periods. Figures for the intermediate years are interpolated by means of the average annual growth rates. Data before 1919 can be found in K. Ohkawa, *The Growth Rate of Japanese Economy since 1878*, Kinokuniya, 1957. Total population figures are taken from Bureau of Statistics of the Office of the Prime Minister, *Japan Statistical Yearbook*.

e) $LE_t$ and $ALE_t$.

Figures of $LE_t$ are taken from *Japan Statistical Yearbook* and the Ministry of Education [4]. $ALE_t$ follows from Eq. (5).

# FOOTNOTES

[1]For detailed arguments, the reader is referred to Cummings [1] for education and Muramatsu [3] for transportation. See also Emi [2] and Nkamura [5] for a general survey of the economic history of Japan since the Meiji Era.

[2]*Shoheiko* started in 1869 as the predecessor of Tokyo University, which was given the name of the Imperial University of Tokyo in accordance with the Imperial University Act of 1886.

[3]Since housing investment needs a separate treatment, we subtract from $IP_t$ the gross private housing investment. See *Data Sources* in the Appendix.

[4]$LE_t$ here includes all the graduates either from the prewar second section of middle schools or from the postwar upper secondary schools, and for institutions higher than these. For a comparison of prewar and postwar systems of school education in Japan, see [1, p. 23].

[5]Substitution of (7) into (6) gives

$$V_t/L_t = Exp[\alpha_0](ALE_t/POP_t)^\beta (KG_{t-1}/POP_{t-1})^\gamma (KP_{t-1}/L_t) \tag{6a}$$

or

$$V_t = Exp[\alpha_0][(ALE_t/POP_t)^{\beta/(1-\delta)} L]^{1-\delta}[(KG_{t-1}/POP_{t-1})^\gamma KP_{t-1}]^\delta \tag{6b}$$

[6]The functional form we employed in the estimation is Eq. (6a) in Footnote 5 above.

[7]Alternatively, one may add $IH_t$ to the numerator in the L.H.S. of Eq. (11) and assume

$$(IP_t + IH_t)/IG_t = \gamma_t \tag{11a}$$

[8]A similar simulation study is given in Tamura et al. [6], where education is neglected, and $KG_t$ and $KP_t$ are assumed to be perfect substitutes.

# BIBLIOGRAPHY

[1] Cummings, W. K. *Education and Equality in Japan*. Princeton: Princeton University Press, 1980.
[2] Emi, K. *Government Fiscal Activity and Economic Growth in Japan: 1868–1960*. Tokyo: Kinokuniya Book Store, 1963.
[3] Muramatsu, I. "A Historical Study in Transport Investment since the Meiji Era," (in Japanese), in Un-yu Keizai Kenkyu Center (ed.), *History of Transportation in Modern Japan*. Tokyo: Seizando, 1979, pp. 169–99.
[4] Ministry of Education. *Japan's Growth and Education* (in Japanese). Tokyo: Teikoku Chiho Gyosei Gakkai, 1962.

[5] Nakamura, T. *The Postwar Japanese Economy*. Tokyo: University of Tokyo Press, 1981.

[6] Tamura, T., Kunihisa, S., Kurasawa, M., and Kaiyama, M. "Social Capital and Economic Development," (in Japanese), *Keizai to Keizaigaku*, No. 47, (October 1981), pp. 45–68.

# 19

# An Examination of the Japanese Direct Foreign Investment Environment

GARLAND KEESLING

## INTRODUCTION: THE DYNAMICS OF DIRECT FOREIGN INVESTMENT

The experience of host countries with direct foreign investment indicates that the problems that result from the presence of foreign affiliates usually involve a combination of economic, political, social, and legal factors. To further exacerbate the problems, a different perception of these factors by individuals in the parent and host countries may frequently exist.

The multinational enterprise is "a chain of companies, operating under different national sovereignties, but under the same management." [7] Figure 1 provides an example of the international business arrangements of a U.S.-based multinational and the structural relationship of the parent with its international headquarters company and its foreign business affiliates, which include a foreign-based company, wholly owned and partially owned subsidiaries, joint ventures, and a licensing arrangement. Figure 1 depicts the U.S. company incorporated in the United States but operating and residing under the laws and customs of eight other nations as well.

The figure also depicts the reciprocal relationship existing between the parent firm and its foreign affiliates. From the parent firm and its international headquarters flow direction and control in such functional areas

FIGURE 1   Multinational Structural Arrangements

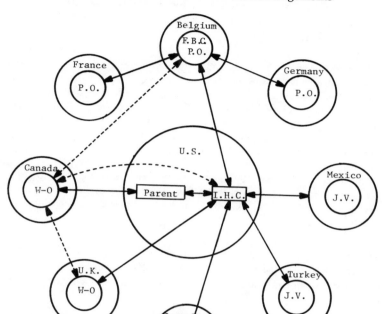

Source: Litvak, Isaiah A. and Christopher J. Maule. "The Issues of Direct Foreign Investment," Foreign Invesment: The Experience of the Host Countries, 1970, p. 5.

as marketing, finance, production, and research and development. In return, the foreign subsidiaries reciprocate by providing profits and vital input regarding marketing and technological considerations.

Each nation-state possesses a business environment which is characterized by certain economic, political, legal, and socio-cultural factors. An example of the complexities of international management is succinctly provided by Litvak and Maule:

> The question of political patronage is an important one. It is often considered by Westerners to be immoral to grease the palm of some foreign government official or businessman. The fact is that business is done like that in all countries . . . in developed countries such activity is called lobbying and thereby receives some aura of respectibility. In addition, the investor must consider whether he is prepared to conform to the attitudes in the host country concerning the hiring and firing of workers, and the appropriate compensation normally paid to fired workers. One of the reasons for French hostility to U.S. investments is the behavior of certain U.S. firms in suddenly dispensing with large groups of French workers without sufficient compensation. Such abrupt actions are rarely undertaken by French businessmen, and are thus not expected by French workers. [7, p. 22]

Management is continually exposed to dynamic forces, to which it must adapt, assimilate, and reconcile conflicting interests. Failure to do so may further compound the problems of international ventures in foreign countries.

Given the complexities of these dynamic factors in the international markets, it is the purpose of this paper to present an overview of the distinguishing idiosyncrasies of the Japanese economic system with the hope that readers will come to possess a better understanding of the dynamics of this island nation that will eventually minimize the problems associated with direct foreign investment. In particular, the investment climate will be examined to include the interplay of the economic goals of Japan with the political, societal, and legal factors that are so uniquely intertwined.

## JAPAN: THE PATH TO INTERNATIONAL PREËMINENCE

The Meiji era (1868–1945) is frequently cited as the beginning of the national restoration that spurred Japan to the economic and military heights that ultimately had to be reckoned with during World War II, and the era's salient features have fundamentally served as the cornerstone of the country's successful progression from complete devastation to economic status once again to be reckoned with.

Primarily motivated by the threat of foreign powers and the desire to provide military protection against dissenting elements within the country, the Meiji government became the major promoter, owner, and administrator of modern industries. The new ruling class placed a high priority on the construction of a dependable military force.

The Meiji entrepreneurship was rooted in the faith of a nation. However, the rapid pace of industrialization had brought about several important changes by the end of the Meiji era. The government commitment had created organizational complexities stemming from the bureaucratization of the business sector. This, in turn, generated corresponding adjustments in the skill qualifications of the labor force, the trend toward urbanization, and the emergence of a proletariat class.

The period between 1880 and 1900 witnessed extensive exploitation of the Japanese worker and tended to undermine the spirit of nationalistic pride so meticulously engineered by the early Meiji leaders. Working conditions were described as primitive and the countless abuses of the sweatshop were commonplace in the nation's factories.

Gradually, the government began to show some concern about the appallingly primitive working conditions. Such concern culminated with the enactment of the Factory Act of 1911. Designed to regulate industrial working conditions, the Factory Act was strongly opposed by the business community as a deterrent to managerial prerogatives and industrial growth. Although a vigorous campaign to defeat the passage of the act was aborted, the first formal articulation of the paternalistic ideology was detected. "Management began to extol the virtues of the traditional family ideology and to emphasize that the problems of employer-employee relations could be approached much more effectively through the application of the familial concepts of benevolence and reciprocity, rather than through labor legislation or organized labor movements." [12]

The pace of industrialization was further accelerated during the decade of the 1910s. This was the period in which the Zaibatsu (large corporate entities controlled by a select few of Japan's wealthiest families) became firmly entrenched in the Japanese industrial system. The Zaibatsu, with the government's endorsement, actively pursued diversification and expansion into capital-intensive and technically oriented fields. Such a basic change in the structure of the Japanese industry necessitated a managerial revision of its traditional personnel practices.

Instability and aberrations in the labor force could no longer be tolerated because of the operating requirements of capital-intensive industry. In order to establish the base for a stable, skilled cadre of employees, the Zaibatsu embarked upon a two-fold mission. First, an attempt was made to persuade the oyakata[1] and their workers to join the ranks of company employees in order to reduce the undesirable mobility of skilled workers. Second, the company began employee recruitment from the secondary schools and established in-house training programs for needed specific skills.

A series of inducements were offered to enlist the oyakata and their workers to become permanent employees of Zaibatsu firms. Incentives included the status of full-time employees, guarantees against dismissal, set salaries, and salary increments. Thus, management began to demonstrate an early concern for employee needs.

Against this background emerged the personnel practices that are considered distinct features of the Japanese managerial system: lifetime employment, a seniority-based reward system, and what some authors term an invasion into the private lives of the workers by management. By linking these personnel policies to the family ideology (management playing the benevolent "father" role and the workers accepting the submissive role of "children"), management sought to optimize its emotional appeal and unity with the workers. However, it is interesting to note that "familial paternalism was used as a deliberate means to solve economic, political, technological, and social problems specific to the era of intense industrialization and urbanization." [12, p. 79]

The decade of the 1920s witnessed some significant political changes. Following traditional oligarchic and autocratic principles, political parties grew in strength and formed close ties with the diverse Zaibatsu interests. Meanwhile, the Japanese economy was plagued by inflationary pressures in the aftermath of World War I, and the impact of the worldwide depression severely crippled Japan. Capitalizing on the prevailing mood of the populace, the ultranationalistic and reactionary elements began to gain momentum.

The 1930s witnessed a surge of militarism and fanatical nationalism and ultimate control of the ruling oligarchy. In the mid-1930s, the government began to socialize control of certain key strategic industries, and continued steadily for the next decade. This had been referred to as the quasi-war economy.

This period of ultranationalism and military supremacy took Japan into World War II and finally ended an era of spectacular economic growth. At the termination of the war, Japan's economy was in shambles. Over 1.8 million lives had been lost, 40 percent of the aggregate urban area was destroyed, and some 2,252,000 buildings were demolished. [12, p. 29]

Immediately after the surrender, the Allied Occupation in Japan, almost exclusively a U.S. operation, took hold and embarked upon a program of economic, political, and legal reformation instituted to disarm the Japanese military and instill democratic values.

Among other things, the Occupation-directed economic reforms included the dissolution of the Zaibatsu,[2] which diffused corporate ownership and shifted corporate control from wealthy families to professional managers who came up through the ranks. The dissolution of Zaibatsu was followed by the passage of the Anti-Monopoly Act, designed to preserve a competitive economic system. In addition, reforms in labor-management relations were initiated and eventually led to unionization of better than half of the nonagricultural labor force by 1949.

Beginning in 1947, the intensification of the Cold War led to a fundamental change in American policy toward Japan. The emphasis in early 1948 took the form of promoting economic recovery and strengthening Japan as an ally in the Cold War. Japan began to recover.

The Korean conflict provided an important stimulus to that recovery. It is estimated that, during the Korean conflict, United Nations forces spent nearly four billion dollars in Japan on strategic supplies for the war effort. Simultaneously, U.S. aid, amounting to a total of two billion dollars, poured into the national economy [12, p. 32]. These payments enabled Japan to amass large dollar reserves, which subsequently were used to reëquip Japanese industries. By 1952, when Japan regained her independence, her industrial output had reached the prewar level and the country was destined to complete its economic rehabilitation a brief four years later.

Japan's phenomenal growth during the decade of the 1960s has been documented many times. The annual growth rate (Japan's fiscal year runs from April 1 through March 31) of the economy averaged 10 percent from 1955 through 1968. It capped the decade with a 13.8 percent real growth for fiscal 1968 and 12.8 percent in fiscal 1969.

The growth figure declined to about 12.2 percent in 1970 and, with the oil embargo crisis of 1973 coupled with the recent 25 percent rate of inflation, Japan's real economic growth slumped to a figure somewhere between four and five percent. As of late, the economic crisis appears to have bottomed-out, and the estimated growth for fiscal year 1981 has been projected to be slightly better than 6 percent. Harvard University professor Henry Rosovsky envisions a "maturing economy" from 1970 to 2000, and a real annual growth for the Japanese economy of no more than 7 percent by the end of the decade [9].

Despite deceleration of its incredible economic recovery, Japan today can proudly boast a GNP outranked only by the United States. Japan now leads the world in shipbuilding and maintains the world's largest fishing industry in terms of value, variety of fish, and areas of operation. In addition, it ranks first in the automobile industry and second in synthetic rubber, tires, caustic soda, plastics and resins, aluminum, refined copper, and zinc; and third in steel, newsprint, pig iron and ferro-alloys, lead, and electronics. On *Fortune's* annual list of the 300 largest foreign industrial firms, nearly one in four is a Japanese concern. Moreover, the Japanese citizenry has enjoyed the fruits of the nation's industrial growth. Something of a consumption revolution has developed, particularly on consumer durables, as evidenced by better than 94 percent of families owning color television sets, more than 75 percent owning washing machines, more than 60 percent having refrigerators, and better than one of every eight driving their own automobiles [12, p. 40].

## JAPAN, INC.

The conventional interpretation by Western analysts attributes Japan's productivity gains mainly to the industriousness and company loyalty of the Japanese worker. However, the essential catalyst is the structure of national coöperation among management, labor, government, and the financial institutions, often dubbed "Japan, Inc."

## Organizational Structure and Groupings

As in prewar years, little public ownership of industry is found. In fact, government ownership of industries has declined, although the government continues to operate the revenue monopolies of tobacco and salt, the telephone and telegraph industry, and the nation's key railroad lines. It also controls a dozen or so financial institutions that are engaged primarily in the field of financing private enterprises. However, key industries, such as oil refining, shipbuilding, steel automotive, as well as power generation and distribution, are completely in the private sector. Once again, economic power has come to be concentrated in the hands of a relatively small number of enterprises.

   Two distinctive types of enterprise groupings are presently dominant in Japan. The most prevalent consists of corporate groups of large independent firms: corporate groupings based on former Zaibatsu ties — the keiretsu; and those molded around major city banks.

   The results of Zaibatsu dissolution proved to be ineffective in some respects. Although family control and ownership of Zaibatsu was totally severed, and the once powerful holding company destroyed, the Korean conflict supplied a strong impetus to the reëmergence of former Zaibatsu firms (keiretsu). The recession that followed the Korean conflict enhanced the keiretsu opportunity to regain their preëminence in a number of key industries — primarily by strengthening their intercorporate ties through increasing cross-holdings of stocks and a resumption of interlocking directorates. Thus, a loose federation of independent enterprises sharing common former Zaibatsu ties and a certain community of interest has charged to the forefront in modern industrial Japan.

   Japan's Fair Trade Commission reported in 1975 that the six largest keiretsu control approximately 40 percent of the nation's corporate capital and 30 percent of its corporate assets. The trading companies of those six groups hold stock in more than 5400 companies in Japan and the groups' banks own even more [9, p. 44]. Unquestionably, these figures have become larger in recent years.

The other important form of corporate group is a loose cluster of large industrial firms organized around a major city bank. This development was primarily attributable to the dependence of industrial firms on bank loans in order tò finance postwar reconstruction and growth.

Being fully aware of their strategic position, the city banks began in the mid-1950s to exert an influence in creating close links with prominent industrial firms by pursuing a preferential loan policy, encouraging its member firms to undertake ventures in new growth fields — jointly, if possible, so as to establish closer ties among themselves, encouraging cross-holdings of stocks among member firms, and by placing some of their executives on the boards of directors of client corporations.

Six major city banks — Fuji, Mitsubishi, Sumitomo, Mitsui, Sanwa, and Daiichi — have been particularly active in this effort. The importance of these six may be seen from the fact that the total capital firms linked to them reached nearly 63 percent of the combined capital of all the firms listed in the first section of the Tokyo Stock Exchange during 1966 [12, p. 142].

The second basic type of enterprise grouping is a loose, vertical hierarchy of small-to-medium-size enterprises organized around a single corporate giant. The parent firm has an intricate network of related subsidiaries, affiliated firms, and subcontractors, which it fosters and directs. Depending on the closeness of their ties to the parent organization, these enterprises are grouped into two major categories: related firms and affiliated firms.

Yoshino points out that these subsidiaries perform a wide variety of functions for the parent firm, ranging from the supply of raw materials to marketing functions to such auxiliary operations as maintenance, transportation, and janitorial services [12, p. 149].

A review of the literature notes yet still other major reasons for the widespread existence of subsidiaries for major Japanese manufacturing firms. In particular, a substantial wage disparity between large and small enterprises, somewhere between 25 and 50 percent, makes it advantageous to the large firms to organize subsidiaries for the performance of labor-intensive operations. Other reasons cited include greater flexibility and freedom of action, and a dumping-ground for managerial personnel either deemed incompetent or beyond the compulsory retirement age of fifty-five. The traditional practice of lifetime employment assures each regular employee a position in the corporation up to a compulsory retirement age, whereupon retired personnel receive a substantial sum in retirement allowance. However, a great majority must locate another source of income after retirement. This usually necessitates placement in the corporation's subsidiaries in an attempt to prolong one's career and, consequently, the managerial and supervisory staff in most subsidiaries of major corporations is made up largely of employees retired from the parent firm.

Large Japanese manufacturing firms in most industries have made rather extensive use of subcontractors. This reciprocal arrangement has become an indispensable element in the total production process, frequently resulting in substantial savings in production costs and providing risk reduction of inventory storage for the parent firm. Subcontractors find such arrangements beneficial in that they promote greater operating stability as well as more opportunities to receive financial, technical, and managerial aid.

In postwar Japan, a managerial career in a large corporate enterprise has carried great societal prestige, and it attracts the most capable graduates from Japan's leading universities. Although the managerial elite occupy a central place in contemporary Japan, their financial compensations, although high by Japanese standards, are not substantial enough to enable them to accumulate personal fortunes.

Another feature, outside the wide disparity in corporate executive salaries, that is uniquely Japanese is the size of the board of directors. A large Japanese corporation is typically somewhat more top-heavy than its U.S. prototype. A study conducted in 1966 of 1,112 leading Japanese corporations revealed that the average number of directors among the firms surveyed was 14, the size of the boards ranged from 5 to 37, and nearly half of the firms had 14 to 20 members on their boards [12, p. 198]. In addition, the role of chairman of the board, a position commonly occupied by a retired president, varies widely among firms. In some, the chairman of the board is the chief executive officer of the corporation, actively involved in its management, whereas in others his functions are only of a ceremonial nature. Today, however, in nearly all firms, the most important operating office is that of the president.

The structure of a large Japanese corporation bears some resemblance to that of a large U.S. firm. However, some clear differences still remain. Yoshino notes that the Japanese corporate organization is structured in terms of collective organizational units such as divisions, departments, and sections rather than individual positions. As a result, there is no way of telling from the organization chart alone how many top management positions exist in the firm. Likewise, reporting relationships between various levels are indicated not in terms of individual positions, but in terms of collective units. The organizational manual also describes assignments and responsibilities in terms of these units. Detailed job descriptions, typically specified in American corporations, are defined in very general terms in Japanese firms [12, p. 202].

As a result, Japanese management tends to perceive the organization in terms of hierarchially related collective units in which a given task is performed by a group and the responsibilities for which are consequently shared by all its members. This concept is filtered down to the plant-floor level and practiced by the rank-and-file.

The major determinants of status in the hierarchy have been level of education, and seniority. Each position has its place in the organization and each member is expected to behave in a manner relative to his hierarchial status. This is where the paradox exists: the relative position of each individual is rigidly defined and observed, but the corresponding functions and responsibilities are not.

Given the tremendous emphasis placed on collectivity as a basis for organization, effective leadership is that behavior that tends to foster an environment facilitating group performance. The commonly accepted role of a leader is one developing a stronger sense of group identity and solidarity and promoting harmonious interpersonal relationships. Technical competence is far less important, and the range of functional authority delegated to the leader is limited. Thus we have a setting where the leader's span of control is typically quite narrow and power is relatively uncertain.

This sense of collectivity is also evidenced by the Japanese decision-making process — the ringi system. The word "ringi" epitomizes the quintessence of the basic managerial philosophy: "rin," meaning "submitting a proposal to one's superior and receiving his approval," and "gi," meaning "deliberation and decisions."

All but a few of the routine decisions that confront a lower-echelon manager must be submitted to top management via a document known as a ringisho. This document includes two parts: a description of the matter to be decided upon and the individual's recommendation. The intent is to solicit top management's approval of the specific recommendation of a subordinate.

It is here that the often laborious task of seeking approval is initiated. The ringisho must be circulated among the various collective units that will be affected by the decision, or whose coöperation will be necessary in its implementation. As each manager evaluates the document, approval is signified by affixing his seal right-side-up. A seal affixed upside-down signifies rejection, whereas a seal affixed sideways indicates indifference to the recommended decision (the absence of a seal is sometimes representative of a deferred decision that will be exercised later once the ringisho is brought before a committee of executives). By complex and circuitous paths, the ringisho eventually reaches top management, and once the president affixes his seal, the decision is final. The ringi document is then returned to the original drafter for implementation, or reconsideration.

Because the system is based on decision making by group participation and consensus, decisions tend to be very slow in forthcoming, taking several weeks, even months, to be made. This method of determining decisions, coupled with a heavy reliance on the intuitive rather than the analytical problem-solving approach, tends to exacerbate crisis management and undermine the concept of management by objectives. This diffusion of the decision-making authority, concludes S. Prakash Sethi, is the cornerstone of an executive's failure to admit an investment is fruitless and should be terminated. As evidence, he points to the fact that one-third of all Japanese overseas manufacturing ventures operated at a loss in the early seventies [8]. Robert Ballon further argues that the Japanese inability to make spontaneous decisions inhibits long-range planning [2]. However, the distinctive advantage of the system is that it allows capable men lacking appropriate status to demonstrate their abilities. This is particularly important where a seniority-based system of promotion may in some cases lead to incompetent top management.

## The Role of Government and Direct Foreign Investment

Why has a trend developed since the mid-1950s toward greater concentration of economic power in the form of large oligopolistic industries? Why has the Japanese government recently taken a more active role in strengthening this economic unity? The answer appears, at least on the surface, in the shape of an old nemesis: the fear of foreign domination. Such fear, in turn, has necessitated cartelization and other collusive actions as a defensive tactic.

The strategy Japan pursued in achieving rapid industrialization was her intense determination to maintain political as well as economic independence. The early Meiji leaders (1868–1912) implemented this philosophy by deliberately restricting the entry of foreign capital — primarily to protect fledgling Japanese industries. Whenever foreign capital was deemed absolutely necessary, solicited loans were preferred.

The Meiji leaders realized in the initial phase of Japanese industrialization that importation of advanced foreign technology could be achieved without foreign ownership or control. This set the basic tone of Japan's attitude toward direct foreign investment throughout the prewar decades.

As in the prewar years, foreign investment, particularly direct investment in Japan, has been comparatively small in postwar decades despite the number of promising features the country offers. The Japanese government, while recognizing the need for foreign capital, strongly resists any foreign domination of the nation's industry. Consequently, the government prefers investments in the form of loans, licensing agreements, and portfolio investments. This objective is accomplished by two important domestic laws: the Foreign Exchange Control Law, which regulates individual foreign transactions completed in one year or less; and the Foreign Investment Law, which regulates foreign investments, licensing agreements, and loans extending for more than one year.

In 1949, Japan enacted the Foreign Exchange Control Law. Article 1 of the law states its purpose as follows:

> To provide for the control of foreign exchange, foreign trade, and other foreign transactions necessary to proper development of foreign trade, and to ensure the balance of international payments and the stability of the currency as well as the most effective employment of foreign currency funds, for the rehabilitation and development of the national economy. [6]

The intent of Article 1 is clearly evidenced by the behavior of Japanese multinationals in the international markets. Unlike more mature multinational enterprises, i.e., those of the United States, many Japanese firms enter foreign markets with their products, sell at competitive prices, and immediately repatriate their earnings to Japan, in order to increase both Japanese foreign exchange reserves (now in excess of twenty-two billion) and the funds for the corporation. This pattern has been followed by most companies for many years and will even have more far reaching implications as Japan's overseas investment continues to expand at a phenomenal annual rate — by 1990 it is projected to grow from the current 33 billion mark to 44 billion.

The Foreign Investment Law, enacted the following year (1950), is more directly concerned with foreign investment control. Article 1 of the Foreign Investment Law properly set the stage: according to it, direct foreign investment is permitted in Japan only when it contributes (1) to the attainment of self-sufficiency and the sound development of the Japanese economy and (2) to the improvement of Japan's balance of payments.

Article 8 of the Foreign Investment Law prescribes the validation conditions which a foreign investor must meet in both affirmative and negative terms. The affirmative terms are that the investment shall directly or indirectly contribute to the improvement of the balance of the international payments, or to the development of essential industries or public enterprises. The negative terms are such that validation will not be accorded to arrangements that are unfair or in contravention of the law, and that are not freely and voluntarily entered into by the Japanese party. Validation can be refused if the arrangements applied for are deemed to have an adverse effect on the rehabilitation of the Japanese economy [6, p. 132].

It must be recalled that both legislative enactments were established during a period when Japan's economic structure was very fragile and the international balance of payments position was a deficit. However, as Japan's economic and international balance of payments improved, gradual relaxation of the government's attitude to validating foreign investment applications was realized.

By 1963, foreign investment was permitted in Japan as long as it did not unduly oppress small-sized enterprises, seriously disturb industrial order, and seriously impede the domestic development of industrial techniques [11]. After 1963, the restrictions were further relaxed. Preceding years permitted a maximum foreign ownership of 49 percent, but by 1963 joint ventures on a 50–50 basis became commonplace. Moreover, the government began to allow joint ventures in vital industries in which only licensing had previously been possible. Still, each application for investment must withstand the test of rigorous examination by the Foreign Investment Council. [3]

Restrictions still prohibit direct foreign investment in utilities, transportation, communications, freight express, banking, fishing, or mining, and the Japanese government also discourages foreign investment in real estate. An examination of the 1980 Foreign Investment Law, however, has liberalized many of the previous restrictions.

Even though public law does not specify any particular limitations on alien ownership and control, investments are not, in fact, approved if the alien holds more than 50 percent of the equity, unless the company is a sales or service firm; then, 100 percent ownership is occasionally permitted. The smaller the amount of equity, the more likely the approval. In addition, the Japanese must control the company's management. Moreover, foreign investors are prohibited from using the profits earned from local operations for purposes other than those for which they were originally granted permission. This measure is designed to prevent foreigners from using locally generated yen for the purchase of Japanese companies.

The question that needs to be asked at this point is why the Japanese government has been so slow in permitting capital liberalization and more active direct foreign investment? Among the major objections to such liberalization, the most frequently mentioned is competitive vulnerability of Japanese industries. Five specific areas of concern are frequently cited. One is the large difference in the size of leading Japanese and international corporations, as measured by such criteria as sales, capital, and overall productivity. An examination of the current *Fortune 500 Directory* shows General Motors' sales to be roughly four times greater than those of Toyota, Japan's leading automobile manufacturer. General Electric's sales are twice as large as those of Hitachi, and E. I. du Pont de Nemours' nearly three times as great as Mitsubishi Chemical Industries'.

The caveat of such an argument is that the phenomenal industrial growth experienced by the Japanese business sector over the past two decades may have made the concern over vulnerability antiquated. As noted earlier, Japan's GNP presently ranks third in the world and her strides in selected industries have been overwhelmingly impressive. Nippon Steel, for example, outpaced U.S. Steel's sales by approximately $1.2 billion in 1980, and exceeded the U.S. steel company's assets by slightly more than $1.7 billion. Moreover, in 1968 General Motors was roughly 18 times as large as Toyota in terms of sales and General Electric's sales were eight times as large as those of Hitachi. These figures have been significantly reduced in the twelve-year interim.

It is also frequently argued that not only is the domestic market small, but for a number of reasons peculiar to Japan its industries are unnecessarily fragmented and suffer from strong internal competition. As a result they are unable to achieve an optimum size of operations. The popular term for this Japanese managerial behavior is "excessive competition."

M. Y. Yoshino describes the development of excessive competition, or 'kato kyōsō,' in his book, *Japan's Managerial System*, by noting:

> Confronted with unprecedented growth opportunities, Japanese business pressed for continued expansion and diversification. Enterprises, especially those in growth industries, competed in a race for advantageous market positions. In the process of this rapid expansion, management became understandably engrossed in the development of productive capacities and the attainment of a greater market share for its products; this, in turn, triggered an investment race. The supply of goods gradually caught up with what appeared to be an insatiable demand. By the early 1960s, a number of industries began to be plagued with excess capacity. The pressure to utilize this excess capacity soon led to what has become known as excessive competition. [12, p. 105]

What clearly has developed in order to utilize this excess capacity has been the Japanese firms more heavy reliance on the pricing mechanism as a competitive weapon in both the domestic and foreign markets. An analysis of the Japanese price behavior must be appreciated in respect to the Japanese business system as a whole, which makes it possible to permit an extraordinary level of debt financing for corporate growth. Japan's business environment reduces the risk and makes tolerable for large Japanese companies a debt level that would be extremely risky in the U.S. context. The following succinctly states the case.

> The financial risks associated with high debt levels are much reduced in Japan by the fact that the central bank stands implicit guarantor of the debt position of major Japanese companies. No American company can assume similar support from the Federal Reserve System. [1]

Another important factor that makes high levels of debt financing possible can be attributed to the generally harmonious relationship between the firm and trade unions. Strikes as we know them in the Western world are practically nonexistent, thus foregoing the necessity of maintaining high corporate liquidity requirements needed to counter long durations of shutdowns.

These low operating margins thus greatly assist in making the price mechanism the competitive weapon in the marketplace. This places enormous pressure on the enterprise to maintain its market share in order to keep pace with cost, and therefore, price reductions. Sizable interest charges, coupled with high unit production costs, contribute to a generally high level of fixed costs for a Japanese company compared with a U.S. company and serves to exacerbate the efforts to continue impressive growth rates at near full capacity. Since growth rates in the west are generally much lower, Western management's appreciation of the effects of market share loss is much less. However, the impact is noticeable upon the smaller, less efficient Japanese producers.

Frequently cited as an example of the highly fragmented market typifying excessive competition is the Japanese auto industry. In 1968, Japan surpassed West Germany and became the second largest manufacturer of automobiles in the world. Although experiencing rapid growth, it remains highly fragmented, with nine firms competing with numerous models at a production cost substantially higher than that in the United States and Western Europe.

As of the end of 1966, the Big Three automobile manufacturers (Toyota, Nissan, and Toyo Kogyo) accounted for 63 percent of the total output. This was considerably less than the ratio of concentration in the three largest firms of other automobile manufacturing countries. The total ratio of concentration for the three largest firms in the United States in late 1966 was 92.1 percent; for West Germany, 82.5 percent; for Great Britain, 83.2 percent; for France, 78.6 percent; and for Italy, 87.9 percent. [12, p. 179]

The degree of fragmentation just described is not unique to the automotive industry in Japan. This tends to support the fear of vulnerability commonly expressed by the Japanese government and why many American exporters have been content to leave the importation and distribution of their products to trading companies.

Another reason given for the competitive vulnerability of the country's industries is the high degree of reliance on debt financing mentioned above. Typically, 75 to 85 percent of the total capital in large Japanese corporations consists of some sort of debt. Figure 2 depicts the 1968 financial structure of the typical large Japanese firm in striking contrast to companies in the United States and Europe. United States companies characteristically tend to finance operations via equity and retained earnings and maintain a much lower (40:60) debt-equity ratio than their Japanese counterparts (85:15). [4]

FIGURE 2    Capital Structure: Manufacturing Industry (1968)

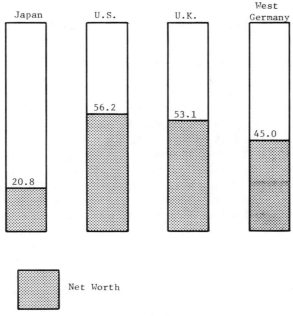

Source: Bank of Japan.

*Business Week* reported in 1975 that, since 1963, the ration of equity to debt among Japan's industrial companies has declined from 27 to 15 percent. The article also points out that the individual creditor has been elbowed out of the nation's credit markets by the insatiable demands of the great manufacturing and trading companies; even though individuals provide 40 percent of bank deposits, they receive only 7 percent of bank credit. [5]

Another strong argument against foreign investment liberalization is the need to protect small firms. Government officials and small business interests argue this sector of the Japanese economy is particularly vulnerable to foreign competition. Small business, still occupying an important role in the Japanese economy, constituted 99.3 percent of the business establishments and were responsible for some 70 percent of the employees and 50 percent of the value of output during 1967 in the manufacturing sector.[4] In distribution, the predominance of small establishments is even more striking. Nearly half of wholesaling and almost 90 percent of retailing establishments had less than four employees during the same year. [11]

A final source of concern lies in what are considered to be the inadequate research and development capabilities of most Japanese firms, compared with their major foreign competitors. As has been previously noted,

Japanese industrial firms have traditionally relied heavily upon importation of foreign technology. Even though significant strides have been made in recent years, Japan still spends only approximately half as much of its gross national product on research and development as does the United States.

To provide assistance in the hopes of stimulating research and development, the Japanese government provides tax concessions, cash grants, and interest-free loans for research in areas of national priority such as energy and defense. "In addition, the cash grants and interest-free loans are available on a selective basis to major industries, such as aircraft, computer, shipbuilding and steel, in order to assist such industries in developing competitive products for the world markets." [3] Such inducements are rarely afforded corporations in the U.S., where a more highly sophisticated, integrated market warrants independent research and development to ensure both maintenance of competitive stature and long-term growth.

The goals and policies established by the Minister of International Trade and Industry are further strengthened by two factors that are commonplace in contemporary Japan. First, the bureaucratic elite and professional corporations are essentially bound by the similar social and academic backgrounds. This tends to facilitate informal communication and understanding between the two groups, which in turn creates a united front that can bring considerable pressure on uncoöperative enterprises.

The second factor that contributes to the fusion of big business and political interests is the financial bond between the two sectors. The corporate generals have been the major and most staunch supporters of the ruling political party — Liberal Democratic Party (LDP). The political power of the business community is largely derived from the fact that the LDP, lacking a broad base of financial support, depends upon business for a major source of its political funds. As a result, large corporations have historically contributed liberally not only to the LDP but to select individual party members. It is rare for major political leaders to make important decisions regarding economic policy without prior consultation with key business leaders. Not only is advice and material assistance afforded, but the aspiring political figure must have the close support of the business leadership in order to win high-ranking political positions.

## CONCLUSION

The business environment in the United States is somewhat different from that of the Japanese and tends not to favor lucrative political contributions by corporate enterprises, or mergers and collusive arrangements (excepting possibly in the transportation industry — particularly in reference to recent administrative and judiciary decisions regarding railroad mergers). The

United States' approach to antitrust regulation in the international arena is governed by four statutes: The Sherman Antitrust Act, The Clayton Antitrust Act, The Webb Pomerene Act, and The Federal Trade Commission Act. The underlying philosophy of all four acts was the maintenance of competitive freedom in both interstate and foreign commerce; and in the case of the Sherman and Clayton Antitrust Acts, the substantive law may be extended to apply to foreign corporations and international markets.

The Sherman Act was passed in 1890 and strives to maintain freedom of competition in interstate and foreign commerce. The Clayton Act was passed in 1914 to supplement the Sherman Act. Section 2 of the Clayton Act is the Robinson-Patman Act of 1936, which generally condemns price discrimination within the United States. Section 7 prohibits corporate mergers that tend to lessen competition. The Federal Trade Commission Act enacted in 1914 gives the F.T.C. jurisdiction in dealing with illegal acts under other antitrust laws. The Webb-Pomerene Act of 1918, although exempting certain firms participating in coöperative export associations from antitrust laws, has been perceived as actually reinforcing the Sherman Act.

The Sherman and Clayton Acts have generated the greatest amounts of litigation and controversy. For example, if the U.S. court can acquire jurisdiction over a foreign corporation,

> case law development demonstrates that American courts will aply Sherman (Act) not only to acts taking place within the United States, but also to Acts occurring outside the United States which have proscribed "effects" on American commerce. Through its reliance on the "effects" test, the Supreme Court has authorized on an almost unlimited extraterritorial application of the Sherman Act. Almost any commercial enterprise operating anywhere on the globe conceivable could have some "effect" on domestic commerce. [10]
>
> A congressional study in 1973 further explains that Section 7 of the Clayton Act does not require that a transaction causing prohibited effect occur within the geographical confines of the United States. All that is required is the anti-competitive effects be felt within "a section of the country." Thus, Clayton can be applied to enforce a U.S. public policy of promoting greater competition in a foreign market if the proscribed activities were found to have an anticompetitive effect within the United States. [10, p. 60]

U.S. efforts to regulate the conduct of domestic enterprises and multinational firms *per se* through application of antitrust laws internally and extraterritorially have in the past generated conflict with the laws of other nations and criticism by foreign and domestic experts. "Although foreign businessmen express anxiety about entrance into the American marketplace out of fear that their worldwide operations will be subject to U.S. antitrust regulation, that fear apparently is groundless or at least substantially overstated." [10, p. 60]

What is apparent and seems to be destined to aggravate judicial anxiety is the evident differences in international law: U.S. law considering dominance as a violation and European, Canadian, and Japanese law making the misuse of a dominant position illegal. As stated earlier, Japanese policy tends to favor concentrations and anticompetitive agreements if they lead to increased productivity, economic growth, technological advancement, or price reduction. Thus, Japan's antitrust laws are not directed at breaking up cartels but at guiding them. And because Japan's approach favors combination and cartelization of domestic enterprises to compete with the U.S.-based multinationals, it seems realistic to profess U.S.-based firms will continue to face ever increasing stiff competition from foreign cartels.

## FOOTNOTES

[1]"Oyakata," or master workmen, were independent labor contractors who provided skilled workers for factories on a short-term contractual basis. Most of the "oyakata" had learned their skills from foreign experts or skilled Japanese workers in government-operated factories. Some influential "oyakata" had as many as several hundred workers under them and they basically performed all the key personnel functions, including recruiting, training, supervising, and rewarding the workers. In addition, the "oyakata" maintained a highly personalized and particularistic relationship with his cadres of skilled workers; and the ideology governing their relationship closely resembled that of the feudal master-artisan ties.

[2]Estimates indicate that a total of over 3600 key executives in Japan's leading corporations and 56 members of the Zaibatsu families were purged.

[3]The formalities and processes of validation, which are necessary for foreign investors to apply for in connection with their acquisition of corporate shares in the Japanese stock market, has been placed under an automatic approval system administered by the Bank of Japan, provided that the percentage of equity ownership by such investors does not exceed certain limits. At present, foreign investors can purchase corporate shares in the market up to 20 percent in general industries and 15 percent in restricted industries, without applying for any formal validation.

[4]Small business is defined as enterprises with less than 300 employees.

## BIBLIOGRAPHY

[1] Abegglen, James C., and Rapp, William V. "Japanese Managerial Behavior and 'Excessive Competition.'" *International Business – 1973, a Selection of Current Readings*. East Lansing, Mich.: MSU Division of Research, 1973.

[2] Ballon, Robert. "Understanding the Japanese." *Business Horizons*, June, 1970.

[3] Ernst and Ernst. *Tax Bulletin*. International Business Series, March 25, 1974.

[4] "Japan's Economy Tomorrow," *Business Week*, January 30, 1978.

[5] "Japan's Economy in Transition." *Business Week*, July 17, 1975.

[6] Kobayashi, Noritake. "Foreign Investment in Japan," *Foreign Investment: The Exterience of the Host Country*, edited by I. A. Litvak and C. J. Maule. New York: Praeger Press, 1970.

[7] Litvak, Isaisan, A., and Maule, Christopher J. "The Issues of Direct Foreign Investment," printed in *Foreign Investment: The Experience of the Host Country*, edited by I. A. Litvak and C. J. Maule. New York: Praeger Press, 1970.

[8] Sethi, S. Prakash. "Drawbacks of Japanese Management." *Business Week*, November 24, 1973.

[9] "Sumitomo: How the 'Keiretsu' Pulls Together to Keep Japan Strong." *Business Week*, March 31, 1975.

[10] U.S. Congress, Senate, Committee in Finance. *Implications of Multinational Firms for World Trade and Investment and For U.S. Trade and Labor*. 93rd Cong., 1st Sess., Washington, D.C.: U.S. Government Printing Office, 1973.

[11] Yoshino, M. Y. "Japan as Host to the International Corporation." *The International Corporation*, edited by Charles P. Kindleberger. Cambridge, Mass.: The MIT Press, 1970.

[12] Yoshino, M. Y. *Japan's Managerial System*. Cambridge, Mass.: The MIT Press, 1968.

# 20

# Computer Auditing in Japan: Lessons and Constraints

RICHARD S. SAVICH

The excellence and rising prominence of Japanese computers is known worldwide. The Japanese management style is discussed as one reason for Japan's sudden rise in international business. Japan's industrious people are also considered a major reason for its rising productivity. But, U.S. standards are typically used when Japanese auditing methods are developed. How then do the Japanese fare when faced with combining Japanese computers and American auditing?

To answer this question and to determine the underlying reasons for the Japanese approach to computer auditing, a research project was conducted involving both Japanese Audit Corporations and U.S. Certified Public Accounting (CPA) firms operating in Japan. This paper discusses the findings of that investigation. Certain caveats, however, should be considered before reading the results.

Japanese people and Japanese business are different from American people and American business. That is, neither group is better or worse than the other, only different. These differences come from a long history of societal and cultural training. Such books as *Japan as No. 1* and *Shogun*, which are popular in the U.S., only touch the surface of these differences. A complete understanding takes many years, and might, in fact, never be achieved. This paper does not pretend to present a total or even logical reasoning for these differences. Instead, it intends to add to a growing body of information that should be read by those interested. Only by experiencing the Japanese way might one come closer to better understanding.

With these warnings in mind, an explanation of the research approach is presented. Interviews were conducted with audit personnel in Japan who were employed by either American CPA firms operating in Japan or Japanese Audit Corporations. While most of the personnel in American CPA firms were of Japanese origin, the top management were usually Americans. Therefore, a blending of American and Japanese styles existed. This mixing caused approaches somewhat different than those of similar firms in the U.S. Seven American firms and five Japanese audit corporations participated. The U.S. firms were all members of what is commonly called the "Big 8," while the Japanese firms were among the largest in the country. These firms, then, could be considered to represent a large percentage of the audit work performed for the major corporations in both the U.S. and Japan.

The firms listed in the various tables are not divided in terms of American and Japanese because of the similarity of approach. That is, the firms' personnel interviewed performed audits of both American and Japanese corporations and had some sort of working agreements with their opposite national counterparts. For example, an American CPA firm operating in Japan would not only audit a branch, subsidiary, or joint venture of an American corporation, but might also audit the local Japanese component of a Japanese corporation or joint venture operating in America. And, conversely, a Japanese Audit Corporation would audit not only Japanese corporations, but might also perform audits of subsidiaries, branches, or joint ventures of U.S. companies in Japan, for compliance with Japanese laws. These complex working arrangements, along with the predominance of Japanese personnel in American firms, precluded division and comparison of American versus Japanese methods. For an explanation of a strictly American approach, see "Organizing Audits in an EDP Environment" (*The CPA Journal*, August 1980) by the same author. Therefore, the research centered around computer auditing in Japan regardless of whether it was performed by American or Japanese firms.

The questions asked involved computer usage by clients, organizational characteristics of, and operational approaches to, computer auditing. While the tables included in the paper present summaries of the answers to the various questions asked, of equal importance are the reasons for the answers. Each of these will be discussed in turn.

## COMPUTER USAGE

To put the impact of electronic data processing (EDP) auditing into perspective, the percentage of clients utilizing computers for significant accounting applications was determined. Table 1 summarizes these results.

TABLE 1    Percent of Clients Using
Computers for Significant Accounting Applications

| FIRM | % |
|:---:|:---:|
| A | 40–50 |
| B | 20 |
| C | 80 |
| D | 80 |
| E | 40–50 |
| F | 10–20 |
| G | 40–50 |
| H | 70 |
| I | 30 |
| J | 75–80 |
| K | 70 |
| L | 80–90 |
| Average | 53–58 |

As can be seen, the percentages ranged from a low of 20 percent to a high of 90 percent with about 53–58 percent being the average. This indicates that in over one-half of the audits conducted an auditor would be confronted with accounting applications which were computerized. The interviewees stated that these figures would be likely much higher if only large publicly-held corporations were considered. Also, the inclusion of minicomputer systems as stand-alones could increase these figures. These results have implications on both organizational and audit technique frameworks, and are discussed later.

## ORGANIZATION

Within the organizational area, questions regarding total audit staff, EDP auditing staff, percentage of time spent on EDP audit areas, use of management advisory services personnel, and the person in charge of EDP audits were asked. The answers to each of these questions are discussed below and a summary is presented in Table 2.

## Audit Staff

The range of total audit staff was from 30 to 400 people, with an average of 175 people. No tax or management advisory services personnel were included in these figures. The numbers did include, however, all juniors, seniors, supervisors, managers, and partners involved in audit work. These titles indicate the management hierarchy commonly in use in auditing firms. The total audit staffs were much smaller than what is usual for the larger CPA firms in the U.S. The implications of these differences in size are discussed later.

## EDP Audit Staff

The number of people capable of performing audits of clients using computers ranged from one to eight, with an average of 4.1. This represents only 2 percent of the average size of audit staffs. Some explanation is necessary, however. Firm A, for example, does not designate anyone within its firm as an EDP audit specialist, and the interviewees in Firms F and L indicated that the numbers shown represented people who were capable of utilizing the firm's generalized audit software packages, but would need assistance to perform all phases of an EDP audit. Therefore, the auditors capable of handling a complete EDP audit, from planning through compliance and substantive testing to issuance of the final report, were the smaller numbers listed for those firms. However, Firm E interviewees stated that all senior auditors were not only capable of handling the firm's software package but could also manage most applications and only call upon the EDP audit specialists for an unusual application or if encountering difficulties on a recurring application. The reasons for the low number of EDP audit staff are explained later.

## Percent of EDP Audit Staff Time

EDP auditors spent a certain percentage of their billable time on performing both EDP and non-EDP audits. The percentage on EDP audits ranged from 10 to 100, with an average of 42. Therefore, a little over two-fifths of the time was spent in computer auditing by these specialists.

## Use of Management Advisory Services Personnel

Occasionally, management advisory services (MAS) personnel were used to assist auditors in performing the EDP portion of an audit. The range of such assistance was from none to equal participation. Some firms did not even have a MAS division. By Japanese law, audit corporations are restricted to auditing financial statements and preparing, investigating, and counseling clients in accounting matters. But many firms do not engage in counseling due to potential conflicts of interest. Instead, separate organizations

TABLE 2   Summary of Results on Organizational Characteristics

| FIRM | A | B | C | D | E |
|---|---|---|---|---|---|
| Total audit staff | 55 | 57 | 400 | 400 | 50 |
| EDP audit specialists | none specified | 3 | 5 | 5 | 4 |
| Percent of time devoted to EDP audits | N/A | 50 | 50 | 50 | 30 |
| Use of MAS personnel | complex and first-time applications | divided equally | none | divided equally | sometimes |
| Person in charge of EDP audit | audit partner | audit partner | audit partner | audit partner | audit partner |

TABLE 3   Summary of Results on Audit Steps and Techniques

| FIRM | A | B | C |
|---|---|---|---|
| Use of internal control questionnaire | detailed | detailed | detailed |
| Use of generalized audit software | firm developed | firm developed | firm developed |
| Other computer assisted audit techniques | custom programs, parallel simulation | custom programs, parallel simulation | custom programs, parallel simulation test data, integrated test facility |
| Audit applications | AR, inventory, depreciation, payroll, retirement allowance | AR, inventory, AP, cash, fixed assets | AR, inventory, AP, depreciation, payroll, retirement allowance, deposits, interest, discounted notes |

TABLE 2 *Continued*

| F | G | H | I | J | K | L |
|---|---|---|---|---|---|---|
| 70 | 30 | 180 | 135 | 175 | 150 | 400 |
| 50–60 are capable | 4 | 3 | 4 | 8 | 2 | basic 150 advanced 3 |
| 20 | 5 | 5 | 10–20 | 50 | 50 | 100 |
| ICQ adm. and design of compliance tests | none | none | none | none | divided equally | only complex applications |
| audit partner | audit partner | audit partner | audit partner | audit partner | audit partner | audit partner |

TABLE 3 *Continued*

| D | E | F | G |
|---|---|---|---|
| detailed | detailed | detailed | detailed |
| firm developed parallel simulation | firm developed custom programs, parallel simulation test data, integrity control test package | firm developed none | firm developed none |
| AR, inventory, AP, cash, fixed assets, notes payable, retirement allowance, sales, purchases, expenses | AP, payroll insurance sales, AR, inventory, AP, payroll insurance policy reserve | AR, inventory, AP, depreciation, payroll, G&A, sales, other income | AR, inventory, sample selection, fixed assets, depreciation |

(continued)

TABLE 3  *Continued*

| H | I | J | K | L |
|---|---|---|---|---|
| detailed | detailed | checklist | detailed | detailed |
| none | firm developed | firm developed | none | firm developed |
| custom programs, program verification | custom programs, time-sharing | custom programs, test data, parallel simulation time-sharing | custom programs, program verification integrated test facility | custom programs, parallel simulation, test data, vendor programs |
| inventory, fixed assets | AR, inventory | sales, AR, inventory, purchases, fixed assets, depreciation, payroll, cash disbursement, pension and retirement allowance | not reported | AR, inventory, fixed assets, depreciation, sales, loans, deposits, interest, retirement allowance, installment sales, foreign exchange |

are created to perform this task. Therefore, the MAS personnel are not, strictly speaking, members of the audit corporation, but could be available for assistance. Table 2 shows that complex applications, first-time audits, and administration of internal control questionnaires were situations where MAS personnel were utilized.

## Person in Charge of EDP Audit

In all firms interviewed, an audit partner was the primary person responsible for decisions regarding EDP auditing. MAS personnel were used in advisory capacities, but not in decision-making situations.

## AUDIT STEPS AND TECHNIQUES

To understand how an auditor performs an audit within an EDP environment, questions were directed to the use of internal control questionnaires, generalized audit software, computer-assisted audit techniques, and applications audited. The answers to these questions are discussed below and summarized in Table 3.

## Use of Internal Control Questionnaires

All firms interviewed utilized an internal control questionnaire (ICQ) to aid in the study and evaluation of internal control. With the exception of one firm which used a checklist of controls, all firms used a detailed questionnaire. The questionnaires were either developed by the firm internally or the firm used the questionnaire designed by the Computer Committee of the Japanese Institute of CPAs. These questionnaires were very extensive and covered controls in general, as well as applications and control areas, similar to those stated in Statement on Auditing Standards (SAS) No. 3 of the American Institute of CPAs (AICPA). Of course, the ICQs were printed in either Kanji, the Japanese character set; Katakana, a syllabary used in Japan for foreign words; Hiragana, the Japanese syllabary; or English, where appropriate.

## Use of Generalized Audit Software

Most of the firms interviewed utilized some type of generalized audit software package. These packages allowed auditors to access clients' data files and perform various calculations, selections, and extractions that could then be printed on special reports for further investigation. Those firms which were American-based used the same package as their counterparts in the U.S., while the Japanese audit corporations either used American firms' packages on a franchise basis or developed their own internally. Those firms that did not have a generalized audit software package used other computer-assisted audit techniques to perform the audit.

## Computer-Assisted Audit Techniques

In addition to generalized audit software, many firms utilized other computer-assisted audit techniques. These included custom-designed, special purpose programs, which access data and perform various other calculations; parallel simulation techniques, which process a client's data on an auditor-prepared program and compare the output with the client's program's output; test data and integrated test facility approaches, which introduce auditor-prepared data to a client's programs to see if stated controls can be bypassed; program verification techniques, where an auditor reviews the source listing of a client's program to determine that expected controls exist; vendor programs, similar to generalized audit software, but only for a particular manufacturer's hardware; and time-sharing, which utilizes existing programs to investigate data available on the system or introduced by the auditor. None of these approaches was used extensively and, in fact, generalized audit software predominated the computer-assisted audit techniques used.

## Applications Audited

The types of financial statement accounts audited included those that might be expected and some that are unique to Japanese businesses. The usual accounts included accounts receivable, inventory, depreciation, payroll, fixed assets, cash, accounts payable, and sales. Of particular difference were the accounts of retirement allowances, loans, deposits, discounted notes, and foreign exchange.

Retirement allowances were audited because of their material effect on the financials. In Japan, lifetime employment, until the age of 55, is the norm. Therefore, a substantial portion of current income is allocated to pension benefits that will be paid to employees upon retirement. The retiree generally receives a large lump sum benefit, which receives favorable income tax treatment. Under funded plans, there is usually an option to receive monthly pension payments, if an individual has had some specified years of service (in many cases twenty years or more), or a lump sum payment. These amounts usually are larger than U.S. retirement benefits, when considered as a percentage of current salary.

Banking relations, which concern loans, deposits, and discounted notes, are also different in Japan. A Japanese corporation's balance sheet might show a debt-equity ratio of 80-20 or be even more debt laden. Therefore, loans are a material account to be audited. Because the Japanese people save approximately 20 percent of their current salary, deposits are also quite large. While the daily Japanese life-style usually requires large sums of cash (checks are rarely written), companies many times issue promissory notes instead of cash in payment for invoices. Suppliers, rather than waiting for the due date, might discount these notes at banks for immediate cash. The volume of these gives rise to audit considerations. And finally, because of the large volume of import and export goods, foreign exchange becomes an account to be audited.

All of the above data concerning organizational and audit considerations were those available that could be categorized for summarization. But, as in many interview-oriented research projects, much of the information gathered could not be generalized. The underlying reasons for the data presented are sometimes more important than the results. Just as an auditor does not rely solely on the books of accounts, but seeks to make an overall evaluation of a company's internal control system, an understanding of the cultural and societal background of Japanese business is necessary. Realization of these differences from Western approaches can ameliorate some of the problems associated with doing business in Japan and help American CPA firms to understand what their expatriate partners face, both now and in the future.

## POSSIBLE REASONS FOR DIFFERENCES

### Historical

Without trying to become a historian, some recognition of the Japanese heritage is necessary. The Tokugawa period, from 1650 to 1867, effectively shut off Japan from the rest of the world. During that time the system of the daimyo, or feudal lords, enforced concepts of duty and loyalty that still exist today in the Japanese companies replacing the former feudal organization. During the Meiji restoration, from 1868 to 1912, international trade was established and the merchant class wrested power from the shoguns. During that 250-year period, belonging was more important than individual excellence. Some people might contend that while the workers adapted this belonging attitude, management was also required to consolidate it into its overall strategies. Top management did so by being able to draw upon extensive bank financing and support, as well as ambitious planning, technological innovation and long-term outlooks. These two forces, labor and management, have utilized group solidarity to such an extent that the usual demarcation between them is negligible. This situation continues to the present day and possibly explains both lifetime employment as well as the low priority placed on the pursuit of profits relative to economic well-being for all constituencies.

Since individual acts are incompatible unless contributing to the overall good, fraud is also almost nonexistent in today's Japanese society. This might allow an auditor to reduce substantially the need for investigation into computer abuse. However, there is another historical trait which, when considered, could cause extensive concern. Because of the group-belonging syndrome, any act by a member of the group reflects on others within the group and they all receive the benefits or face the consequences. So if a fraud is committed, others in the group, such as the defrauder's family, will make restitution to the company. Therefore, since no loss has been incurred by the company, there is no need to report fraud. This scenario could be an explanation as to why very few instances of fraud have ever been reported publicly in Japan.

But there are other, more modern, reasons for the current status of computer auditing in Japan. The period after World War II saw the Japanese people traveling the globe researching Western business practices and technology. They took an eclectic approach, borrowing the best from America and Europe and applying an Eastern philosophy to it. The current prominence of Japan in computer hardware is evidence of such learning. But it is mainly an imitative rather than a creative skill. While hardware development rivals and, in many cases, surpasses Western techniques, software development in business applications, such as accounting, is lagging. This, however, could change as the Japanese government, in connection with the larger computer manufacturers, such as Fujitsu, Hitachi, Nippon Electric (NEC), and Toshiba, is beginning to support more software development. However, the benefits from these efforts will take a few years to be realized. This lag, in addition to the scarcity of overall management information systems networks within companies, has led to very little being done currently in Japanese companies in terms of sophisticated computer usage for accounting applications. Many of the present applications performed by computers are simple input-output tasks, without an integration of all elements into a cohesive whole. This means that EDP auditors do not need extensive knowledge of distributed networks or data base systems, because very few exist in Japan. Batch processing or elementary on-line systems knowledge suffices.

However, this might change in the near future as indicated by many Japanese banks introducing on-line systems for deposits and withdrawals. In fact, a recent defalcation of 130,000,000 yen by an employee of a Japanese bank indicates both the advances in computer technology and the opportunities for fraud. Also, with the advent of Kanji processors, much of the handwritten work currently performed might be amenable to computer processing. But the underlying social structure described above must still be considered.

## Educational

The educational system is also a reason for the state of computer auditing today. Male graduates of colleges and universities generally plan to work their entire lives for the first company they join. Many job offers are made only after examinations, which the company administers, are passed. This examination syndrome permeates the educational system. Exams are given for company, university, high school, elementary school, and even kindergarten admission. While the pressures for admission are intense, once admitted, a student is almost guaranteed graduation. So learning becomes a pursuit for knowledge to be shown on an entrance exam, not for a single course grade. And, of course, group learning predominates because of the need for belonging rather than individual excellence. This learning continues after graduation and an individual is rotated through many different departments in a company, sometimes regardless of prior experience or a particular college major. To find an accounting major spending three years in the personnel department, or a marketing major handling accounting records, is not unusual. Extensive company training promotes this practice.

Even those individuals who decide to concentrate on a particular aspect of learning, such as becoming a recognized expert on accounting for foreign exchange, and spend an entire lifetime in this area, also have other pursuits such as bonsai or golf or the study of some other topic that provides respite from the detailed study. This approach to life may be traced back to the samurai, who in addition to being warriors became excellent poets, artists, or calligraphers. Therefore, one can be both a specialist and generalist at the same time.

## Philosophical

What all this has to do with computer auditing might appear obtuse to the Western mind. But in Eastern philosophy, logic is not paramount, emotion is. A reasoned, logical decision is not always necessary to issue an audit opinion in Japan. What concerns Westerners is that a feeling is needed that the financial statements are fairly presented. Therefore, in-depth computer auditing will not remove doubts as it does in the U.S., and consequently, might not be necessary to the Japanese way of thinking.

## Professional

Of a more concrete nature in explaining the state of computer auditing in Japan is the current accounting profession's framework. There are approximately 6,000 CPAs in Japan. Comparing this figure to the U.S., where there are approximately 200,000 CPAs, indicates substantial differences. Both the population and Gross National Product of Japan are about half that of the U.S. The number of CPAs compared to the population shows that there is one CPA for every 20,000 persons. In the U.S., there is one CPA for every 1,200 persons. Even if tax accountants, which are not usually CPAs in Japan, and nonpracticing CPAs are omitted from the U.S. figures, the comparison is still astounding. Also there are only about fifty audit corporations (*kansa-hojin*) in Japan, compared to approximately 14,000 CPA firms in the U.S.

Those persons desiring to become CPAs in Japan must pass three examinations. The preliminary exam, which covers basic Japanese reading and writing skills, is waived for university graduates. The intermediate exam, which covers bookkeeping, accounting theory, cost accounting, auditing, business administration, economics, and commercial law, is usually taken as soon as possible after graduation. The pass rate usually is less than 10 percent. The final examination is taken after three years of experience and has a pass rate of less than 20 percent. Therefore, less than 2 percent of the applicants to the intermediate exam ever become CPAs. The severity of the exam results in few CPAs.

None of the exams have ever had questions on computers or computer auditing. Compare this to the U.S. where, ever since 1969, there have been questions related to computers or computer auditing in the auditing section of the CPA exam.

Until recently, government employment was considered the optimal job opportunity in Japan. Trading companies now head the list of desired job applications. CPA firms are very low on the list of priorities. Compared to the U.S., where many accounting graduates have a desire to work for CPA firms, this reverse situation also causes differences in the accounting profession. The CPA firms' personnel interviewed all expressed a need for more employees. But most college graduates in accounting do not want to work for CPA firms. And even those that do have difficulty passing the intermediate examination. And until they pass the exam, they do not consider themselves fully qualified to work for a firm and might spend an entire extra year studying for the next exam. If they pass, they then become junior CPAs and are required to work for three years before taking the final exam. Since there is so much pressure to pass the final exam, the third year of the three-year experience period is devoted almost entirely to studying for the final exam. What this leads to is a person who might not want to concentrate on computer auditing until after passing the final exam. Therefore, almost five years after graduation might pass before a CPA would be willing to emphasize computer auditing as a career path. This time lag could also be a reason for the low number of computer auditors in Japan.

All these explanations are possible reasons for the current state of computer auditing in Japan. No one reason predominates. They all blend to form the pattern of a long-term outlook. A computer auditing philosophy takes many years to develop. In the U.S., computer auditing began seriously in the mid-1960s and evolved over the past two decades to what it is today. In Japan, it is still a relatively new idea. But the Japanese are accustomed to long-term views.

# FUTURE OF COMPUTER AUDITING IN JAPAN

Reporting and auditing of consolidated financial statements has been required in Japan only since 1977. The number of computers in Japan totals over 70,000, and is growing rapidly. The Business Accounting Deliberation Council of the Ministry of Finance is currently revising the generally accepted accounting principles to conform with the Commercial Code of Japan. All these circumstances will have a great effect on the future of auditing and computer auditing in Japan.

All CPA firms' personnel interviewed expressed a strong desire to increase the amount of computer auditing performed and the size of their computer audit staffs. They also saw much more training being performed utilizing U.S. CPA firms' continuing education programs, more in-house instruction, as well as that provided by the major computer vendors such as IBM and Fujitsu.

What will happen in the decade of the '80s is speculative. What is certain is the increased use of computers in businesses of all sizes. To match the Japanese methods of conducting business with the Western methods is a task requiring in-depth knowledge of all countries' societal, cultural, and technological circumstances. Such a task is not insurmountable, but needs a cautious approach. The background and current state of computer auditing presented in this chapter hopefully provide one step along the path.

# Index

# About the Contributors

**Robert Angel** is currently President of the Japan Economic Institute of America. He earned his B.A. in Political Science, magna cum laude, and his M.A. from Columbia University. He has taught at Columbia University and American University on International Relations. He is a frequent contributor to various publications on East Asia and Japan.

**Allan S. Baillie** is currently Professor of Management at California Polytechnic State University. He has contributed to a number of publications on various management related topics.

**Howard W. Barnes**, Associate Professor of International Business at Brigham Young University, received a doctorate in political economy from the Technical University of Brunswick in West Germany. Formerly a marketing research analyst with an international foods manufacturer, he has conducted market and business feasibility studies in the U.S., Europe, and Japan.

**C. S. Chang** is an Associate Professor of Management at Lander College in Greenwood, South Carolina. He earned a Ph.D. in business from American University in Washington, D.C. and an M.B.A. from the University of South Carolina. He studied at Yonsei University in Seoul, Korea, where he earned B.A. and M.A. degrees in Economics. He has published a book, *The Japanese Auto Industry and the U.S. Market*, through Praeger Publishers in New York. He has also published several articles and presented many papers at various conventions.

**David M. Flynn** is Assistant Professor of Management at Baruch College, The City University of New York. He received his Ph.D. in International Business and Policy from the University of Massachusetts. His research has included the following areas: long-range planning in the public sector; free trade between Canada and the U.S.; cultural values and behavior; personal values and strategy; commitment and strategic implementation; and cultural values as they affect management processes.

**Steven B. Johnson** is Assistant Professor of Accounting at the University of Florida. He received his Ph.D. from the University of Wisconsin–Madison and holds a J.D. degree from Washington University School of Law. His current research interests include tax policy, institutional analysis, and information economics. He has published papers in these areas in the *Journal of Accounting, Auditing and Finance, Managerial Finance,* and other journals.

**Garland Keesling,** Ph.D., is currently an Assistant Professor at the School of Business Administration, Stetson University, Deland, Florida. His research interests are in the Japanese foreign investment strategies and marketing research.

**Lane Kelley,** Ph.D., is Professor of Management at the University of Hawaii at Manoa. He has been a frequent contributor to various publications dealing with comparative management.

**Sohtaro Kunihisa** was born in 1938 and finished undergraduate and graduate work at Waseda University. He joined the Institute of Behavioral Sciences in 1967 and has been a chief researcher of the economic section thereof since 1977. Among his articles are: "Application of the Spatial Econometric Model (SPAMETRI) to the Evaluation of the Economic Effects of Shinkansen and Expressway Construction," (in Japanese), *Chiiki-Gaku Kenkyu,* Vol. 8, 1977; "Time Distance and Regional Production Function," (in Japanese), *Tokyo Keidai Gakkaishi,* Mar. 1977.

**Robert Lange** is Assistant Professor of English at the University of Hartford. He earned his B.A. from Tufts University and M.A. from Harvard University. He also studied European literature at the Sorbonne and organizational behavior at the Barney School of Business.

**Joseph W. Leonard** received his B.S.B.A. from Missouri Southern State College (1970), an M.S. in Economics from Kansas State College (1971) and an M.B.A. from Drury College, Missouri (1979). After his military service, he joined Eagle-Picher, Inc., as a Contract Administrator (1973–1979). Presently, he is finishing a Ph.D. at the University of Arkansas, where he has served as an instructor in management. He has published numerous case studies and papers, and his main research interests are in Japanese management systems.

**Leonard Lynn** has lived in Japan for a total of seven years as a Fulbright Research Fellow, businessman, university instructor, and an interpreter in the U.S. Army. He received his Ph.D. in Sociology from the University of Michigan and has degrees in East Asian Studies from the University of Oregon. He is now an Assistant Professor in the Department of Social Science at Carnegie-Mellon University. His current research concerns various aspects of technology and society in Japan, including labor relations in the steel industry and the development of industrial robotics. Lynn's recent book, *How Japan Innovates* (1982), reports his research on the adoption of new technology in the U.S. and Japanese steel industries.

**Magoroh Maruyama** was born in Japan in 1929 and worked in Japan until 1950. He studied at the University of California, Berkeley; the Universities of Munich, Heidelberg, Copenhagen, and Lund; and has received a Ph.D. in cultural epistemology. Currently he is a research professor at Southern Illinois University-Carbondale. He has authored numerous articles, including "The Second Cybernetics" (*American Scientist* 1963), "Heterogenistics" (*Cybernetica* 1977), and "Mindscapes and Science Theories" (*Current Anthropology* 1980). He has taught at the University of California, Berkeley and Stanford University, has worked in Africa and the Middle East, and has been a consultant to NASA, NSF, the U.S. Department of Commerce, and several Japanese, Canadian, and American corporations.

**Motofusa Murayama**, Ph.D., is Professor of International Management at Chiba University. He studied at Columbia University and holds an M.B.A. degree from Seton Hall University. He has taught Japanese management at the International Division of Sophia University in Tokyo. He has published a number of books and journal articles dealing with a variety of management topics.

**His Excellency Yoshio Okaware** is currently the Ambassador of Japan to the United States. He is a graduate of the University of Tokyo and has had a distinguished career as a diplomat.

**Clayne L. Pope**, Associate Professor of Economics at Brigham Young University, received his Ph.D. from the University of Chicago. An economic historian and Research Associate from the National Bureau of Economic Research, he has published *The Impact of the Antebellum Tariff on Income Distribution* and is currently at work on a book concerning the distribution and mobility of income and wealth.

**Richard S. Savich**, Ph.D., C.P.A., is an Associate Professor, School of Accounting, and Director of the Doctoral Program, Graduate School of Business Administration, University of Southern California. He is also a member of the American Institute of CPA's Computer Education Subcommittee. He has written many books and articles on the topics of computers, accounting information systems, and systems auditing. He is also a consultant to many multinational corporations, financial institutions, and accounting firms both in the United States and abroad.

**Anson Seers** is an Assistant Professor of Organizational Behavior in the College of Commerce and Business Administration of the University of Alabama, in Tuscaloosa, Alabama. His research interests include the integration of work design and interpersonal interaction in organizations and the process of organizational change. He recently completed his Ph.D. in business administration at the University of Cincinnati, after receiving an M.S. in organizational psychology from the University of Illinois at Urbana-Champaign.

**Martin H. Sours** is Professor of International Studies at the American Graduate School of International Management (Thunderbird) in Phoenix, Arizona. He received his B.A. degree from the University of California, Berkeley, and M.A. and Ph.D. degrees from the University of Washington. His recent publications include "ASEAN and U.S. Foreign Policy" in *Asia and U.S. Foreign Policy* (Praeger, 1981) and "Trans-pacific Interdependencies" in *Region Building in the Pacific* (Pergamon, 1982).

**Toshiyuki Tamura** was born in 1941 and studied economics and econometrics at Hitotsubashi University. He has been an associate professor at Tokyo Metropolitan University since 1974, and was a visiting fellow to the Institute of Economic Research, Seoul National University, Korea in 1979. Among his writings are: "Economic Analysis of Market Societies" (in Japanese), *Shin-Hyoron*, 1977; "Negative Income Tax and the Governmental Budget Surplus," (in Korean), *The Korean Economic Journal*, Dec. 1978; and "Pre-War Korean Population in Japan Based on the Police Bureau Data," (in Japanese), *Keizai to Keizaigaku*, Feb. 1981.

**John Thanopoulos** received his B.A. from the Athens Graduate School of Economics (Greece, 1971) and his M.S. from City University, London (England, 1973). After his military service, he joined Voktas, Inc. (Greece) as a planning officer, assistant to the CEO, and finally as sales manager. He has served at the University of Arkansas as a Research Scholar in Business, where he is presently finishing his Ph.D. and teaching economics and marketing. He has published several works and his research interests are geared towards social marketing.

**Ezra Vogel** is Professor of Sociology and Director of the East Asian Research Center at Harvard University. He received his B.A. degree from Ohio Wesleyan University and his Ph.D. from Harvard University. He is a widely known expert on East Asian societies. Although he is best known to the general public because of his book *Japan as Number One*, he has numerous other publications to his credit. He has received honorary degrees from Kwansei Gakuin University in Japan and Wittenberg College in Ohio.

**Reginald Worthley**, Ph.D., is a professor at the College of Business Administration, University of Hawaii. He has done much research on the Japanese management systems.

# About the Editors

**Sang M. Lee** is a Regents Professor of the University of Nebraska system; the First National Bank, Lincoln, Distinguished Professor; and Chairman of the Management Department. He received his MBA from Miami University of Ohio and his Ph.D. in Management Science from the University of Georgia. He is the author or co-author of 17 books, including *Goal Programming for Decision Analysis, Introduction to Decision Science, Linear Optimization for Management, Management Science,* and others. He has published over 130 research papers in various leading journals of management. He has been an expert referee for the National Research Council, National Academy of Sciences, National Academy of Engineering, and National Science Foundation. He is a consulting editor for the publishers of two book series and is on the editorial boards of 16 journals. He has been a distinguished visiting scholar at Ohio State, University of Minnesota, University of Georgia, Rutgers, Michigan State University, and many other universities in the U.S., England, Japan, and Korea. He won the Outstanding Research Award at the University of Nebraska System in 1980. He was the founder and first president of SE AIDS, from which he received the First Distinguished Service Award. He has been a member of the Council, Chairman of the Publication Committee, Vice President, Secretary, and Nominee for the President-Elect of the National AIDS. He is a Fellow of AIDS. He received the Distinguished Service Award from National AIDS in 1980 for his contribution to AIDS and the management profession.

**Gary Schwendiman** is Dean of the College of Business Administration and Professor of Management at the University of Nebraska–Lincoln. A specialist in the area of Management Psychology, he earned his Bachelor's degree with honors from Washington State University and his Master of Science and Ph.D. degrees from Brigham Young University. In 1969 he joined the faculty of Marshall University in West Virginia, where he taught courses in management and psychology. He joined General Motors Institute, the Educational and Management Development division of the General Motors

Corporation, in 1972, where he was Associate Professor of Organizational Behavior and Communication. His research and consulting activities have been mainly with financial organizations. He recently completed a survey of the nation's 300 largest banks to determine future directions for the effective management of human resources. He has developed the Individual Assessment Profile, which is used in the development of supervisory personnel, and the Organizational Profile, which assesses organizational and management effectiveness. He has published numerous research papers in scholarly journals of psychology and organizational behavior.